Stress in Young People

Related titles

Maurice Chazan, Alice F. Laing, Diane Davies and Rob Philips: *Helping Socially Withdrawn and Isolated Children and Adolescents*
Dennis Child: *Psychology and the Teacher* (6th edition)
Sue Cowley: *Starting Teaching*
Steve Decker, Sandy Kirby, Angela Greenwood and Dudley Moore: *Taking Children Seriously*
Raymon Flannery: *Preventing Youth Violence: A Guide for Parents, Teachers and Counsellors*
Janet Kay: *Protecting Children*
Michael Jacobs (ed.): *The Care Guide: An Interdisciplinary Manual for the Caring Professions and Other Agencies*
John McGuinness: *Counselling in Schools*
Angela Thody, Barbara Gray and Derek Bowden: *The Teacher's Survival Guide*

STRESS IN YOUNG PEOPLE

What's New and What Can We Do?

Sarah McNamara

CONTINUUM
London and New York

Continuum

The Tower Building   370 Lexington Avenue
11 York Road   New York
London SE1 7NX   NY 10017–6503

First published 2000

British Library Cataloguing-in-Publication Data
A catalogue record for this book is available from the British Library.

ISBN 0 8264 4920 4 (paperback)

Designed and typeset by Ben Cracknell Studios
Printed and bound in Great Britain by The Cromwell Press, Trowbridge, Wiltshire

Contents

Acknowledgements

I would like to thank the following people for their help and support in compiling this book. First, I would like to thank Continuum for their decision to publish and in particular Anthony Haynes, who provided essential advice, encouragement and guidance. Second, I would like to thank those who kindly agreed to review early drafts of the book and whose suggestions proved invaluable. These include Paula Mayock, Lucette McNamara, Veronica O'Doherty, Katie Baird and Molly Byrne. I would particularly like to thank Veronica for her persistent interest in the book's development. I am also grateful to the EU Training and Mobility of Researchers Fund and the Economic and Social Research Council for funding the initial research upon which the book is based. Finally, I would like to thank Michael Plumb for his support and love.

Introduction

In recent years there have been major increases in stress-related disorders in young people, including suicides, substance abuse, depression, anxiety and eating disorders. Young people are experiencing more social and psychological problems than ever before. These trends indicate an increase in the pressures faced by young people, together with a general decline in coping skills and absence of social support. Such patterns have emerged worldwide and represent a challenge to policy-makers, service providers and families alike.

Adolescence is an exciting but vulnerable time, and the experiences of young people throughout this period of transition have extremely important consequences for their adult lives. Because children and young people represent our most valuable resource, we need to prioritize their needs. It is up to us to support them and to teach them the necessary skills to cope, and to provide them with a safe and stimulating environment in which they can learn and grow. It is important to understand young people, the difficulties they face, and the types of interventions that are effective in reducing adolescent stress.

Understanding adolescence will help to explain some of the emotional and behavioural tendencies that parents and practitioners witness in their communications with young people. It will help them to find a key to that behaviour and to relate more effectively. In this way, sources of stress, ways of coping and stress-related outcomes can be discussed in a constructive way with insight and understanding.

To this end we first need to acknowledge the importance of youth. We also need to recognize that although young people share many experiences, difficulties and challenges, they are also individuals whose lives resemble tapestries as different from each other as they are from adults. We need to create a more positive environment for young people.

There are books that describe teenage stress, but there are far fewer that offer suggestions as to what one can do to help young people to navigate this difficult transition. This book aims to help you to develop a more informed understanding of the causes and consequences of stress. It goes further, however, in providing a practical guide to help you equip young people with skills that will be of real value in negotiating their adolescence.

Similarly, there are books that offer advice as to what you, as a concerned adult, can do in response to difficulties that have already developed. This book, however, will enable you to pass on skills that are preventive. In other words, these skills are aimed at preventing problems from arising in the first place. Learning how to communicate, solving problems constructively, learning how to relax and manage time properly, taking care of your health and nurturing self-esteem are examples of generic coping skills that will prove invaluable to young people in a wide variety of situations, both now and in the exciting future that lies ahead.

Many practitioners and parents want to improve their knowledge about stress and coping. They want to offer advice, but are often at a loss to understand the way in which young people are thinking about their lives. This book will help to develop an understanding of coping skills and stress management for young people. It aims to equip the reader with the understanding and tools to provide essential direction, advice and support to young people.

The book helps the reader to see things from a teenager's perspective, and to have respect and understanding for that perspective. Young people have little power or experience and limited knowledge, yet making decisions is a crucial part of their transition to adulthood. They need guidance, skills, and enough space to develop and acquire knowledge based on their own experiences.

All those seeking to understand the stress process in young people and to help young people cope better with stress will find this publication invaluable. It answers questions such as: Why do some young people suffer depression following a parental separation and not others? Why do some young people develop eating disorders as a result of exam stress and not others? Why do some young people see no other option than suicide as a solution to the building pressures in their lives?

It is a text that should be read by everyone who is in contact with teenagers, as well as those who are concerned about particular individuals or groups of individuals under stress. There is much to be learned from the book for adults too, as many of the causes and consequences of stress are shared by both adolescents and adults alike. Similarly, many of the stress-coping strategies that are effective for young people are equally effective when used by adults.

This is a general text on adolescent stress. It identifies the pathways within the stress process, and links coping, self-esteem, social support and other key factors. It also provides advice and guidelines for those who wish to design or deliver stress reduction interventions to groups of young people. It explains how these programmes should be set up, facilitated and evaluated to aid in their development or maintenance within the specified context. It therefore represents an essential guide to the many practitioners working with young people, such as teachers, counsellors, psychologists, youth workers and so on.

Hence, this book is important in many ways: in developing issues of relevance to today's young people, in providing insights into a time of life that many of us have ceased to remember, in helping parents and practitioners to understand their unique challenges, in outlining the types of interventions that work, and in taking the findings from risk and resiliency research and providing the information and techniques necessary to teach these skills to young people.

It was not the author's intention to provide an assessment tool, but to provide a general text on stress. Those working with young people should be aware of professional services available to young people prior to raising issues around stress. They are advised to contact their local youth centre, health authority, GP or school counsellor for more specific advice and follow-through.

The book is divided into two parts. The aim of Part 1 is to discuss the theories of stress, current research on stress in young people, sources and symptoms of stress, and whether stress reduction interventions are effective. Suggested reading will allow readers to explore specific issues further. Our current knowledge and understanding of stress in young people is explored. The question is raised: Is it inevitable that adolescence is a time of turbulence or is adolescent stress more prevalent in contemporary society? Part 1 critiques traditional views of adolescent psychology and asks how these account for the rising figures in adolescent suicide, depression, substance abuse, eating disorders and so on. It also provides advice on designing, delivering and evaluating stress reduction interventions.

The aim of Part 2 is to provide professionals with a practical guide for helping young people to cope with stress. Chapter 4 will help practitioners introduce young people to the area of stress and the different factors involved. Chapters 5 and 6 provide information on mental and physical ways of coping with stress. Mental ways include useful advice on how to keep things in perspective and how to keep stress levels low, as well as problem-solving and coping skills. Physical techniques of coping with stress include looking after sleep, exercise, nutrition and relaxation patterns as well as cutting down on alcohol use. Chapter 7 is devoted to study skills and time management, as many students in their exam years (and other years) find this difficult to deal with. It includes suggestions to help students to study more easily and efficiently.

The stress which arises from relationships can be the most difficult form to deal with for some people, and so ideas and issues for discussion on how to get the most out of our relationships, communication, assertiveness and negotiation skills are discussed in Chapter 8. Finally, none of these techniques will work without the self-esteem and self-confidence to carry them through, and Chapter 9 discusses ways in which young people can learn to treat themselves with respect and compassion to get the most out of their lives. A section on coping with depression and anxiety has also been included, as these may be a cause of stress in our lives or the direct consequence of our difficulties in dealing with stress. Chapter 10 discusses the meanings of the findings outlined in the book and their implications. It explains why tackling stress in young people has become so important, and why we must invest in primary prevention methods if we are to help young people to cope in the increasingly demanding world in which they live.

This book is timely in the light of the growing concern in most Western countries of increasing malaise and stress in young people. Stress is a fact of life for many of today's teenagers. Having read this book, teachers, practitioners and parents will be able to provide practical and health-promoting advice on a wide range of relevant and contemporary issues.

PART ONE
What's New?

Theory and Research on Stress in Young People

The aim of Part 1 is to present an overview of our current understanding of stress. Models of stress are examined with particular reference to life events, personal and social factors and stress-related outcomes. A detailed discussion is provided on the nature of adolescence, followed by the causes and consequences of adolescent stress. Finally, stress reduction interventions are reviewed, together with resources for practitioners in delivering interventions.

Due to different aims and emphases, the tone of Part 1 is intentionally different from that of Part 2. Part 1 sets out the context in theory and research to the second part of the book, which guides the reader more informally in applying this knowledge to real life.

CHAPTER 1

The stress process

Introduction

As most research on the stress process has focused on adult stress, this book begins with a chapter on general definitions, models and research on stress. The remaining chapters relate specifically to stress in young people.

This chapter begins with a discussion on definitions of stress. It examines three ways of looking at stress, or 'models' of stress. Having argued that stress is not one single thing, but a process, it introduces us to the various components which make up this process. These include life events and daily hassles, ways of coping, social support, personality and social factors, and symptoms or outcomes of strain.

Early research on young people in their teen years focused mainly on psychoanalytic and developmental processes. The advent of stress and coping literature within the adult domain has, however, caused a large number of researchers to seek to integrate findings regarding adult adaptation with the developmental tasks or challenges faced by young people. Although the majority of theoretical and research advances in this area pertain to the adult population, there is much evidence to suggest that these findings are of equal relevance to young people. This book therefore combines conceptualizations of stress in adults with those of adolescents. It then marries these with empirical research conducted with young people.

The literature reviewed in this chapter presents an overview of our current understanding of the stress process. Rather than looking at stress as a unidimensional variable, that is a 'stressor' (an event that happens to young people) or 'strain' (the way they feel as a result), the most exciting of current research outlines the mechanisms and pathways through which change occurs. In order to understand this, it is useful to know about different models of stress.

What is stress?

Definitions of stress

In a book on stress and stress management, it is often useful to begin with a definition of stress. What exactly do we mean when we talk about stress? It is obvious that stress means different things to different people, and what is stressful for one person is not necessarily stressful for another. Although stress as a term is used frequently and relatively unproblematically, academics see stress in very different ways. Stress can refer to the internal state of the individual, an external event, or the interaction between a person and his or her environment. It is common to divide ways of looking at stress like this. Despite the different ways of defining stress, what is clear is that stress is an important issue for professionals in many disciplines. Looking at stress as a process represents a useful framework which consists of environmental, psychological and physiological variables and processes.

The term 'stress' in this book refers to the general stress process in its entirety or to the overall area of research. The terms 'stressors', 'stresses' or 'demands' are used to represent the environment (objective or perceived), and 'strain', 'stress responses' and 'stress-related symptoms' depict emotional, biological or behavioural outcomes. 'Appraisals' or 'perceptions' depict the subjective and personal evaluations of the stressfulness of a situation.

SUMMARY

Stress can be conceptualized within three main models:

- the environmental model
- the medical model
- the psychological model

It is useful to understand the different ways in which stress is depicted in each of these three models, although the third model of stress is by far the most commonly accepted and is used for the rest of the book.

Environmental model of stress

This model treats stress as an independent factor which arises from characteristics of disturbing or noxious environments. Analogous to Hooke's Law of Elasticity in metals, stress is viewed as the load or demand which is placed upon an individual. Strain is the resulting outcome when deformation occurs. This model attributes an 'elastic limit' to an individual within which a certain degree of strain is tolerated allowing the individual to return to homeostasis. If, however, the individual is subjected to an intolerable amount of stress, psychological and physical damage may occur. In parallel to the varying degrees of elasticity demonstrated in metals, individuals also vary in their levels of resistance to stress.

An outcome of the popularity of this approach to stress was seen in the proliferation of stressful life events inventories which began with the Schedule of Recent Experiences.[1] In order to calculate the level of stress an individual was experiencing, events were assigned a standardized weight. The weighted sum of events provided a score measured in 'life change units' which were believed to place the individual at risk of illness.

Ongoing research, however, has failed to find consistent, generalized effects of stressful events in keeping with the laws espoused by the environmental model. It has been shown, for example, that human performance levels decline with departures from an optimum level of demand. In other words, low levels of stress can result in negative outcomes akin to high levels of demand. A growing awareness of the role of individual differences in the stress process saw the introduction of a cognitive or psychological component into stressful life event measures, together with the expansion of the range of experiences included and the design of measures targeted at particular populations.

Medical model of stress

The medical model defines stress mainly as an outcome variable, emphasizing the responses of the individual. Originating in the writings of Hans Selye (1956), stress is described as a general physiological response of the body to any demand made upon it. This response, Selye believed, was independent of the nature of the stressor, and invariably underwent a three-stage pattern.

The 'General Adaptation Syndrome' consists of three stages:

- alarm
- resistance
- adaptation or exhaustion

According to Selye, stored energy supplies were mobilized by physiological responses which protected the individual in the short term but were harmful if prolonged.

The main criticism of this approach lies in its assumption that all stressors evoke the same response pattern in all individuals. Research shows that people respond differently to the same levels of stress. There are individual differences in patterns of physiological reactions to stress which involve heart rate, respiratory rate and galvanic skin response. Furthermore, different types of stress elicit different types of physiological response. It also appears that the type of coping strategy employed will affect the pattern of physiological responses. Active coping results in catecholamine release (e.g. adrenalin) and sympathetic nervous system activation and passive withdrawal results in the production of stress hormones such as corticosteroids. Situations that evoke anxiety have been linked to increased adrenaline release, while those which produce aggression appear to stimulate the release of noradrenaline. Another, perhaps more damning criticism of this model, is the finding that some hormonal responses disappear when individuals are re-exposed to acute stressors or are exposed to chronic stressors; that is, stress over a long period of time.

The fact that we respond differently to different types of stress and that each of us responds in an individual way makes it clear that our psychological processes play a very important role in the way stressful events affect our emotions, physical health and behaviour.

Psychological model of stress

Today, it is most common to view stress as a relationship between the events which happen to us, our attitudes to them and the way our body reacts. This assumes that there is an interactive relationship between us and our environment. Our environment has an effect on us, we have an effect on our environment, and we can determine the effect the environment will have on us through our interpretations of the world we live in.

The most influential proponent of the psychological model of stress is Richard Lazarus, whose book *Psychological Stress and the Coping Process* (1966) heralded a new direction for stress research. This approach awarded central precedence to cognitive functioning, namely appraisal, within the stress process. Lazarus produced a rich theoretical formulation of the stress process which proved to account for much of the existing data. Stress was defined as 'a particular relationship between the person and the environment that is appraised by the person as taxing or exceeding his or her resources and endangering his or her well-being'.[2]

According to Lazarus, two fundamental processes mediate this relationship: those of cognitive appraisal and of coping. Cognitive appraisal consists of two types of appraisal: primary and secondary. Their function is to ascertain respectively whether the individual's well-being is at risk and, if so, what resources are available to deal with this risk. Primary appraisal may lead the individual to evaluate the situation as harm or loss, threat, challenge or benign. Secondary appraisal takes into account access to coping options, their applicability and chances of success. It is common for individuals to re-appraise the situation as it unfolds and they receive more information.

Of equal importance to the psychological viewpoint is coping, defined as 'the process through which the individual manages the demands of the person–environment relationship that are appraised as stressful and the emotions they generate'.[3] Coping may comprise actions which aim to manage or alter the problem (problem-focused coping), or actions or thoughts targeted at regulating emotional responses to the problem (emotion-focused coping).

While generally regarded as the most satisfactory model, the psychological model of stress has also received some criticism. First, researchers with a sociological approach to the stress process object to the centrality which Lazarus awards to subjective appraisal. This, they believe, denigrates the real impact of objective stressors such as unemployment. While it is likely that involuntary unemployment represents a formidable source of stress, researchers such as Warr (1989) have reported significant individual differences in responses to unemployment, which support the psychological position.

Second, from a biological viewpoint it appears that cognitive appraisal is not always required to mobilize physiological reactions. Some researchers have discovered that the effort involved in actively coping with stress may affect many of the same biological processes influenced by the emotional response. This may influence the development of disease independently of the way we respond emotionally.

The division of stress models into the three described above is in some ways an academic pursuit, as most approaches to stress employ a broader and more integrative model than do any one of these models.

Psychological theories elaborated
The transactional model
For many researchers, the comprehensive breadth of the psychological model of stress has resulted in its adoption as an almost consensual paradigm within which to conduct research on stress and design interventions. As mentioned above, the approach originated in the perceived inadequacies of conventional approaches to stress. These deficiencies included a focus on the environment as always the

objective cause. In addition, research on stressful events was vague in its criteria for the duration, intensity and type of stressful event necessary to induce a stress-related outcome. The treatment of stress responses as homogenous entities, while ignoring the importance of sequencing and response pattern in individuals, has also been criticized as a failure to take a holistic approach to the stress process. Laboratory-based experiments were dismissed in favour of more naturalistic studies of stress which more adequately encompassed contextual factors and the availability of normal resources for people in coping situations. In summary, Lazarus challenged the integrity of stimulus-response models. This approach seemed to epitomize an absence of concern with the processes mediating between the environment and the stress response.

Researchers seeking to understand and examine stress within a psychological approach try to include cognitive as well as objective measures of stress. They also combine a cross-sectional approach (looking at differences between people) with a longitudinal approach (looking at change over time). Changes within people over time can reveal the way that our perceptions of events and our physical and mental health affect each other in a two-way relationship. In other words, it is hard to separate the way we think from the way we feel. Stress, then, may be seen as a dynamic interaction or 'troubled commerce' between the person and the environment involving two-way relationships which operate via a complex set of feedback processes. When we successfully negotiate the demands in our environment, this interaction remains untroubled, and we do not experience major mental and physical stress-related outcomes. This approach is represented in Figure 1.1.

Within this model, daily hassles or the 'stress of daily living' are strongly believed to predict outcomes more effectively than stressful life events *per se*. Furthermore, this model seeks to progress from simply employing one factor to represent stressful life events. Rather, stress is represented as a dynamic, ongoing and changing process mediated by cognitive appraisals which are flexible by nature.

Criticisms of the transactional model

As mentioned above, the centrality of appraisal to the development of symptoms has failed to secure unequivocal agreement. Debate also remains concerning whether we need to appraise something as stressful to have stress-related emotions. In other words, sometimes we can react in a certain way without ever having thought about an event in a particular light. This version of stress also assumes that there are general

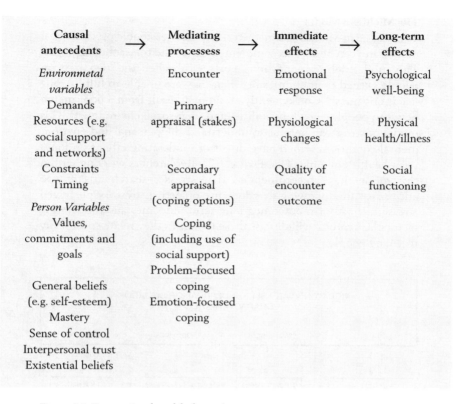

Causal antecedents	→	Mediating processess	→	Immediate effects	→	Long-term effects
Environmetal variables		Encounter		Emotional response		Psychological well-being
Demands		Primary				
Resources (e.g. social support and networks)		appraisal (stakes)		Physiological changes		Physical health/illness
Constraints		Secondary		Quality of		Social
Timing		appraisal		encounter		functioning
Person Variables		(coping options)		outcome		
Values, commitments and goals		Coping (including use of social support)				
		Problem-focused				
General beliefs		coping				
(e.g. self-esteem)		Emotion-focused				
Mastery		coping				
Sense of control						
Interpersonal trust						
Existential beliefs						

Figure 1.1 *Transactional model of stress*[4]

personalities with certain traits and patterns of behaviour. However, some would argue that we do not always respond to stress in a predictable way according to our personality type. Research suggests that we use different coping strategies in different situations.

Perhaps most importantly, it is difficult to prove the transactional model of stress as this requires a combination of epidemiological and personality oriented, in-depth and longitudinal studies of large cohorts of individuals in their natural environment. This has led researchers to suggest that rather than always trying to capture the dynamic interplay between various factors, we should look at everything on its own and then work out the relationships between the factors. This would focus on more simplistic models of stress, which look at causes, moderators and outcomes, to examine stress in the dynamic, bi-directional way proposed by a transactional perspective. The Michigan Model aims to provide such a model.

The Michigan Model

The Michigan Model has emerged as a more measurable psychological model, and can be seen as complementary to the transactional model. This model defines conditions as stressful when the 'demands on people exceed their abilities or when they are unable to fulfil strong needs or values'.[5] Consequently, strain may result from a poor match between people's needs or abilities and their social environment. This model of stress can help us to understand the personal and environmental conditions which have direct or moderating effects on long-term health outcomes (see Figure 1.2). Researchers working within this model have recommended that stress research attempt to encompass the following five domains: objective stressors, perceived stressors, short-term outcomes, long-term outcomes and moderating factors.[6] Chapter 2 will discuss these factors as they relate specifically to young people.

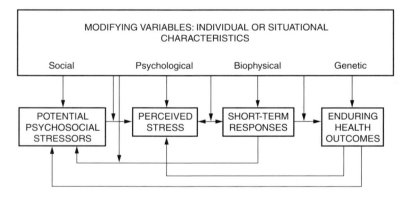

Figure 1.2 *The Michigan Model of stress (adapted from Israel* et al. *(1992))*

SUMMARY

The transactional and Michigan models rely on a multi-stage process or chain of associations, whereby stressors, through mediating and moderating variables, may develop into short- and then long-term illnesses. As a result, interventions such as stress inoculation and other cognitive skills-based programmes have emerged which focus intervention efforts on appraisal and perceptions of reality.

The remainder of this chapter will present in more detail the literature emphasizing the significance of each of these domains, as well as the role of coping in psychological well-being.

Stressful life events

Voluminous literature has accumulated regarding the role of stressful life events in the aetiology of disease and psychological disorder. The aim of this section is to provide an overview of various ways of categorizing stressful life events. This is followed by a review of the major findings which support their significance for physical and psychological health together with the main criticisms of this research.

History of life events research

Epidemiological research concerning the association between environmental stress and adaptational outcomes has its roots in the work of Adolf Meyer in the 1930s. Following his suggestion that physicians complete a life chart when assessing patients, a large body of evidence evolved implicating life events in the aetiology of illness. This led to the development of the Schedule of Recent Experiences, mentioned earlier, which was later modified by Holmes and colleagues (1974) as the Social Readjustment Rating Scale. Each event listed was given an objective weighting based on the degree of adaptation or adjustment which the event required. It was assumed that any change, positive or negative, which necessitated adjustment could potentially endanger well-being. Following its apparent success in demonstrating a causal relationship between life events and negative outcomes, this scale was followed by a succession of similar measures each seeking to cover a broad range of life events with a view to predicting illness. These took the format of checklists and stress rating scales.

Sources of environmental stress may be manifold. Aldwin (1994) distinguishes between physical stressors, which include both trauma and aversive conditions such as pollution and noise, and sociocultural stressors emanating from the distribution of social resources. Furthermore, the demands which arise from primary sources of stress, termed 'secondary stressors', may surpass the former in their impact on well-being. Aldwin draws attention to the timing characteristics of the stressor, as there are large differences between short-term, chronic and intermittent stressors.

Three major sources of stress have been outlined by Lazarus and Cohen (1977):

1 Cataclysmic phenomena or 'sudden, unique, and powerful single life-events requiring major adaptive responses from population groups sharing the experience' (p. 91). These may include natural disasters, bombings, imprisonment and relocation.

2 'Changes affecting fewer persons or a single individual but nonetheless having the same powerful and sudden impact on the individual or persons involved.' These include bereavement, terminal illness, divorce, giving birth, parents being laid off work and going away to school for the first time.

3 Daily hassles which are described as 'stable, repetitive or chronic' stressors. Much evidence suggests that these daily hassles play a larger role than life events in the aetiology of symptoms.

Main findings in life events research

Despite the controversy surrounding its use, the life events approach represents the traditional and still dominant research procedure for assessing variations in stress exposure. This approach has indicated a reliable association between life stress and the occurrence of both psychological distress and psychiatric disorder. The role of life events has also been demonstrated in connection with physical outcomes such as tuberculosis, cancer, arthritis and diabetes,[7] and has been shown to be related to allergies, hypertension and a greater risk of sudden cardiac death.[8] Researchers on stress and immunology have concluded that stressful situations and events are associated with changes in immunity in humans. These writers refer to literature which links bereavement, marital discord and examination stress to substantial immune system changes including decreased lymphocyte proliferation and decreases in natural killer cell activity.

Not all studies have shown such a direct link however. As noted by Wagner and his colleagues, studies on major life events can only partially predict the onset of symptoms, and:

> although the results of studies in the area have provided a description of the relationship between major life stressors and symptoms, they have not adequately explained the process through which the relationship operates. (Wagner, *et al.*, 1988, p. 190).

As already mentioned, the study of daily hassles has shown them to be better predictors of symptom development, overall health status and energy levels. DeLongis and her colleagues (1988) have found support for the predictive relationship between daily hassles and negative mood but report significant individual differences in this relationship. This seems to be largely accounted for by social support, self-esteem and neuroticism which substantially moderate the relationship.

A further moderator in the hassles–outcome relationship concerns the degree of centrality or salience which the event invokes, i.e. how important it is to the individual. In outcome terms, research has demonstrated an increase in hydrochloric acid in the stomach under conditions of ongoing and prolonged anxiety but not episodic anxiety. A possible explanation for the divergent findings on the relative contributions of life events and hassles lies in the findings that daily events provide a mediating relationship between life events and psychological symptoms.

Evidently, age and life stage dictate the sources of environmental stress individuals are likely to encounter and their relative capacity to cope with these demands. Adolescence, in particular, is a period of great transition and change. Specific stressors and ways of coping associated with adolescence will be discussed in detail in Chapter 2.

Criticisms of life events research
Methodological issues are particularly salient in the field of life events research. Without strong research designs and valid, reliable measures, much of the literature relating stressful events to long-term health outcomes may be spurious. The most frequent criticism levied against life events measures lies in their omission of appraisal in favour of objective, standardized weighting of items. This, according to some researchers, violates the central lesson in our understanding of the stress process, whereby stress which is not perceived to exist does not exert a negative influence. In defence of the method, however, many researchers prefer the objectification of stress exposure to the confounding effects which result when appraisal is considered.

The return of a call for measuring stress as an independent variable may be seen to reflect the frustration for some researchers in disentangling appraisal of events or hassles from the symptoms of stress. Thus, symptoms may become stressors, as in myocardial infarctions (MIs) which are known effects of cardiovascular disease, or hassles may be more readily perceived depending on existing vulnerabilities within the person. Among the most vociferous critics of the life events approach to the measurement of stress are Schroeder and Costa (1984), who dismiss much of this literature as prone to 'memory, perception and response tendencies' which undermine the validity of all findings.

Another assumption of the original research espoused by Holmes *et al.* (1974), that all change necessitating adjustment heightened the risk of developing negative symptoms, has been challenged by recent literature. Not only have positive events been shown not to induce negative symptoms, but positive life events have actually been reported to exert a 'buffering' effect on outcomes.

SUMMARY

Debate continues concerning the superiority of objective measures of environmental stress and methods which encompass an individual's subjective appraisal of environmental stress. In summary, exposure to stress is most adequately measured using both life events and daily hassles. The biological costs involved in coping with chronic or ongoing stressors appear to be greater than those for acute or episodic stressors. Repeated and unsuccessful attempts to cope with a chronic stressor can produce feelings of helplessness and distress. The additional likelihood that individuals may become socially avoidant while trying to cope with chronic stressors may remove social support, an important resource for dealing with stress.

The role of coping

A large body of research exists focusing on the role of coping in the stress process. One explanation for the growth of interest in this field may be the major social changes witnessed during the past two decades, including the entry of women into the workforce, social mobility, racial integration and changes in family structure. Literature concerning the function of coping in the stress process can be divided into two main themes: that which attempts to develop a typology of coping processes, and that which explores the relationship between coping processes and adaptational outcomes. As mentioned earlier, a large proportion of studies on adolescent coping utilize the general paradigms provided by the literature on adult coping processes.

Background to coping research

The precursors to modern-day coping research can be found within early psychoanalytic psychology, where coping strategies received much attention as defence mechanisms aimed at resolving internal conflict. These included suppression, denial, projection, reaction formation, hysteria, obsessive-compulsive behaviours and sublimation. This approach was embedded within a person-centred view of coping which contrasted with the later development of situational approaches to coping. These aimed to identify those aspects of the environment which engendered differential coping efforts. There is much evidence to suggest, from this latter approach to coping, that individuals vary in the way they respond to different types of stressor. Situational variables which influence choice of coping strategy include level of controllability, life domain and whether the outcomes potentiate loss, threat or challenge.

The majority of coping researchers currently use the transactional model. This model sees coping as constantly changing cognitive and behavioural efforts to manage specific external and/or internal demands that are appraised as taxing or exceeding the resources of the individual. It assumes that the way we appraise situations is central to our choice of coping strategy, and that we tend to be flexible in their choices.

Under this approach there are two types of coping: problem-focused coping and emotion-focused coping. The first is aimed at doing something to alter the source of the stress. The second refers to efforts aimed at reducing or managing the emotional distress associated with the situation. Although there are other ways of classifying coping efforts, this approach is most prevalent in the coping literature. More details will be provided on coping processes during adolescence in Chapter 2.

What we know about coping

The majority of studies examining the effectiveness of different coping strategies have related more adaptive outcomes to the use of problem-focused coping. Problem-focused coping when representing the majority of the individual's total coping efforts is associated with reduced depression.[9] Conversely, emotion-focused coping has shown a positive association with maladaptive functioning and strain.[10] Personality styles have been linked to these coping strategies. Perceptions of personal control have been demonstrated to influence coping. When situations contain a degree of controllability, 'internals' (those individuals who attribute success to their own efforts) employ more direct coping efforts while 'externals' (those who attribute success to circumstances beyond their control) use more indirect coping. Socioeconomic factors have also been reported to play an important role in choice of coping strategy. There is much evidence to suggest that individuals who are better educated and have higher socio-economic status are more likely to use adaptive ways of coping, involving problem-focused coping, and are less likely to employ defence and avoidance as ways of relieving stress.[11]

The dichotomization of coping into problem- and emotion-focused coping may be too simplistic however. Many studies have reported a broader range of coping strategies which diverge significantly from this model. Thus an active reconstrual or denial of events can be found within emotion-focused coping. Within problem-focused coping, refraining from acting is just as likely to be found as taking active measures to resolve the problem. Furthermore, seeking social support has been reported to represent another independent category of coping response.

Avoidance, *per se*, rather than emotion-focused coping has been linked by numerous authors to deleterious outcomes. Avoidance may include wishful thinking, escapism, self-distraction, denial, and mental or behavioural disengagement. On the positive side, focusing on tasks and the positive reframing of situations appear to have beneficial adaptational consequences.

Criticisms of coping research

A central debate in the coping literature lies in the distinction between coping styles or dispositional coping and coping strategies or situational coping. In other words, do we use the same coping styles in different situations, or does it depend on the situation? A transactional approach assumes that coping emerges as a product of the particular situation and person variables at that time and cannot be divorced from the context in which it occurs. While, empirically, it appears that a broad range of situational factors influence choice of coping strategy, some authors continue to favour a 'trait' approach to coping which focuses on preferential patterns in coping style.

In addition, the treatment of situations as unidimensional phenomena has been criticized. It appears that many encounters unfold in various stages which are different in nature from each other. In summary, it would appear that people have dispositions towards particular coping styles, and that individual situations also play an important role in determining the type of strategy used.

Researchers working within the Michigan Model see coping *resources* as relatively stable characteristics, attitudes or skills, while coping *strategies* are specific to situations. There is some evidence to suggest that while coping strategies do vary greatly across situations, these strategies may be surprisingly stable within life domains (e.g. home, work or school).

SUMMARY

Both personality and situational factors are known to influence coping processes. Fairly consistent coping patterns have been seen to operate within life domains. As will be discussed in Chapter 2, for some groups, such as adolescents, the psychological distinction between these domains may have yet to emerge, resulting in a more uniform employment of coping strategies across domains.

Moderating factors in the stress process

Psychological and social factors, such as social support, perceptions of control and personality factors, exert a direct and indirect influence on both the short-term and enduring outcomes of stress. A direct effect refers to a causal relationship between two variables (e.g. parental divorce leading to an eating disorder in an adolescent girl). An interactive effect refers to the modifying influence of a variable on the relationship between two other variables (e.g. the role of social support in intervening to prevent this outcome). The importance of identifying specific pathways in which environmental and individual variables operate within the stress process is important, as an understanding of their individual roles is essential to the design of appropriate and effective stress-relieving interventions. A more detailed discussion of their role in the adolescent stress process is provided in Chapter 2.

Social support
Background to social support research

A majority of the literature on moderating effects concerns the relationship between social support and health outcomes. Definitions of social support vary. It has been described as interpersonal transactions involving tangible help, emotional support and affirmation. House (1981) refers to emotional, instrumental, informational and appraisal social support. There is evidence to suggest that social support may influence the relationship between stressful events and health in many ways (see Chapter 2). There is also evidence to suggest that emotional support may have a 'buffering effect' on physical and mental health.

Social support may have an impact on stress-related symptoms by:

1 preventing stressful life events and daily hassles from occurring

2 making the individual feel less vulnerable when they do occur

3 reducing the impact, intensity and duration of the symptoms

4 providing help, advice and support to remove the stressor or the strain

What we know about social support

High levels of emotional support, together with high levels of self-esteem, have been found to moderate the relationship between daily hassles and physical symptoms both on the day those hassles occurred and the following day. Consequently, lack of social support has been linked with increased rates of morbidity and mortality. Much evidence suggests that social support has a buffering effect on mental health. In a summary review of research, Kahn and Byosier (1992) found that lack of support produced direct and interactive effects on strain outcomes in twenty of the twenty-two studies reviewed. Potential stressful events may be directly influenced by social support, therefore affecting levels of strain.

Support may be conceptualized and measured subjectively or objectively; that is, by the *perception of* or *actual* availability of support. Cohen and Hoberman (1983) reported that perceived availability of social support and accumulated positive life events both moderated the relationship between negative events and depression and physical symptoms. These authors support the hypothesis that 'perceived availability of support wholly or partly protects one from the pathogenic effects of high levels of life stress' (p. 116). Further classifications involve a distinction between emotional and practical support or between support which increases our sense of belonging, improves our material situation, helps us to see things in a different way or that which boosts our self-esteem. These distinctions may provide more in-depth explanations for the protective role of social support in mental and physical health outcomes.

The pervading influence of social support was further illustrated by Rudolph Moos (1995), who examined the relationship between social resources and coping processes. Moos found that social resources influenced adaptation by 'facilitating the use of more active coping strategies' such as positive reappraisal (p. 10). Tangible aid may be coupled with the reinforcement or discouragement of particular coping strategies, and self-esteem may be enhanced through the reassurance of worth which social support can provide.

Further variables which influence the effects of social support in the stress process may include age, perceptions of control and neuroticism. Gender differences appear to be quite marked in the seeking and mobilization of social support in times of stress, with women being more likely to engage social support.

Finally, there is some evidence to suggest that increases in perceived social support may produce slight increases in strain, possibly due to the additional demands which these relationships place on an individual's resources, the lack of agreement between recipient and provider perception of what constitutes helpful support, or the increase in emotional coping this may encourage.

In summary, much evidence has been provided to suggest that social support may be one of the most important factors in mitigating or buffering the effects of potentially stressful situations. It does this by altering initial perceptions of situations, allowing them to appear less threatening, and thus reducing the likelihood of the development of disease-provoking outcomes. This is even more true for young people than it is for adults. It is likely that social support exerts direct and moderating effects which, in the main, reduce the number of stressful events and limit the distress caused as well as alleviating short- and long-term responses.

Personal control
Perceived control has proved to be the most extensively examined personal factor within psychological models.

Background to personal control research
Like the concept of stress, the term 'control' represents an integration of a variety of concepts. These include mastery, self-efficacy, learned helplessness, locus of control, hardiness, fatalism and personal competence. Individual differences in personal control beliefs have important implications for motivation, attitudes, adaptation and behaviour in many life domains.

Control is a 'multifaceted construct' which has been classified in various ways. The most frequently used classification is provided by Steptoe (1989), where he defines three aspects of control.

Control can be:

• behavioural or objective control over environmental events

- subjective or perceived control
- individual differences described as need for control or belief in control

Frequently, in health-related research, 'control' refers to 'perceived control' as opposed to 'actual' control.

Much of the interest in perception of control as an individual difference originated in the work of Rotter (1966). Rotter distinguished between those individuals who had an internal orientation of control ('internals') and those who possessed an external orientation of control ('externals'). The former held beliefs that outcomes were contingent upon their own efforts, while the latter believed that outcomes were contingent upon forces outside themselves, such as fate, luck, chance or powerful others. According to Rotter, generalized control beliefs tend to have the greatest effect on control perceptions when environmental characteristics are ambiguous or novel.

Although Rotter's (1966) scale has been used extensively to assess locus of control, subsequent studies have led to a growing recognition of the inadequacies associated with such a broad dichotomization of control orientations. This has led to the development of more sophisticated measures of control beliefs. One example is the 'Spheres of Control' Scale[12] which assesses control in the personal, interpersonal and sociopolitical domains. The assumption is that people may differ in their control beliefs in each of these spheres.

What we know about personal control

The main findings arising from research on perceived control may be summarized thus:

- a lack of control may act as a source of stress and exert direct, negative effects upon health outcomes
- enhanced perceptions of control may have a buffering effect against stressors
- an increased sense of control may encourage health promoting behaviours

Specifically, a majority of early research on locus of control reported superior outcomes for those individuals with an 'internal' orientation. Studies have indicated that internals are more likely to engage in information searches regarding disease and health maintenance.

Internals have also been found to be more likely to engage in task-centred (problem-focused) coping behaviours, while externals employ more emotion-directed coping. Internals appear to exhibit greater resistance to influence, and to handle success and failure in a more realistic fashion than do externals. Also, successful performance has also been found to strengthen an individual's current orientation.

There are a number of processes through which control may influence health outcomes. Biologically, there is now substantial evidence for altered autonomic functioning together with changes in endocrine response and immunological activity. Psychologically, appraisals may modify cognition and emotion shifting as the encounter unfolds, while on the behavioural level health-related behaviours may be affected. Furthermore, the provision of social support may bolster internal locus of control beliefs, but only up to a certain threshold.

There is evidence to suggest, however, that adaptation does not improve as someone becomes more 'internal'. Rotter (1966) alluded to this when he referred to extremism of orientation and potential psychopathology. More adaptive responses to stress have been reported in men with moderately internal locus of control beliefs than in those classified as extreme internal, extreme external or moderately external. Research has shown a link between extreme internal beliefs and anxiety and depression.[13] Furthermore, uncontrollable events may produce maladaptive coping efforts in 'internals', which has been referred to as 'hysterical rigidity'.

Criticisms of personal control research

Control remains a central concept in the study of the stressor–strain relationship, but criticisms of its use pervade the literature. There is evidence to suggest that though formally accepted as a stable trait, locus of control may change with age, life experience and situation. Feelings of control are also difficult to define.

A marked preference for more refined, specific scales, such as the MMCS[14] and the Spheres of Control Scale,[15] have emerged following findings which indicate their greater relevancy and predictive power. In addition, a shift towards person–environment match has replaced more simplistic within-individual models. In other words, both situational and personality factors influence the degree of perceived control. The result is that most contemporary research on control attempts to integrate situational features, such as controllability. Findings also suggest that perceptions of uncontrollability do not necessarily lead to increased strain, and are currently receiving more empirical attention.

The appeal of this construct may lie in its applied value, as, following its demonstrated role as a moderating variable in the stress process, interventions may aim to enhance perceptions of control. To establish this role with certainty, longitudinal research is essential. In addition, the coinciding of both external and internal control beliefs in stressful situations merits further exploration.

In summary, there appears to be good evidence for the 'prevailing view of the relationship between locus of control and life stress, that individuals who define events in their lives as outside their control will be less able to cope effectively with stress, and therefore more likely to experience physical and psychological distress than persons with internal locus of control beliefs'.[16]

Personality factors

Personality factors of relevance to stress-related outcomes include extroversion and introversion, social desirability and levels of self-esteem and self-competence. Extroversion in particular has been closely linked to subjective well-being. The most well-documented personality factor in the stress process is neuroticism or negative affectivity.

Background to research

Negative affectivity is a personality trait and is also referred to as 'neuroticism'. It has been defined as a mood-dispositional dimension representing individual differences in the experience of negative emotion and self-concept. It has been shown to exert a direct effect on measures of strain. It can be measured using trait anxiety[17] or neuroticism and has been highlighted as an important potentially confounding factor in the relationship between stressful life events and adaptational outcomes. In other words, high levels of neuroticism can influence the *reporting* of stress-related symptoms and not necessarily reflect a higher level *per se*.

What we know about neuroticism

People scoring highly on negative affectivity also tend to report more stress-related symptoms. Research has also found that individuals scoring highly on neuroticism demonstrate poorer adaptation to demanding situations and are more prone to distress than those with low scores. In a major longitudinal study, Eysenck (1991) found that high rates of neuroticism correlated with higher death rates.

Stressful life events and daily hassles appear to be more likely to translate into symptoms for those with high levels of negative affectivity. It is useful to give a measure of this trait when evaluating the impact of stress reduction programmes, as it will indicate whether aspects of the programme failed or succeeded due to a high level of neuroticism in individuals as opposed to aspects of the course itself.

Criticisms of neuroticism research

The precise role of negative affectivity in the stress process has been the subject of much debate. Schroeder and Costa (1984) have argued that the consistently demonstrated relationship between life events, neuroticism and outcomes results from a content overlap in these scales. The inclusion of the Eysenck Personality Questionnaire – Revised[18] in a research design permits an exploration of the exact role of neuroticism in the stress process.

SUMMARY

Social support, perceptions of control and negative affectivity are just a few of many modifying variables (along with extroversion and self-esteem) which may mitigate the relationship between objective and perceived stress, and the development of physical and mental symptoms. The attention which they receive in this chapter is due to their heavy representation in the stress literature and their recommended measurement when evaluating the impact of stress reduction interventions designed for young people.

The final section of this chapter will present an overview of the main findings regarding physiological, psychological and behavioural responses to stressful events.

Stress-related outcomes

The final stages of all stress models represent psychological and physical efforts to cope with stresses which may manifest in transient or enduring outcomes.

Physiological outcomes
Physiological processes

The perception of stress is accompanied by an organized set of physiological responses. These aim to help the individual to reduce or remove the source of stress in the short term. If psychological responses are viewed as coping strategies, then physiological responses may be seen as mechanisms which aim to facilitate coping. In reviewing the physiological response to stress, it is usual to begin with the contributions of Walter Cannon whose work proved highly influential in this field.

The adrenal medulla was identified by Cannon (1932) as the pivotal organ associated with the stress response. This response, which he termed the 'fight-or-flight' reaction, exhibited autonomic nervous system and endocrine characteristics and represented the mobilization of the body in preparation for muscular activity in response to a perceived threat. The activation of the sympathetic nervous system was seen to coincide with catecholamine secretions from the adrenal medulla. Immediate alterations in cardiovascular functioning were initiated by the SNS, while catecholamine secretions supported these changes through metabolic processes.

THE EMERGENCY REACTION

This has been referred to as the 'emergency reaction'. Its symptoms include increases in blood pressure, heart rate, respiration rate and perspiration, the release of glucose stored as glycogen in the liver which leads to increased blood sugar, blood clotting (which results from an enhancement of the blood coagulation process), the re-routeing of blood from the skin, digestive tract and viscera to the striated muscles and brain, dilation of the bronchi, dilation of the pupils to enhance vision, stimulation of lymphocyte production (goose-pimples), decreases in saliva, mucus and gastrointestinal fluids and the contraction of the spleen. These rapid changes result in the mobilization of bodily resources, the majority of which are directed towards the brain, muscles and enhanced immunity.

The findings of Hans Selye (1956) borrowed largely from Cannon's work. According to Selye's general adaptation syndrome, initial alarm reaction represented the activation of the sympathetic-adreno-medullary axis, followed by the resistance stage, which is characterized by enhanced adrenocortical activity. The adrenal glands are situated on the apices of the kidneys and within the peritoneal membrane. The inner adrenal medulla is regulated by the splanchnic nerve, which is a sympathetic nerve. It consists of chromaffin cells, which produce two types of catecholamine, norepinephrine and epinephrine. The outer adrenal cortex is responsible for the production of three different groups of steroid hormones: the mineralcorticoids, the glucocorticoids and the androgens. These are all active during the stress response. Of particular importance are the glucocorticoids, an important member of which is cortisone. As a result of stress, these may inhibit inflammatory processes and protein manufacture, deplete the kidneys of calcium and phosphate and increase levels of blood sugar.

Catecholamine excretion has been linked with changes in psycho-social stimulation, including the absence of situational control, overstimulation and understimulation and anticipation and uncertainty. It is clear that autonomic nervous system activation takes place in human beings during states of emotional arousal. In summary, physiological activation occurs following the complex neocortical and limbic integrations which occur when a stimulus is appraised as 'threatening'. The dorsomedial-amygdalar complex seems to be the highest point of origination for the 'fight-or-flight' response and represents a functionally discrete psychophysiological axis. From here, neural impulses are transmitted to the lateral and posterior hypothalamus and then on to the thoracic spinal cord, converging at the celiac ganglion, then innervating the adrenal gland, more precisely, the adrenal medulla.

Physiological effects on health
The stress-related disorders which have received most attention in the scientific literature include gastrointestinal disorders (including stomach and duodenal ulcers, ulcerative colitis and irritable bowel syndrome), cardiovascular disorders, respiratory disorders (including allergies, bronchial asthma and hyperventilation), musculoskeletal disorders and skin disorders.

Other disorders which have been linked to stress include diabetes, strokes, migraine, indigestion, heartburn, headaches, cancers and rheumatoid arthritis.[19] States associated specifically with altered hypothalamic–pituitary–adrenal (HPA) axis activity include chronic stress, melancholic depression, anorexia nervosa, obsessive-compulsive disorder, panic disorder, excessive exercise, chronic active alcoholism, alcohol and narcotic withdrawal, diabetes mellitus, central obesity and premenstrual tension syndrome.[20] Decreased activity in the HPA axis is associated with adrenal insufficiency, atypical/seasonal depression, chronic fatigue syndrome, fibromyalgia, hypothyroidism, post-chronic stress and rheumatoid arthritis.[21]

These disorders may be exacerbated or caused by the overactivation of the stress response over prolonged periods. Excessive catecholamine production has been implicated in the aetiology of coronary athero-sclerosis.[22] Cortisol is also believed to compromise the immune system, resulting in an increase in colds and minor infections, and possibly even cancer.[23] Noradrenaline (often produced during aggressive behaviour) is believed to assist in the development of plaque rupture, coronary thrombosis, coronary spasm and arrhythmia, all of whose culpable role in the onset of heart attacks has been well documented.

With regard to cancer, Faragher writes, 'the possibility of a direct, and potentially causal, relationship between psychological factors and all forms of cancer has been hypothesised for centuries. Nevertheless, this premise remains controversial.' He laments the methodological problems which have hindered attempts to link stressful life events with cancer. He concludes, however, that

> the results obtained suggest that stress tends to break down the effectiveness of the immune system, creating an environment that can cause a tumour to be formed or, if already present, can cause its development to accelerate. (Faragher, 1996, p. 171)

The existence of a cancer–personality link is also highly controversial but continues to receive some support[24]. Similarly, Theorell (1996) writes that 'critical life changes are undoubtedly important potential stressors to patients and others and seem to have both specific and non-specific importance to the cardiovascular disorders' (p. 156).

SUMMARY

Critics of the framework which Cannon espoused point to individual differences associated with stress response and disease outcomes. While stressors may produce similar patterns of response, individuals who experience these events do not react in a uniform manner suggesting that important psychological processes intervene between stimulus and response.

Psychological outcomes

Psychological responses to stress have been discussed in the section above on coping. As noted, coping may prove adaptive or maladaptive in navigating the individual successfully through a stressful event. As mentioned, physiological responses and psychological responses may overlap, as is the case with myocardial infarctions (MIs) which are known effects of cardiovascular disease. Similarly, research has shown that the homeostatic, neuroendocrine 'fight-or-flight' response can be activated in human beings by numerous and diverse psychological influences.

The psychological effects of stress are studied within the area of psychosomatic research, which examines the mechanisms through which life stress and its subsequent appraisal can ultimately affect a target organ to such a degree as to result in dysfunction and disease. The field of psychoneuroimmunology has provided a great deal of evidence to support stress-induced alterations in immunological reactivity, and conversely, immunological influences on behaviour. In 1989, the US Institute of Medicine reported that the empirical data support the premise that the nervous system, either directly or through neuroendocrine mechanisms, can affect the immune system.

Placebo effects are the most commonly observed indicators of psychological effects on the physiological functions of the body. These are seen when the physiological processes in the body respond (usually on the basis of expectation) as if they had been given an active treatment, when in fact the treatment contained no active components (e.g. a sugar pill).

Stressful situations which have been shown to compromise immunological functioning include examination stress, coping with divorce and the stress of caring for unwell family members. Some of the psychological disorders believed to originate in stressful events include post-traumatic stress disorder, panic disorder, depression, anorexia nervosa and schizophrenia.[25] Furthermore, evidence is beginning to emerge that stressful lifestyles may render certain individuals vulnerable to chronic fatigue syndrome.

Personality styles have also been implicated in immune-related disease, and are believed to activate changes in the autonomic nervous system and neuro-endocrine functioning. The cancer–personality theory has already been mentioned. The most well known of these theories is 'Type-A behaviour pattern' which has been independently associated with the incidence of heart disease in numerous prospective studies.[26] Classic symptoms include hurried manner and speech, eating while doing other things, impatience, and behaving in an over-assertive manner. There is, however, a paucity of well-designed longitudinal studies with any predictive power.

Behavioural outcomes

It is possible that the association between psychological appraisal and physical outcomes is mediated through behaviour. In the short term, sympathetic nervous system arousal results in the changes in behaviour which include increased arousal and alertness, increases in cognition, vigilance and focused attention, and the suppression of feeding and reproductive behaviour. If the source of stress is prolonged, however, performance-related activity will show a decline, accompanied by behavioural changes in eating, sleeping, drinking, smoking, physical activity and social functioning. These behaviours have been implicated in the onset of many disorders such as eating disorders, alcoholism, heart disease and lung cancer. Health-endangering behaviours are particularly pertinent to young people, and the form this behaviour takes may differ somewhat from the adult population. A more detailed discussion of the effects of stress on adolescent behaviour is provided in Chapter 2.

CONCLUSION

This chapter presents an overview of current understanding of the stress process. Most theoretical and empirical advances in this area pertain to the adult population. It was therefore necessary to review the adult research and models which provide a unifying framework upon which an examination of the adolescent stress process may be based. The psychological model of stress was seen as the most appropriate, given that it acknowledges the inter-action between people and their environment.

Within the psychological approach, the two major models reviewed were the transactional model and the Michigan Model. Although it is acknowledged that the former provides a richer theoretical framework and is employed extensively throughout the adolescent stress literature, the Michigan Model provides a thorough and comprehensive framework through which the occurrence and appraisal of stressful life events, psychological, physical and behavioural outcomes as well as modifying and mediating variables may be examined. Rather than looking at stress as a unidimensional variable, through appraisal or outcomes (as is often the case), this book aims to also explore the mechanisms and pathways through which change occurs.

Notes

1 Hawkins, N. G., Davies, R. and Holmes, T. H. (1957) 'Evidence of psychosocial factors in the development of pulmonary tuberculosis'. *American Review of Tuberculosis and Pulmonary Diseases*, **75**, 768–80.

2 Lazarus, R. S. and Folkman, S. (1984) *Stress, Appraisal and Coping*. New York: Springer, p. 19.

3 Ibid.

4 Although not shown here, the model is bi-directional. Note also, the parallelism between short- and long-term effects. Lazarus, *et al.*, 1985, p. 777.

5 House, J. S. (1981) *Work Stress and Social Support*. Reading, MA: Addison-Wesley, p. 37.

6 Adapted from Israel, B. A., Schurman, S. J., Hugentobler, M. K. and House, J. S. (1992) 'Case Study No. 3: A participatory action research approach to reducing occupational stress in the United States'. *Conditions of Work Digest*, 11(2), 152–63.

7 Holmes, T. H. and Masuda, M. (1974) 'Life change and illness susceptibility', in B. S. Dohrenwend and B. P. Dohrenwend (eds) *Stressful Life Events: Their Nature and Effects*. New York: Wiley.

8 Jemmot, J. B. and Locke, S. E. (1984) 'Psychosocial factors, immunologic mediation, and human susceptibility to infectious diseases: how much do we know?' *Psychological Bulletin*, 95(1), 78–108.

9 Parker, G., Brown, L. and Blignault, I. (1986) 'Coping behavior as predictors in the course of clinical depression'. *Archives of General Psychiatry*, 43, 561–5.

10 Terry, D. J. (1991) 'Stress, coping and adaptation to new parenthood'. *Journal of Personality and Social Psychology*, 8, 527–47.

11 Billings, A. G. and Moos, R. H. (1981) 'The role of coping responses and social resources in attenuating the stress of life events'. *Journal of Behavioral Medicine*, 4, 157–89.

12 Paulhus, D. L. and Christie, R. (1981). 'Spheres of control: an interactionist approach to assessment of perceived control', in H. M. Lefcourt (ed.) *Research with the Locus of Control Construct Assessment Methods*, Volume 1, pp. 161–88. New York: Academic Press.

13 Phares, E. (1976) *Locus of Control in Personality*. Morristown, NJ: General Learning Press.

14 Wallston, K. A., Wallston, B. S. and DeVellis, R. (1978) 'Development of the multi-dimensional Health Locus of Control (MHLC) scales'. *Health Education Monographs*, 6(2), 160–70.

15 Paulhus, D. L. (1983). 'Sphere-specific measures of perceived control' *Journal of Personality and Social Psychology*, 44, 1253–65.

16 Krause, N. and Stryker, S. (1984) 'Stress and well-being: the buffering role of locus of control beliefs'. *Social Science and Medicine*, 18, 783–90 (p. 788).

17 Spielberger, C. D., Gorsuch, R. L. and Lushene, R. E. (1970) *Manual for the State-Trait Anxiety Inventory*. Palo Alto, CA: Consulting Psychologists Press.

18 Eysenck, H. J. and Eysenck, S. G. B. (1975) *Manual of the Eysenck Personality Questionnaire*. San Diego: EDITS. See also Eysenck, J. J. (1991) 'Type A behaviour and coronary heart disease: the third stage', in M. J. Strube (ed) *Type A Behaviour*. Newbury Park: Sage.

19 Gregson, O. and Looker, T. (1994) 'The biological basis of stress management'. *British Journal of Guidance and Counselling*, 22(1), 13–26.

20 Tsigos, C. and Chrousos, G. P. (1996) 'Stress, endocrine manifestations, and diseases', in C. L. Cooper (ed), *Handbook of Stress, Medicine and Health*, pp. 61–85. London: CRC Press.

21 Ibid.

22 Wright, L. (1988) 'The Type A behavior pattern and coronary heart disease'. *American Psychologist*, 43, 2–14.

23 Gregson, O. and Looker, T. (1994) 'The biological basis of stress management'. *British Journal of Guidance and Counselling*, 22(1), 13–26.

24 Eysenck, H. J. (1996) 'Psychosocial stress and cancer', in A. H. Bittles and P. A. Parsons (eds) *Stress: Evolutionary, Biosocial and Clinical Perspectives*. Basingstoke: Macmillan.

25 Moore, K. A. and Burrows, G. D. (1996) 'Stress and mental health', in C. L. Cooper (ed.) *Handbook of Stress, Medicine and Health*, pp. 87–100. London: CRC Press.

26 Rosenman, R. H. (1996) 'Personality, behavior patterns and heart disease', in C. L. Cooper (ed.) *Handbook of Stress, Medicine and Health*, 217–31. London: CRC Press.

CHAPTER 2

The stress process in young people

Introduction

This chapter presents key theoretical and research findings regarding stress in young people and highlights the mechanisms through which potentially stressful events may lead to negative psychological, physical or behavioural outcomes.

What is 'adolescence'?

Definitions of adolescence

Adolescence is, for many, a confusing concept with uncertain definitions, contradictory characteristics and inconsistent behavioural patterns. Lay usage of the term 'adolescence' often refers to the teenage years from ages 13 to 19. This definition, however, belies the fact that puberty may begin at 10 or 11 years, and those remaining in higher education or living at home in their early twenties may display regressive-like confrontational or over-dependent behavioural tendencies.

Adolescence may be defined as the period of transition from childhood to maturity with universal changes in morphology, physiology and cognitive ability. It is characterized by rapid processes of change in social and psychological functioning, as well as marked physical growth. Few developmental periods with the exception of infancy feature the same degree of change on so many levels, including changes due to pubertal development, changes in emotions, values and behaviour, self-image, social role redefinitions, intellectual development, school transitions, gains in social and psychological autonomy and the emergence of sexuality. Changes which occur in these domains are interrelated and occur in most societies.

Despite sharing these common characteristics, there are wide individual variations in this stage of development which indicate the pervasive influence of social and economic factors. According to Emler (1995), the extent of these changes and the way in which they manifest is a product of the 'social ecology' within which they occur, including the 'immediate family environment, community, social structure, geography as well as political, cultural and historical context' (p. 9). In fact, it has been argued, that the emergence of 'adolescence' as a specific and distinct life phase is largely a result of cultural, political and economic developments of the twentieth century, evoked by industry and the establishment of mass compulsory education.

Theories of adolescence
Psychoanalytical theories of adolescence
Two classical theories have emerged to explain the observed developmental processes described above. The psychoanalytic approach focuses on the psychosexual development of the individual, with concurrent upsurges in instinctual behaviour, emotional upheaval and resurgence of drives. This increase in libidinal energies occurs at a time when the super-ego is striving for autonomy from parental authority. According to this view, psychic imbalance and increased vulnerability result in the employment of psychological defence mechanisms, which serve to increase psychological disengagement. Behaviours indicative of this process include mood fluctuations, inconsistent and ambivalent social behaviour, and nonconformity and antipathy towards parents. In addition, identity formation and crisis are emphasized as characteristic of this stage. The influential theories of G. Stanley Hall (1940) did much to propagate the depiction of adolescence as a time of storm and stress, conflict and confusion.

Sociological theories of adolescence
The sociological approach seeks to explain adolescent characteristics as a function of socializing forces, role conflicts and societal expectations. While acknowledging the reality of physiological developments during puberty, sociological theories propose that adolescence is an institutionalized social construct, and that over time the organization of adolescent development has changed far more radically than have the biological and psychological aspects of development. These changes have been attributed to the rise of modern capitalism and the modern welfare state, equal opportunities, changes in legislation, the extension of schooling, population patterns, improved health and living

conditions, the growth of mass media, fluctuations in international migration, changing employment opportunities, accommodation availability, entry into further education, and changing family and network patterns. These developments have resulted in a move from traditional normative patterns towards a more prolonged and increasingly individualized transition process.

Contemporary theories of adolescence

While each of these theories has contributed greatly to our understanding of psychological and social factors associated with this life phase, a shift has occurred in the way in which adolescence is conceptualized and portrayed. As a result of empirical findings, current research emphasizes transitional processes rather than stages. It also focuses on the interaction between characteristics in the young person and their social environment rather than studying these separately. A life-span developmental approach is favoured by many researchers which encompasses developmental and ecological systems within a multi-disciplinary framework. This approach represents for many a more realistic, refined representation of teenagers as active agents who shape their environments as well as being influenced by them, and accommodates dynamic, reciprocal and individualized transitions through adolescence.

It has been increasingly argued that transactional stress and coping theory may be fruitfully applied to the study of adolescent development. Robson and colleagues (1993) have suggested that the model developed by Lazarus and Folkman (discussed in Chapter 1) is the most suitable model for examining developmental issues and designing appropriate interventions.

Is adolescence important?

Contrary to traditional psychoanalytic thinking, it has been argued that adolescence is of equal significance to infancy in determining personality development in later life.[1] Coleman and Hendry write:

> For many years it has been widely believed that what happens in infancy represents the foundation stone for later personality development, and that many of the effects of the experiences of these early years are irreversible. However, it is increasingly recognised that experiences during other critical phases of development especially during adolescence, have an equally important bearing on what happens later in life. This realisation

that adjustment in adolescence has critical implications for adult development, as well as for the health of society in general has led to a new surge of interest in the adolescent years. (Coleman and Hendry, 1990, p. 2)

The decisions made in adolescence hold important and often irreversible consequences for occupational and social status in adulthood. Furthermore, there is a growing conviction that many mental health problems experienced in adulthood have their roots in adolescence. Behaviours adopted during adolescence, such as smoking, alcohol, substance use and physical activity patterns are believed to contribute greatly to the consolidation of health-endangering values, attitudes and behaviours in adulthood. According to Hamburg and Takanishi (1989), experimental behaviours such as drug use, risky driving, risk-taking sexual activity and disengagement from school carry high long-term risks. Jessor and colleagues (1990) conclude that 'among biomedical and social scientists [there is] now considerable consensus that adolescence is something of a crucible for the shaping of health in later life' (p. 25).

In addition to the longitudinal risks to which this group is vulnerable, many psychosocial disorders reach their peak during the teenage years. These include crime, suicide, depression, eating disorders and the abuse of alcohol and psychoactive drugs. Adolescence is therefore a key life stage and formative period in the life-course. Frydenberg (1997) agrees, and writes that 'adolescents are on the threshold of adulthood and, as a result, the ways in which they cope establish the patterns for the future and impact on the community at large' (p. 2).

Stress in young people
Is adolescence naturally a time of 'storm and stress'?

Human life is a continuous thread which each of us spins to his own pattern, rich and complex in meaning. There are no natural knots in it. Yet knots form, nearly always in adolescence.
Edgar Z. Frydenberg.

To be normal during the adolescent period is by itself abnormal.
Anna Freud.

As discussed above, 'storm and stress' characterized the prevailing view of adolescence for some time. Siddique and D'Arcy write:

> In a rather rare agreement, both popular notions and academic thinking consider adolescence as a time of major changes in all areas of functioning. Adolescence is said to involve dramatic transitions in the physical, social, sexual and intellectual spheres and transitions of this order must be stressful. (Siddique and D'Arcy, 1984, p. 460).

These authors cite recent research which indicates a greater prevalence of minor psychiatric morbidity among adolescents than among children and adults. Other researchers attribute this view to inappropriate generalizations made from clinical observations, and point to the largely successful adjustment made by the majority of adolescents.

Although most adolescents traverse the period without major difficulties, 10 to 20 per cent of adolescents do manifest severe emotional disturbance.[2] This figure, however, is approximately the same as that found in the adult population.[3] In general, the inevitability of 'storm and stress' has been replaced with a view which emphasizes diversity and the potential for constructive adaptation, while acknowledging that a significant minority do experience distress and turmoil.

Increase in adolescent stress literature

During the past ten to fifteen years there has been a dramatic increase in the academic attention devoted to adolescence. In particular, developmental and clinical psychologists have become increasingly aware of the importance and value of studying stress and coping mechanisms in teenagers. Although still representing a fraction of total research on stress and coping, adolescent stress research has made much progress in unravelling the relationship between stressful events and symptoms in young people. Although earlier research tended to focus on clinical cases, examining events with low incidence and using self-report and cross-sectional designs, recent research increasingly employs prospective studies with larger samples from the non-clinical population.

Is stress increasing for young people?

Many researchers believe, given the results which have emerged from the research findings of the last two decades, that today's adolescents are experiencing more distress than previous generations.[4] According to Heaven (1996), it has become 'widely accepted that teenagers and even children face stressful events that have the potential to severely disrupt their lives and negatively affect their psychological adjustment and health' (p. 44). Raised concerns regarding the well-being of young people are reflected in statements such as that of the Carnegie Council

(1989), who report that in the US alone, 'the future of about 7 million youth – 1 in 4 adolescents – is in serious jeopardy'. In the UK, the NSPCC has reported an alarming increase in the number of calls it receives from adolescents seeking help. Between 1980 and 1993, the incidence of symptoms of psychological distress and anxiety in late adolescence demonstrated dramatic increases[5] together with other stress-related problems including eating disorders and depression.[6]

Illness and mortality have decreased in all populations except the 10- to 25-year age group where an increase has been documented.[7] A rise in adolescent suicide is also in evidence.[8]

The three primary causes of mortality during adolescence are:

- accidents
- homicide
- suicide

Other causes of death include alcohol and drug abuse, sexually transmitted diseases and malnutrition. Observable outcomes of the increase in adolescent distress are seen in the rise of physical disease and psychiatric disturbance.[9] Millstein (1989) points out that 'in contrast to mortality among children and adults, the causes of adolescent mortality are not diseases, but are primarily related to preventable social, environmental, and behavioural factors' (p. 837). Between early and late adolescence, mortality rates increase by more than 200 per cent, mortality due to motor vehicle accidents by almost 400 per cent, homicide rates by over 400 per cent, and suicide rates by 600 per cent.

Why is stress increasing for young people?

Traditional theories of adolescence, even those which assume that this transition will be marked by turmoil, fail to account for the documented increase in adolescent symptoms of distress. Hamburg and Takanishi (1989) suggest that the adjustment required by rapid changes in the physiological, biochemical and neuroendocrine systems may be exacerbated by historically recent events. These, they argue, 'have drastically changed the experience of adolescence, in some ways making it more difficult than ever before' (p. 825). Although all social changes have not been for the worse for young people, several societal developments of possible aetiological significance to these changes have already been mentioned. Others may include changes in legislation, the growth of a mass youth consumer market and growth of youth cultures, earlier onset of puberty, earlier sexual initiation and later completion of education, increases in female employment, changes in moral concepts and values, instability within family units and the changing constellations of family networks.

In particular, the alleged 'atomization' of family life has been heavily implicated in the manifestation of adolescent distress, through the removal of normative frameworks which serve to guide social action. Some evidence for this appears in statistics provided by the NSPCC, which show that 30 per cent of calls received cited marital discord as the primary cause of distress.[10]

It has also been argued that reported increases in strain are the result of the increasingly individualized nature of adolescent transitions, which remove from young people their social status, social orientation and sense of identity. Hamburg and Takanishi (1989) attribute rises in distress to the lengthening period of adolescence (resulting in increases in adolescent uncertainty), the disjunction between biological and social development (allowing young adolescents to make fateful decisions which affect their lives when they are still cognitively immature and lack sufficient experience), the absence of adult role models (depriving young people of sufficient assistance), the erosion of family and social support networks (which leads to the absence of support during stressful periods), and increasingly easy access to potentially life-threatening activities (including sexual behaviour, alcohol, drugs, smoking, vehicles and weapons). For some authors, the answer lies in the failure of our educational and training environments to adequately provide for the changing needs of young people.

SUMMARY

Contemporary theories of adolescence refute the inevitability of emotional turmoil during the teenage years, and refer instead to natural but resolvable conflicts which only a minority of adolescents fail to manage successfully.

There is, however, evidence that today's adolescents are experiencing higher levels of psychological distress and disorder. Various explanations for these increases have been propounded. In order to gain a clearer picture of the causes and consequences of adolescent stress a thorough examination of component aspects of the stress process is necessary. This chapter examines normative and non-normative stressors, moderating variables such as social support, perceived control, gender, age and socioeconomic variables, together with psychological, physical and behavioural outcomes. The overall aim of this review is to highlight potential risk factors which could be targeted within intervention programmes.

Sources of stress for young people

Advances made in the adult literature connecting stressors to physical illness have stimulated similar research into adolescent stress. Recent research has found support for a relationship between major life stress and depression and suicide, decreased levels of self-esteem, antisocial behaviour and poor school performance.[11] In summary, the growing body of evidence supports the causative role of life stressors and social resources in adolescent functioning. While this section looks at tangible sources of adolescent stress, it is important to note that anxiety may arise in adolescents due to general fears and abstract concerns.

There have been numerous attempts to classify the range of stressful events which adolescents may encounter. The resulting categories may represent the domain in which the stressor occurs or the relative frequency with which it occurs. Examples of the former include Frydenberg's (1997) finding that student concerns fall into three categories, namely achievement (success in examinations, finding a good job and finding a suitable partner), relationships (including family and peers), and altruistic issues (such as nuclear war, poverty in the Third World and issues relating to sexual equality). Seiffge-Krenke and Shulman (1993) describe adolescent stressors as comprising developmental tasks, normative demands and critical life events. Gore and colleagues (1992) identify the five main classes of adolescent stressors as direct to self, direct to family, direct to friends, between self and friends, and between self and family.

A second and more consensual method is the classification of events in terms of their frequency and severity. Stressors are hereby categorized as normative, non-normative and daily stressors. Normative stressors comprise generic developmental challenges which all adolescents encounter. These include physical changes, school transitions, emerging sexuality in oneself and one's peers, changing peer relations and negotiations with parents. Non-normative stressors represent unexpected demanding events which may exacerbate the transitional experience. These may include parental divorce, family deaths, parental mental illness, bullying or physical disability. Finally, daily hassles represent irritating minor events which, when accumulated, have been shown to be strong predictors of psychological symptoms.

Common sources of stress

In a large survey of adolescents, Frydenberg (1997) found that normative student stressors concerned appearance, school grades, employment, relationships, vocational and educational plans, personal health, self-esteem, parents' physical and mental health, dating and sexual relationships. In fact many of the challenges which adolescents face are an inherent part of the adolescent transition, including social (transitions to new schools and the formation of friendships), cognitive (acquiring the ability to think abstractly) and physical (neuroendocrine and biological) change. It has been suggested that many normative stressors, including school and relationship stress and concerns regarding the future and self-identity, peak during early adolescence.

Developmental tasks

Developmental tasks were previously conceptualized as imperative tasks, the resolution of which was necessary for progression to the next developmental stage. They are now viewed as ongoing challenges and hurdles, or 'normal crises' arising from social and biological changes which prepare the adolescent for adulthood. Young people must adapt to changes in schools and possibly residence, changing body status, increasing separation from family, increasing peer contact, changes in financial responsibilities and academic expectations, and shifting values, personal norms and perceptions of identity.

According to Chisholm and Hurrelmann (1995), stress-related symptoms may be a signal of biosocial tension arising from the overloading of personal and social developmental tasks. Advanced sexual development which occurs prior to economic independence and psychological autonomy may also prove challenging for the adolescent. In an interesting theory put forward by Coleman (1995) known as 'focal theory', it is suggested that adolescents may be naturally adept at pacing the timing of these tasks, thus enabling adjustment to take place before new challenges are confronted. Following stressful events and normative transitions, developmental tasks may include discerning the meaning and importance of the event, problem-solving, maintaining positive relationships with family and peers, and preserving emotional balance, self-image and feelings of competence.

Puberty

The mean age at which menarche is experienced has decreased from 16 to 13 years during the twentieth century and boys now experience their 'voices breaking' on average at 14 rather than 18 years old. This has been attributed to improvements in the nutritional status of adolescents. Puberty is important for several reasons. First, enormous physiological changes occur. Second, individual variation may have significant psychological consequences for those who are early or late in experiencing puberty. Third, integral aspects of psychological well-being, such as self-esteem and self-concept, are deeply influenced by physical maturation. Physical changes during this time are not only sexual by nature, but also occur in cardiovascular and respiratory activity, muscle size and physical strength. It has been suggested that body changes occurring in puberty may prove more stressful for girls than for boys, with boys tending to exhibit a more positive body image. Furthermore, ongoing aspects of family functioning may impact the onset and development of pubertal change.

Transitions

Transitions presuppose vulnerability at any age and the progression from childhood to adulthood includes multiple developmental transitions. These transitions may be biological, social or psychological by nature, and can be perplexing and disquieting for many teenagers. School transitions may be particularly stressful due to tangible discrepancies between the relative security of the primary school and the more anonymous, detached atmosphere of the secondary school. Recently, the changing and increasingly varied nature of contemporary adolescent transitions has received much attention. It is argued that as transitions become decreasingly normalized, their successful negotiation becomes more difficult. Changes in the structure of education, the family and the labour market have been most heavily implicated in this process.

Relationships
Family

> When I was a boy of 14, my father was so ignorant I could hardly stand to have the old man around. But when I got to be 21, I was astonished at how much the old man had learned in seven years.
> Mark Twain.

The pervasive influence of the family on adolescent psychological and physical development has received much empirical support. Family stressors have been reported to exert a stronger negative impact on adolescent health than school or peer-related stressors. As already mentioned, its impact may even extend to pubertal processes by shaping adolescent responses to stress and behavioural patterns. In recent decades family structures have undergone fundamental changes due to social and economic developments. Within the nuclear family, traditional research assumed that conflict would occur and this was attributed to the so-called 'generation gap'. Recent research has, however, failed to find evidence to support the inevitable development of rifts between parents and adolescents.

I am not young enough to know everything.
Oscar Wilde.

Although familial relations vary depending on cultural background, adult behaviour, age and social class, conflicts, when they occur, usually concern relatively trivial issues. These may include conflicts over chores, relationships, activities, personality, homework, bedtime, curfews and appearance. Despite the superficiality of many arguments, minor disagreements can prove stressful for adolescents and parents alike, and may escalate into more serious conflicts. The transition from early to late adolescence may witness a growing resentment of parental restrictions and rules, particularly in boys. The rigid adherence of family members to certain beliefs may incite anger and frustration in adolescents who are seeking increased psychological and physical autonomy.

Furthermore, parental reports of perceived stress and their own psychological symptoms have been shown to influence behavioural and emotional adjustment in adolescents. Interestingly, this association appears to be more significant for paternal symptoms. This has been attributed to the lower frequency and thus potentially higher saliency of paternal symptoms, which may carry more negative implications than maternal symptoms. Distress arising from family relationships has been implicated in the aetiology of several disorders, including anorexia nervosa.[12]

Peers

When I look back on those years when I was neither fish nor flesh, between the ages of 16 and 22, I remember them as an uncomfortable time, and sometimes a very unhappy one. Now . . . I may at last be allowed to say: Oh dear, Oh dear, how horrid it was being young, and how nice it is being old and not having to mind what people think.
Gwen Raverat, Period Piece.

Adolescent peer groups are highly influential in determining the sources and outcomes of stressful life events for young people. Although providing social support, peer relations may also prove stressful, particularly, it appears, for young girls. Cliques emerging in early adolescence tend towards exclusion and social prejudice, and great importance is placed on issues of loyalty, confidentiality, trust and generosity. Lapses in these prerequisites may disqualify the young adolescent from the clique, causing much distress and potential alienation. Coleman (1995) describes the peer group as the source of 'a wide range of potential conflicts in values and ideals' (p. 26). With the decline of the stable family unit, adolescents may turn increasingly to the peer group as a means of support and emotional stability.

Compared to earlier friendships, adolescent relations are characterized by increased intimacy, reciprocal exchange of thoughts and feelings and shared activities. With regard to adolescent stress, the relative impact of peer and family stressors is the cause of some debate. According to Coleman's (1961) book *The Adolescent Society*, pressure from peers constitutes the main source of adolescent distress and maladaptive coping. The findings cited above, however, indicate that family stressors may be potentially more distressing to adolescents.

School
Feeling unhappy at school can cause significant stress to young people as well as having important consequences for their prospects for personal and career development. There is now impressive evidence for the power of school stress to affect adolescent psychological growth and health. School stressors have been found to include concerns over grades, teachers, homework, comprehension, isolation and general worries about the future. More specifically, they may include unclear lessons, impatient teachers, class tests, public examination on comprehension, fear of loss of friends, public criticism by teacher or classmates, unjustified suspicions, work overload, needless rules and peer pressure. Girls frequently cite more school stressors than boys, but these often decrease between the ages of 16 to 18 to a level comparable with boys.

Furthermore, parental pressure towards scholastic achievement may combine with certain pressures generated by the school environment itself. Many characteristics of the secondary school may prove distressing including increased academic demands, pressure to fit in with peer groups and to form friendships, reductions in status, heightened possibility of the occurrence of bullying (see Chapter 8), more formal and possibly less positive relations with multiple teachers, loosened structure and guidance, possible reductions in discipline and increased exposure to sexual activity. Separation from parents and the introduction to mixed-sex schooling are other factors which may prove challenging to the young adolescent. In addition, second level may bring a decreased emphasis on higher-level thinking skills at a time when cognitive development requires more complex and interactive academic tasks.

These pressures may produce negative psychological outcomes in adolescents with low self-efficacy, and impact self-esteem, motivation and achievement. The consequences of unsupportive school environments have been conceptualized within the person—environment fit theory as an organizational failure on the part of the school to appropriately match the growing needs of adolescents and to afford them the necessary opportunities. This theory predicts that declines in adolescent motivation, interest, performance and behaviour will result from this mismatch.

As well as contributing to individual strain, failure at school is likely to exacerbate relations between young people and their parents and cause considerable tension at home. According to Hurrelmann *et al.* (1992), 'poor school performance may constitute a source of considerable tension that can interfere with satisfactory relations between adolescents and their parents' (p. 48). Furthermore, it has been suggested that the increasing tendency towards testing in schools, with its specification of standards at different levels, constitutes an additional school stressor. This may, according to some researchers, produce stress responses in adolescents not previously thought to be 'at risk'.[13] Competition for tertiary places together with a rise in the number of young people staying on at school due to declining employment opportunities can produce more pressure on adolescents to compete with peers and achieve at school. The stakes for academic failure are higher than before, and doubts concerning ability to attain career goals can generate substantial distress.

Exams
Alarming rates of adolescent distress have been recorded associated solely with approaching exams. The rise in educational qualifications necessary to enter third-level institutions and the work place (credential inflation) is well documented. It is not surprising then, that increasing numbers of young people are displaying stress symptoms in response to increased pressure to achieve. Furthermore, adolescent exam anxieties may be compounded by parental worries concerning the reproduction of the social status of their family.

In addition to the manifestation of symptoms before and after exams, positive relationships have been found between academic failure and psychosocial disorder, antisocial behaviour and conduct disorder. Exams may constitute significant elements of other environmental stressors, in the preparation required, confrontation with the event, and coping with unpredictable and sometimes negative consequences. Thus, the way in which adolescents confront exam stress may in turn influence the way in which they respond to stress in other domains in their lives.

Sexuality

As children move into the adolescent years, sexual relations become more salient and contribute to increased levels of vulnerability within the sexual domain. According to some researchers, the way in which adolescents come to terms with their sexuality is one of life's most important developmental tasks. Early theories of adolescence viewed stress and conflict as natural responses to the emergence of sexual impulses and physical changes within the body. Findings from cross-cultural studies have demonstrated considerable variation in responses to sexual development. This undermines the view that stress is an inherent feature of sexual development, and suggests that societal norms, restrictions and expectations contribute greatly to the experience of emerging sexuality. Adolescent anxieties concerning sexual development may be exacerbated by cultural norms and media images of models with prepubescent figures together with promiscuous story-lines.

There is evidence to suggest that adolescents are becoming sexually active at an increasingly younger age.[14] Furthermore, it is believed that a significant percentage of young people engage in sexual activities against their will. A study by Erickson and Rapkin (1991) found that 15 per cent of adolescents, mostly female, had undergone unwanted sexual experiences. This may prove a formidable source of stress for individuals of this age. Intolerant or religious attitudes towards auto-erotic or homosexual behaviour by family and society may also prove stressful to teenagers.

Further sources of stress
Divorce

Non-normative stressors are described as unexpected or unusual stressful events, and include the experience of family disruption, divorce and marital separation. Given the rising divorce rates in Europe and the US, it may be inappropriate to classify divorce as a non-normative event. At present, the UK has the highest divorce rate in

Europe with one in three marriages ending in divorce. There has been extensive literature associating parental divorce with negative mental health outcomes in young people.[15] Zill *et al.* (1993) reported that children with divorced parents were twice as likely to use psychological services as children from two-parent homes. Adolescent children from divorced lone-mother families and in stepfamilies score consistently lower on indices of adaptive behaviour, competence and education. Children from divorced families are also more likely to suffer from psychiatric illness,[16] problem behaviour and delinquency,[17] anxiety, depression, hyperactivity, dependency and inattention[18] and low educational attainment.[19]

There are two points, however, which are important to note with regard to these findings. First, in most studies parental conflict is compounded with divorce outcome. Psychosocial risks associated with divorce can result from parental tensions and conflicts rather than the separation itself.[20] Second, it has been suggested that rather than treating divorce as a single, discrete event, the stages which ensue in the aftermath of the event contribute more directly to psychological adjustment in adolescents.[21] These may include familial tension, changes in residence and school, adjusting to a new step-parent and step-siblings, potential changes in financial status, separation from friends and the possibility of alienating custodial disputes.

Prior to divorce, children whose parents have divorced have been found to score lower on a range of psychological measures compared with children whose parents remained married.[22] This indicates that factors other than divorce may also be responsible for the negative outcomes so often cited in the literature. These may include parental conflict, social class and age at time of parental breakup, and reiterates the need to view marital breakdown as a multi-dimensional and complex process. Other factors such as lost contact with extended family may contribute to adolescent distress following a divorce.[23]

Parental characteristics

The role of parental characteristics in adolescent stress has received much attention. In one study, suicide was shown to be directly related to the level of parental absence and abusiveness.[24] Similarly, Schaffer (1974) lists among the correlates of suicide changes within the nuclear family, parental death, discord and divorce. Other risk factors for adolescents include child abuse, local authority care, paternal criminal record, low level of parental education,[25] family disorganization, poverty and parental drinking.[26]

Unemployment

Many researchers agree that increases in youth unemployment represent a powerful source of stress for young people. In 1997, youth unemployment affected nearly three million young people in Britain. Although youth unemployment is not as high as it was in the mid-1980s, Chisholm and Hurrelmann (1995) suggest that this decade endowed a legacy of anxiety and uncertainty for those growing up in the 1990s. As mentioned above, uncertainty regarding future work situations may act as a stressor for school students. Falling cohort sizes and an improved economy in many Western countries have alleviated the problem to some degree, but for a marked percentage of the population unemployment continues to be a real threat. The young unemployed face marginalization and economic disadvantage.

Through the deprivation of employment, one is denied access to an opportunity structure which in turn affords access to status, respect, income and power. Thus, young people who fail to find employment may become disaffected, frustrated and angry against the society which has obstructed this access. Research has shown that failure to secure employment constitutes a major concern among 15-year-olds. Furthermore, a link has been demonstrated between youth unemployment and poor psychological adjustment and social isolation. Following numerous studies investigating this subject, Donovan *et al.* (1986) conclude that unemployment may have far-reaching effects on the social and psychological development of the young adult due to the inextricable link between occupation and identity in modern society. The unemployed school-leaver is denied the opportunity to establish an occupational identity, gain social contacts, become financially secure and confident in his or her ability and often to obtain his or her own home.

Difficulty in finding a first job may exacerbate the process of identity formation, increasing the possibility of negative outcomes and hampering the cultivation of positive self-esteem. It has also been suggested that prolonged parental dependence may render the establishment of long-term relationships more difficult.

There is evidence to suggest that personal beliefs, the availability of social support and a constructive societal response may moderate the influence of unemployment on individual outcomes. However, there is supportive evidence in the literature to indicate that foreseen or actual difficulties in obtaining work may produce psychological strain in school students and school-leavers.

Social context

Non-normative stressors may also include more general attributes and consequences of the macro-environment of which the adolescent is a part. These may include minority group membership, social class status, having unemployed parents, poverty, disruption of the neighbourhood, moving to a new neighbourhood and racial prejudice. Many of these impact the developing adolescent through ongoing strain or chronic stress.

Daily hassles

There is growing recognition within adolescent psychology of the importance of everyday stressors in the aetiology of psychological and physical disorders. These have been described as irritating, frustrating, distressing demands that to some degree characterize everyday transactions. It is believed that persistent, daily stressors may contribute to adjustment problems in youth if they are experienced in a cumulative manner. These may include parent–adolescent disagreements, academic, parental and peer pressure, career and education goals, dating worries or financial concerns. Daily stress appears to represent a more powerful predictor of psychological and somatic symptoms in adolescents than life events.

Furthermore, in a review of the evidence, it was found that ongoing hassles within the family, school and peer relationships correlate highly with depression, anxiety and behavioural dysfunction in young people.27 Daily hassles appear to exert a greater influence on feelings of strain than do life events. Sociologically, chronic stressors are linked to negative life events by the restructuring of ongoing life conditions which they initiate and maintain. The experience of poverty, for example, may originate in a single event but will impact the well-being of the adolescent in an ongoing, varied and pervasive manner. The experience of boredom at school and in leisure time can also be a key cause of psychological unrest and malaise among adolescents.

The importance of timing

An important factor in the way in which life events affect coping and outcomes is how their occurrence coincides with other salient events in the lives of young people. Research suggests that young people who encounter several significant events simultaneously will experience greater levels of distress. The cumulative effects of such events as school change, pubertal development, dating, neighbourhood change and family disruption have been shown to have maladaptive outcomes in young people. These include lower grades and self-esteem and a decrease in extracurricular participation.

Furthermore, if the timing of the initial occurrence of the event departs significantly from the norm, as in early or late menarche, negative consequences may ensue. The impact of non-normative pubertal development may, however, differ significantly according to gender. Evidence suggests that, relative to girls who mature at a normative age, early maturing girls exhibit lower self-esteem, lower self-confidence, have a poorer body image and are more likely to develop eating problems, experience conflictual relations with their parents and become frequent users of alcohol and cigarettes.[28] Early maturing boys, on the other hand, appear to develop more confidence than their peers and report feeling more attractive and 'sporty'.[29]

The withdrawal of social support, which often accompanies divergence from the social norm, may be heavily implicated in the development of maladapted outcomes. Others have attributed negative outcomes to an over-dependency on friends which early maturing girls tend to develop. It is argued that these intense and often conflicting relationships may undermine perceptions of self-efficacy and competence. Furthermore, pubertal status of female adolescents at the time of transition to secondary school has demonstrated clear associations with subsequent psychological and academic adjustment. This has been attributed to the failure of the secondary school to meet the heightened needs of mature adolescents for input and opportunity.

Coping and adaptation

Rising figures for teenage stress, for many researchers, represent problems in coping on a grand scale. Together with other important social and personal resources, access to adaptive coping skills often determines whether exposure to stressful events manifests in positive psychological or behavioural outcomes. It is essential that we try to understand the factors that determine the young person's choice of coping strategy as this has crucial implications for his or her outcome. For example, why are young women more likely to seek support from others, while males choose distraction? This section discusses different ways adolescents may choose to respond to stressful events in their lives, and explores the relationship between their choice of coping strategy and their ultimate well-being.

Research has indicated that certain coping skills are particularly constructive when used in particular situations (e.g. problem-solving, talking to others, cognitive restructuring and so on). This section forms the basis for Part 2 of the book in which those coping strategies which have been shown to be adaptive are discussed in more detail, with specific reference to teaching these skills within intervention programmes.

Theories of adolescent coping

The declining adherence to the 'storm and stress' model of adolescence has contributed to a theoretical shift from adolescent crisis to adolescent coping. Adolescent coping has been described as the 'flexible orchestration of cognitive, social, and behavioral skills in dealing with situations that contain elements of ambiguity, unpredictability, and stress'.[30] Many of the current methodologies and issues concerning adolescent coping are based on theoretical and research findings from within adult coping research outlined in Chapter 1. Studies have supported the utility of the adult stress and coping paradigm in adolescent research, showing significant relationships between coping and adjustment indices.

In the past two decades, the importance of coping in adolescence has also been established through resiliency research, which has linked positive adjustment to successful coping with developmental challenges. According to Olbrich (1990): 'how [young] people cope with stress is more important for their adaptation, their health and their development, than is the stressful impact itself' (p. 40).

The success of adolescent coping is also important due to the high-risk status of this age group, with their intense energy combined with minimal experience. Coping styles which emerge in adolescence appear to have far-reaching consequences, but empirical investigations into the long-term effects of coping are somewhat rare. The majority of studies on adolescent coping have focused on actual stressful events. However, it is important to note that the emergence of anticipatory anxiety in adolescence may challenge coping efforts, as this is less amenable to constructive coping and relies on the development of cognitive and emotional strategies often emerging at a later age.

For some researchers, there is evidence to suggest that successful coping is no longer an 'inherent capacity' for many young people (e.g. Allen and Hiebert, 1991; Phelps and Jarvis, 1994; Frydenberg, 1997). There has been a documented rise in severe depression and suicide,[31] underachievement, bullying, eating disorders, drug abuse, vandalism and hopelessness concerning the future in the current generation of young people.[32] These statistics indicate large-scale problems in coping in this age group. The transactional model of coping provided by Lazarus and Folkman (1984) has achieved most consensus in the adolescent literature.

Measuring adolescent coping

A large proportion of early research on adolescent coping focused on small, homogeneous groups of adolescents coping with acute events and serious illness. More recent research has examined the way in which young people cope with normative and ongoing developmental challenges. Growing interest in normative stressors and coping has necessitated the development of more appropriate multi-dimensional coping instruments, which have increased in recent years. Questionnaires are the most well-researched measuring technique (but see Knapp *et al.*, (1991) for a review of projective, observation and interview techniques).

Measures may be distinguished by their emphasis on situational or trait-based coping. Much of the adult literature and some adolescent research indicates that the former approach may be more appropriate for coping measurement. There is, however, evidence to suggest that within the adolescent population, trait-based coping is likely to predominate. Frydenberg (1997), while favouring a situational approach, writes that 'adolescents have an underlying pattern of coping responses that are utilised for all concerns' (p. 39). Other researchers have also found stability in adolescent coping styles across varying situations.

Classifying adolescent coping

Corresponding to developments in the adult literature, the original categorization of coping responses as emotion- or problem-focused has been extended to include a broader range of coping categories. Frydenberg and Lewis (1993b), for instance, have identified eighteen coping strategies employed by adolescents. These include: seeking social support, problem-solving, working harder, worrying, investing in close friendships, seeking to belong, wishful thinking, social action, tension reduction, not coping, ignoring the problem, blaming oneself, keeping to oneself, seeking spiritual support, focusing on the positive, seeking professional help, seeking relaxing diversions and physical recreation. According to Frydenberg and Lewis, these may be grouped more parsimoniously as:

- problem-solving
- non-productive coping
- reference to others

Three main modes of coping have been identified by Seiffge-Krenke (1993a); namely, active coping, internal coping and withdrawal. The results of research by Patterson and McCubbin (1987) produced twelve categories of coping, including: ventilating feelings, seeking diversions, developing self-reliance and optimism, developing social support, solving family problems, avoiding problems, seeking spiritual support, investing in close friends, seeking professional support, engaging in a demanding activity, being humorous and relaxing. These can be categorized as problem-focused coping, appraisal-focused coping and emotion-focused coping.

While categorization provides a useful heuristic guide to assist the measurement of adolescent coping, there is an acknowledged overlap between strategies employed with adolescents likely to use both problem- and emotion-focused coping in a range of stressful situations.

Age differences in coping
The study of age differences in adolescent coping is relatively rare in comparison to gender differences, but existing research does suggest that age moderates choice of coping strategy. The emergence of formal operations enables adolescents to empathize, predict consequences and view alternative perspectives, and may affect coping. Logical analysis and positive reappraisal are increasingly evident in older adolescents, as are self-blame and tension-reducing techniques. Emotion-focused coping has been found to increase with age while functional coping decreases. Some studies, however, have failed to achieve consistent evidence for the increase in emotion-focused coping with age. Willingness to compromise appears to develop in later adolescence.

Studies have also indicated a wider repertoire of coping strategies in older adolescents when compared to younger ones. Research by Allen and Hiebert (1991) found fewer coping resources and lower coping effectiveness in adolescents compared to adult norms. Some researchers have argued that differential use of coping strategies occurs due to the changing nature of stressors experienced through the life span rather than developmental change. Much of the existing evidence, however, supports the existence of developmental differences in coping styles.

Gender differences in coping
Differential rates of depression, anxiety and well-being which emerge in adolescence between boys and girls have been largely attributed to gender differences in coping styles. Young women consistently report higher rates of depression and anxiety and poorer perceptions of well-being.[33] An established finding is the propensity for female adolescents to seek peer and institutional social support at times of stress. Emotion

venting or catharsis, acceptance, religion and positive reinterpretation, together with wishful thinking and consumptive habits, such as shopping and eating, have been indicated as more frequently used coping strategies in young women. Female adolescents have also been shown to employ a wider use of coping strategies, both active and avoidant.

Male adolescents have been found to show a stronger preference for using humour, alcohol and drugs, sporting activities, hobbies and diversions as coping strategies. Male adolescents are also more likely to present themselves as stable and hard to irritate.

Higher rates of depression in females have been attributed to the emotional attentiveness they give to their depressed state (rumination), which triggers negative memories, self-evaluations and explanations for current events. Affiliative behaviour in females may also heighten vulnerability to depression, as events which are stressful for family and friends ('network events') may in turn become personal stressors. Gendered socialization patterns and structural influences on sources of stress may also contribute to the development of different coping styles in males and females. Male coping strategies which tend towards distraction and alcohol use may in turn be associated with higher rates of aggression, alcoholism and substance abuse. Hormonal factors may also contribute to higher rates of reported depression in women.

Much of the above research has been dismissed as flawed and biased conjecture. Using a student daily report form, Hamilton and Fagot (1988) failed to find significant gender differences in coping, concluding that 'the apparent instrumental–expressive dichotomy suggested by earlier studies may be due, in part, to differential recall of female-specific events using retrospective methods' (p. 822). Frydenberg and Lewis (1991) also found gender differences only for closed data (multiple choice), with open-ended data displaying 'remarkable similarity in the relative use of different coping strategies by boys and girls' (p. 131).

Cultural differences in coping

In an integrative review of adolescent coping, Rosella (1994) found that 'much of the research did not report or possibly consider the social and economic situations when identifying coping behaviours' (p. 486). Most of the studies examined in this review focused on white, middle-class, suburban or rural schools rather than inner cities. Rosella asserts that by ignoring race, 'a social and human division, [which] surpasses all others, even gender, in intensity and subordination' (p. 487), insights into the shared coping repertoire of different populations will continue to elude researchers.

Those studies which have explored ethnicity have largely found support for its influence on coping. Minority group membership increases the likelihood of experiencing poverty, unemployment, underemployment, racial discrimination, language barriers and migrant status. Adolescence is a particularly vulnerable time for minority group members, as identification shifts from the family to the peer group. Cultural values and beliefs may also influence coping efforts during adolescence.

Coping and adjustment

Despite the relative lack of standardized data concerning adolescent adjustment, findings have emerged which demonstrate a clear link between adolescent coping styles and adaptation outcomes. Avoidant coping has been associated with depression, physical symptoms and social incompetence. Although not differing in their use of approach coping, depressed adolescents and those with conduct disorder have been found to employ a greater use of avoidant coping strategies, including ventilating feelings, resigned acceptance and distraction. Similarly, in a study by Seiffge-Krenke (1993a), adolescents in a clinical sample reported using higher rates of dysfunctional coping, such as withdrawal, than those in a non-clinical sample. An over-reliance on avoidance strategies may itself become a source of stress for adolescents (e.g. drug abuse). Emotion-focused coping has been found to predict poor adaptation to general stress and exam stress in particular.[34]

The documented use of withdrawal and defence strategies in adolescent clinical populations may, according to Olbrich (1990), represent *underdeveloped* coping potential rather than qualitative differences in the coping styles of these individuals. Although the association between positive adolescent adjustment and problem-solving has received much support, there is some evidence to suggest that instrumental and expressive coping are unrelated to psychological outcomes. Timko *et al.* (1993), for example, failed to find a predictive relationship between approach coping and chronic stressors.

Coping strategies may have differential protective effects depending on gender. For example, 'being humorous' and 'ventilating feelings' have been shown to have protective effects for girls against depression and anxiety, while the former alone showed protective effects for boys.[35] In addition, turning to religion and friends appears to be predictive of good adaptation in girls but poorer adaptation in boys.[36] Furthermore, the effectiveness of a chosen strategy may be largely determined by the controllability of the stressful situation and other contextual factors. Access to stable resources such as family support appears to facilitate approach coping, such as problem-solving and seeking social support. Exploring the individual and contextual variables which affect adolescent coping styles and strategies is essential in order to identify those young people who are at greatest risk.

Moderating factors

Investigations into the complex relationship between stress and illness have resulted in a heightened interest in the individual and social differences which moderate this relationship, producing vulnerability or resilience to disorders. Mitigating factors which have been explored in adolescent research include social support, perceptions of control, gender, age and cultural differences. Risk and resiliency is also a major field of exploration.

Risk and resilience

Resiliency factors may be described as personal and social resources in young people which enable them to cope with stress in a constructive manner, even in adverse conditions. Psychosocial vulnerability changes throughout the life-course with protective and risk factors tending to cluster; that is, some adolescents are exposed to many protective/risk factors and others to very few. Personal resources may include interpersonal and coping strategies, while social resources include formal and informal networks. Inherent in resiliency research is the assumption that through identifying and promoting constructive profiles, adolescents may be supported in their transitions to adulthood. With its roots in epidemiology and medicine, resiliency research seeks to identify the mechanisms and processes through which physiological, psychological and behavioural variables contribute to resiliency.

Protective factors

Thus far, empirically derived protective factors include stable care, problem-solving abilities, attractiveness to peers and adults, competence and perceived efficacy, identification with competent role models, planfulness and aspirations,[37] the development of self-esteem, scope and range of available opportunities, environmental structure and control, patterning of stresses, compensating experiences, the acqusition of coping skills (or percentage approach coping) and the availability of personal bonds and intimate relationships.[38] In general, low anxiety and high self-worth are associated with more efficacious coping responses and competence in resolving stressful situations.

Risk factors

Risk factors include having a schizophrenic parent, low birth weight, low socioeconomic status, minority group membership, disorganized family background, prematurity, poor nutritional status, physical handicap, organic brain damage and having a young, unmarried, poor mother.[39] In other words, if the preconditions for self-efficacious and self-regulated behaviour are lacking, problem behaviour is more likely to develop. Adolescents at risk are more likely to experience chronic school failure, come from abusive or neglectful families, be vulnerable to peer pressure and adopt a bravado attitude to risky behaviours which are often deemed acceptable by parents. In general, high levels of emotionality and low sociability have been linked to long-term difficulties.

Specific risk factors for depressive symptoms in adolescents include gender, socioeconomic status and the unavailability of internal and external resources. The reliance on broad variables evident in early studies of risk, such as single parenting and socioeconomic background, has been replaced with more complex, ambitious and nuanced research aiming to account for the high rates of recorded individual differences in outcome development. Some researchers, however, continue to attribute risk and resiliency to the broad sociodemographic indices of age, gender, and social and economic class. These variables are discussed below, following a brief review of findings concerning the moderating influences of social support and locus of control.

Social support

Social support has been highlighted as a key protective mechanism in adolescence and may constitute parent, sibling, extended family, school, friend and boy/girlfriend resources. Family support may act as a buffer against stresses experienced in school and with peers, while peer support mitigates the depressive consequences of family stress.

There is evidence that a direct link exists between adolescent depressed mood and poor communication with parents, together with the absence of family stability and cohesion. Evidence also exists for the positive effects of family and social resources on reducing depression and increasing self-confidence, enhancing self-esteem, shaping coping behaviour and in contributing to general resiliency in children and young people.

An exploration of the mechanisms through which social support exerts its protective influence has revealed the following: social resources bolster mastery, involve the direct help and advice of family and friends in coping with stressors, may contribute to the avoidance or reduction of potential stressors, provide an outlet for cathartic relief in a domain not directly associated with the stressor itself and facilitate employment of effective coping strategies.

In addition, distressed adolescents are more inclined to manifest behavioural patterns which result in the reduction of available supportive resources and subsequent increase in experienced stress. Ideally, support offered by familial sources will enable the adolescent to achieve the balance between enmeshment and disengagement which is associated with positive adaptation. Furthermore, it appears that the provision of tangible and other resources by the family, as well as socialization patterns which shape values, aspirations and goals, contributes directly to superior levels of scholastic attainment.

The established link between familial support and adolescent adjustment is supportive of theories which relate the reported rise in adolescent stress to increasing family instability and atomization. This has led, according to Chisholm and Hurrelmann (1995), to a dramatic reduction in the time that adolescents now spend with their parents and siblings and may deprive young people of adequate nurturing at this vulnerable time. Furthermore, the increasing trend towards truncated and often disparate families may intensify problems which arise, as extended family and siblings may not be available for support. Dual worker parenting may also reduce time spent with family, and trends towards older parenting may contribute to conflict when pubertal development coincides with mid-life crises.

Finally, social support appears to be particularly salient for girls during adolescence. Relative benefits compared to the costs of social stress are debatable. While identity formation and subjective well-being are closely associated with quality of relationships for young women, they are also more reactive to social losses, more vulnerable to social stress, more open to personal feedback and more reliant on the protective functions of social networks.

Perceptions of control

Research suggests that deep-seated perceptions of control (or 'locus of control') moderate the impact of school and peer stressors rather than family stressors, and that adolescent girls exhibit greater externality. Females who go on to attend university have been shown to have higher internal locus of control scores than other females. As discussed in Chapter 1, 'internals' attribute outcomes to themselves, whereas 'externals' attribute outcomes to other factors. Higher scores reported by male adolescents in internal locus of control have shown positive correlations with high levels of self-esteem. Low scores correlate highly with depression, low self-esteem, low aspirations and risk-taking behaviour. Some evidence suggests that young people from ethnic minorities and those from lower socioeconomic backgrounds have more externalized orientations of control.[40]

Teenage boys who have experienced physical punishment demonstrate higher externalization of control[41] and a relationship has been found between family conflict (in intact and divorced families) and external locus of control.[42] Adolescent girls who attribute events to outside causes are more likely to show negative attitudes to authority and to experience teenage pregnancy.[43] Those who accept responsibility for their own successes and failures are more likely to show more advanced academic achievement.[44] Despite the tendency for locus of control to be described as a trait, there is strong evidence to suggest that it is influenced by environmental factors, such as youth unemployment.

Gender differences

The pervading influence of gender is in evidence throughout the stress process. One consistent finding is that adolescent girls report experiencing greater levels of stressful events than do their male counterparts. This has been found for school stress as well as interpersonal stress. The debate remains as to whether exposure or appraisal are at the root of these differences. Subsequent levels of distress in females correspond with lower levels of subjective well-being, lower self-esteem, more frequent negative moods and greater depressive affect and anxiety. Adolescent males, on the other hand, have been shown to display more behavioural problems and substance abuse. These findings have caused Siddique and D'Arcy (1984) to conclude that 'while both males and females experience the stresses that normally accompany adolescence, this developmental phase is considered to be more stressful for female adolescents' (p. 460).

The mechanisms which produce and maintain these differences are not yet fully understood. Genetic, biological, endocrinal, social, historical and political arguments abound. It is known, however, that the impact of 'network stressors' is far greater for females than males, and that their heightened social vulnerability may be a major contributor to the outcomes described above. Identity formation may be too closely reliant on peer approval for adolescent girls and frequent ruminative conversations may serve to exacerbate distress.

Reporting biases may be occurring here and significant class differences operate within these findings, with working-class women being more likely to report depression. It has been argued that methods of psychological measurement are to some degree responsible for producing these consistent findings, given that fewer measures are used which examine positive well-being, optimism and good mood. It may be, then, that these results fall prey to a measurement artefact, and that females are more likely to experience and report a greater range of psychological states across the spectrum. Furthermore, there are recent indications of a slight levelling off of sex differences, with increases in depressive disorders among male adolescents, while female rates remain stable.[45]

Differential outcome states have been attributed to inequitable affordance of opportunities to males and females, particularly in the area of employment. Nevertheless, studies have shown that females cope better with unemployment, exhibiting greater hardiness. Another theory purported for existing gendered outcomes in adolescence is the concurrence of school transitions with menarche for females, while for male adolescents these two transitions are usually staggered. Inadequate coping styles have been implicated, as have disparities in the employment of stress-relieving extracurricular activities as the potential cause of observed gender differences.

On the positive side, the prevalence of sociotropic concerns in female adolescents may be preventive of the development of aggressive, destructive or violent behaviours. In concluding an extensive review of current understanding of gender-linked vulnerabilities to stress-related outcomes, Leadbeater *et al.* (1995) urge researchers to 'look beyond existing differences in individual personality dimensions to the sociocultural causes of gender-linked psychopathology', pointing to the 'culturally based and pervasive' nature of gender stereotyping (p. 21).

Cultural differences

Many stressful experiences typically can be traced back to surrounding social structures and people's locations within them. (Rosella, 1994, p. 485)

Gender, race and socioeconomic status would appear to influence the stress process at every stage. Those adolescents from minority groups or lower-income families are at heightened risk of experiencing poverty, familial homelessness, violence, marginalization, inadequate education and health services and troubled home lives, and manifest differential resiliency patterns to those from other groups. It is likely that the advent of high levels of youth unemployment in the UK and elsewhere has had a more negative impact on working-class young people. In terms of moderation effects, socio-economic status of an adolescent's family has been shown to have significant effects on educational and career achievement and psychological indices, though its impact on objective stress exposure is a matter of some debate.

Finally, ethnic group membership appears to affect the perception, appraisal and frequency of stressful events. In a recent American study, white students rated being chosen for important school events as more stressful, black students reported experiencing more frequent school suspension, while academic difficulties were more frequently reported by Mexican-Americans.[46]

Age differences

This section focuses on the differences between younger and older adolescents. Again, some of the main moderating effects of age operate through the coping strategies which are used at different developmental levels. Other developmental skills which are of advantage to the older adolescent are greater control and knowledge and the ability to nurture relationships. This may contrast with the sense of 'role captivity' in younger adolescence, characterized by limited choices, greater restrictions and the negotiation of several transitions.

Sources of stress also vary according to age. Older adolescents experience, in general, more parental problems, but fewer difficulties with peers and siblings, while it is within friendship networks that the most distressing difficulties arise for younger adolescents. Academic stressors can produce a good deal of distress for 18–20-year-olds or sometimes younger students. There are wide individual differences in these developments.

The findings regarding developmental differences in stress-related outcomes emphasize positive development in older adolescence. Winefield and Tiggemann (1993) found no evidence for psychological distress increases between age 10 and 12, and Rodriguez-Tome and Bariaud (1990) report large decreases between 12- and 16-year-olds in their fear of failing school and of parental punishment. These findings may be domain-specific, as it has been shown that although negative emotions in older adolescents drop significantly for non-school activities, negative emotions regarding networks increase during this period.

Other moderating factors which serve to protect the growing adolescent from negative outcomes and maladjustment include self-esteem and self-concept. The remainder of this chapter focuses on psychological, physical and behavioural outcomes of stress in adolescence.

Stress-related outcomes in young people

The main feature of mortality during adolescence is its preventability. Accidents, homicide and suicide represent the three main causes of death.[47] Other factors, largely behavioural, contribute to the morbidity rates, including injury, risky driving, sexual promiscuity leading to the transmission of sexually transmitted diseases and substance abuse. The overlap therefore between psychological, physical and behavioural outcomes is of particular relevance during this developmental phase.

Psychological outcomes

One-third of adolescents experience some form of psychosis, emotional disturbance, conduct disorder or depression.[48] Depression appears to be the most common psychological outcome, and its links to stress are well documented.[49] This section therefore focuses on depressive disorders together with the more extreme outcome of suicide in adolescents.

Depression

Rates of depressive conditions in adolescents, particularly males, have increased over other psychiatric disorders in recent decades.[50] Current prevalence rates vary between 1.8 and 8.9 per cent with most studies reporting an average of 5 per cent of adolescents with a depressive disorder.[51] This may vary cross-culturally. There appears to be some evidence to suggest the attrition of traditional gender differences in depressive disorders, although females remain approximately twice as likely to experience depression as males.[52] In addition, recent research suggests increased vulnerability in younger adolescents. The concurrence of depression with other disorders is well documented, including alcohol and drug abuse, eating disorders, anxiety and behavioural problems.[53] Clinical depression has been implicated in 60 per cent of adolescent suicides in England and Wales.[54] Its symptoms include changes in eating and sleeping patterns, suicidal ideation and feelings of worthlessness. Interestingly, irritability rather than sadness may characterize adolescent depression.

Genetic, hormonal and social risk factors have received empirical attention. The role of inadequate coping skills has been discussed above. Although theories on the aetiology of depression vary, the most consensus exists regarding the probable role of parental psycho-pathology, adverse psychosocial and familial circumstances and stressful life events in the development of unipolar depressive disorders. Parental rejection appears to be a particularly strong predictor of depression in adolescence. Changes in family functioning leading to increased conflict and instability, and changes in family structure leading to increases in older, single, divorced or step-parenting have also been heavily implicated as causes in the development of depression in adolescents.

Added to this are prolonged and more competitive school careers, larger cohorts, unemployment, increased urbanization, rapid changes in living arrangements and increased female participation in the workforce. According to Frydenberg (1997), 'the evidence of youth stress is shown in the incidence of depression.' All in all, the evidence would seem to suggest that increases in depressive outcomes in adolescents are direct reflections of the increased stressfulness of this period at the end of the twentieth century.[55]

Suicide

Suicide has been described as a failure in coping and the most extreme response to stress. The past two decades have witnessed a documented rise in adolescent suicide, particularly in young, white males. Between 1970 and 1990 the number of young suicides trebled.[56] Suicide is six times more likely to occur in adolescence than in childhood, particularly in older adolescence, making it the second leading cause of death in 15- to 24-year-olds.[57] Male adolescents are three times as likely as females to commit suicide, whereas female rates of attempted suicides remain higher. Correlates include emotional or psychiatric problems, experience of suicidal behaviour, parental absence or abusiveness as well as immaturity, disturbed family background, depression and often a humiliating precipitating experience. Cumulated stress and societal stress have been linked to suicide. Other psychological disorders which show increases in adolescence include anxiety, social dysfunction and anergia (lack of energy).

Behavioural outcomes

Adolescence has long been the period of greatest risk for the development of behaviours such as delinquency and crime, risk-taking sexual activity and risky driving. However, there has been a recorded increase in these behaviours in recent years.[58] Epidemiological studies indicate a current prevalence rate of 15 per cent of adolescents with a severe emotional or behavioural disturbance.[59] Accidents account for more than half of all deaths among teenagers, increasing by 400 per cent in this age group. Attributed causes include the growing number of concurrent developmental tasks faced by young people, exposure to high levels of parental conflict and cumulated stress. Educational failure is highly correlated with psychosocial disorder, antisocial behaviour, and conduct disorder. As suggested by DuBois and colleagues:

> according to transactional-ecological perspectives, children and youth who are faced with significant levels of hazardous environmental conditions, as well as those who experience difficulty in their transactions with others, are at increased risk for disorder. (DuBois *et al.*, 1992, p. 542)

Physical outcomes

Psychosomatic complaints frequently experienced by adolescents include headaches, nervousness, lack of concentration, asthma and allergies. These have been linked directly to educational difficulties and disagreements with parents. Furthermore, stress may combine with other developmental processes, such as experimental behaviour and rebelliousness. This can lead to the adoption of unhealthy behaviours, such as smoking, drinking and drug use, together with the development of eating disorders and unhealthy lifestyles well documented to originate in adolescence.

Alcohol and substance use

Secular trends in alcohol and drug use vary cross-culturally. While the US and some parts of Europe have witnessed a partial decrease in their use, the developing countries as well as Central and Eastern Europe have seen a rise in consumption.[60] Furthermore, there is evidence for increases in the use of certain drugs in recent years, including hallucinogens, particularly MDMA ('ecstasy') and nitrates.[61] With regard to trends in alcohol use, Silbereisen and colleagues (1995) conclude that 'there is no indication of any substantial increase or decrease in the proportion of young people with alcohol problems during the past decade or so' (p. 501). Overall substance use, however, has been shown to have doubled in the 15- to 24-year-old age group between 1989 and 1992,[62] with a subsequent doubling of mortality attributed to use of solvents during this period. Drugs and alcohol are used more heavily by males than females (five to one for heavy drinking), though evidence exists for a convergence between the sexes in these behaviours during the past twenty years.

Correlates of alcohol abuse include parents who drink heavily, and families characterized by inconsistent discipline and low levels of control. Religiosity and occupational achievement demonstrate negative relationships with alcohol abuse, leading Silbereisen and colleagues to conclude that:

to the extent that the importance of religion declines and the opportunities for occupational achievement by young people decrease in society, one can expect an increase in use of substances. Similarly if the quality of parenting deteriorates one would expect the attachment to parents to be weaker, and thus the likelihood of substance use and abuse greater. (Silbereisen *et al.*, 1995, p. 518)

This conclusion is borne out by a study by Magura and Shapiro (1988), who found clear evidence for a predictive relationship between divorce rates and alcohol consumption. This demonstrates again the link between stress and negative adaptational outcomes.

Eating disorders

Although prevalence rates are difficult to ascertain, there is now substantial evidence to indicate that eating disorders, including anorexia nervosa and bulimia nervosa, have increased in recent years. Statistics vary cross-culturally and also within cultures. According to Fombonne (1995), anorexia rates for girls in private schools in the UK are, on average, one per 1,000, compared to 0 per 1,000 in Japan and 1.08 per 1,000 in Sweden.

Rates for bulimia nervosa are slightly higher at 2.7 per 1,000. Eating disorders peak during adolescence. According to a study by Bushness and colleagues (1990), eating disorders are experienced by 4.5 per cent of 16- to 24-year-olds, 2 per cent of 25- to 44-year-olds and 0.4 per cent of 45- to 64-year-olds. Female vulnerability is well documented, with 1.9 per cent of adolescent girls and 0.2 per cent of male adolescents manifesting some form of eating disorder. Eating disturbances are far more common than eating disorders, and refer to regular binge eating, fasting, vomiting, laxative consumption and dieting. It appears that normative discontent with weight is now part of the daily psychological life of most adolescent girls.

The explanations and social implications of these statistics have been examined by many writers. The particularity of eating disorders to Western women has implicated sociocultural factors in its aetiology. In a recent study of American women, 90 per cent of women were found to have been on a slimming diet at some time.[63] Writers have identified cultural pressures on girls and women to appear in control and strong, while feminine and attractive at the same time. The media have been accused of portraying consistently unrealistic images of thin women and associating this with success.

CONCLUSION

This chapter began with a discussion of definitions and theories of adolescence. The inevitability of stress in teenagers was debated. It was argued that today's young people are experiencing more stress than previous generations. Evidence and possible explanations for this increase were presented. Sources of stress for young people were discussed. These include developmental tasks, puberty, transitions, relationships, school, exams, divorce, parental characteristics, unemployment and their social context. This was followed by a discussion of coping, age, gender and cultural differences, social support and personality factors. The chapter ended with a discussion of stress-related outcomes in young people. These can be psychological, behavioural or physical.

The common aim of Chapters 1 and 2 is to describe and illustrate a process whereby stress, actual or perceived, precedes psychological and physical well-being through pathways and mechanisms orchestrated by moderating variables. Thus young people who appraise their family, school or peer group life to be stressful may be expected (and have been shown) to display symptoms of emotional and physical distress, including depression, anxiety, social dysfunction and anergia.

It is to be expected that the rapid changes involved in adolescence will bring with them increasing risks and potential for positive and negative outcomes, and although the majority of young people proceed to positive adaptation, a significant minority have been shown to experience scholastic failure and reductions in self-esteem and self-confidence.

With regard to the adolescent stress process, Johnson (1982) concludes that 'various studies support a relationship between life stress, assessed in various ways, and problems of both health and adjustment' (p. 245). Daniels and Moos (1990) concur, finding that in young people 'negative life events are predictably associated with more depression, anxiety and behavior problems and less self-confidence' (p. 285).

Chapter 3 examines the role of preventive psychology in tackling the outcomes discussed above, with a particular emphasis on intervention studies. These programmes aim to provide young people with the skills necessary to cope with specific and general stressors as well as dealing with the psychological and physical outcomes of stress.

Notes

1 Stattin, H. (1995) 'The adolescent is a whole person'. *Journal of Adolescence*, 18, 381–6.

2 Graham, P. and Rutter, M. (1985) 'Adolescent disorders', in M. Rutter, E. A. Taylor and L. Hersov (eds) *Child and Adolescent Psychiatry: Modern Approaches*, pp. 351–67. Oxford: Blackwell Scientific Publications.

3 Hauser, S. and Bowlds, M. K. (1990) 'Stress, coping and adaptation', in S. Feldman and G. Elliott (eds) *At the Threshold: The Developing Adolescent*, pp. 388–414. Cambridge, MA: Harvard University Press.

4 See Colten, M. E. and Gore, S. (1991) *Adolescent Stress: Causes and Consequences*. New York.: Aldine de Gruyter; Compas, B. (1987) 'Coping with stress during childhood and adolescence'. *Psychological Bulletin*, 101, 393–403; Jones, R. W. (1993) 'Gender specific differences in the perceived antecedents of academic stress'. *Psychological Reports*, 72, pp. 739–43.

5 Winefield, A. H. and Tiggemann, M. (1993) 'Psychological distress, work attitudes and intended year of leaving school'. *Journal of Adolescence*, 16, 57–74.

6 Elkind, D. (1984) *All Grown Up and No Place to Go: Teenagers in Crisis?* Reading, MA: Addison-Wesley. Frydenberg, E. (1997) *Adolescent Coping: Theoretical and Research Perspectives*. London: Routledge. See also Klerman, G. L. and Weissman, M. M. (1989) 'Increasing rates of depression'. *Journal of American Medical Association*, 261(15), 2229–35.

7 Hurrelmann, K. and Losel, F. (1990) *Health Hazards in Adolescence*. Berlin: Walter de Gruyter.

8 Murphy, G. E. and Wetzel, R. D. (1980) 'Suicide risk by birth cohort in the U. S.'. *Archives of General Psychiatry*, 37, 519–23.

9 Hurrelmann, K. (1990) 'Health promotion for adolescents: preventive and corrective strategies against problem behavior'. *Journal of Adolescence*, 13, 231–50.

10 Robson, M., Cook, P. and Gilliland, J. (1993) 'Stress in adolescence: theory and practice'. *Counselling Psychology Quarterly*, 6(3) 217–28.

11 Hains, A. A. and Szyjakowski, M. (1990) 'A cognitive stress-reduction intervention program for adolescents'. *Journal of Counselling Psychology*, 37(1), 79–84. (p. 79)

12 Olbrich, E. (1990) 'Coping and development', in H. Bosma and S. Jackson (eds) *Coping and Self Concept in Adolescence*, pp. 35–47. London: Springer-Verlag.

13 e.g. Robson, M., Cook, P. and Gilliland, J. (1993) 'Stress in adolescence: theory and practice'. *Counselling Psychology Quarterly*, 6(3), 217–28.

14 Wielandt, H. and Boldsen, J. (1989) 'Age of first intercourse'. *Journal of Biosocial Science*, 21, 169–177.

15 Reese, F. L., and Roosa, M. W. (1991) 'Early adolescents' self-reports of major life stressors and mental health risk status'. *Journal of Early Adolescence*, 11 (3) 363–78; Robson, M., Cook, P. and Gilliland, J. (1993). 'Stress in adolescence: theory and practice'. *Counselling Psychology Quarterly*, 6(3) 217–28; Hauser, S. and Bowlds M. K. (1990). 'Stress, coping and adaptation', in S. Feldman and G. Elliott (eds.), *At the Threshold: The Developing Adolescent*, pp. 388–414. Cambridge, MA: Harvard University Press; Mechanic, D. and Hansell, S. (1989) 'Divorce, family conflict and adolescent well-being'. Journal of Health and Social Behaviour, 30, 105–16.

16 Wadsworth, M. E. J. (1984) 'Early stress and associations with adult health behaviour and parenting', in N. R. Butler, and B. D. Corner (eds) *Stress and Disability in Childhood*. Bristol: John Wright and Sons.

17 Dawson, D. A. (1991) 'The impact of divorce on children', in *Contemporary Families: Looking Forward, Looking Back*. Minneapolis, Minnesota: National Council for Family Relations.

18 Guidubaldi, J. and Perry, J. D. (1985) 'Divorce and mental health sequel for children; a two year follow up of a nation wide sample'. *Journal of American Academy of Child Psychiatry*, **24**, 531–37.

19 Aro, H. M. and Palsaari, U. K. (1992) 'Parental divorce, adolescence and the transition to young adulthood: a follow-up study'. *American Journal of Orthopsychiatry*, **62**, 412–28.

20 See also Amato, P. R. and Keith, B. (1991) 'Parental divorce and the well-being of children: a meta-analysis'. *Psychological Bulletin*, 110(1), 26–46.

21 Wallerstein, J. S. (1985) 'Children of divorce: preliminary report of a ten year follow up of older children and adolescents'. *Journal of American Academy of Child Psychiatry*, **24**, 545–53.

22 Elliott, B. J. and Richards, M. P. M. (1991) 'Children and divorce: educational performance and behaviour before and after parental separation'. *International Journal of Law and the Family*, **5**, 258.

23 See for review: McFarlane, A. H., Bellissimo, A. and Norman, G. R. (1995) 'Family structure, family functioning and adolescent well-being: the transcendent influence of parental style'. *Journal of Child Psychology and Psychiatry*, **36**(5), 847–64.

24 Hauser, S. and Bowlds, M. K. (1990) 'Stress, coping and adaptation', in S. Feldman and G. Elliott (eds) *At the Threshold: The Developing Adolescent*, pp. 388–414. Cambridge, MA: Harvard University Press.

25 Rutter, M. (1979) 'Protective factors in children's responses to stress and disadvantage', in M. W. Kent and J. E. Rolf (eds), *Primary Prevention of Psychopathology*. Volume 3. *Social Competence in Children*, pp. 49–74. Hanover, NH: University Press of New England.

26 Reese, F. L. and Roosa, M. W. (1991) 'Early adolescents' self-reports of major life stressors and mental health risk status'. *Journal of Early Adolescence*, **11**(3), 363–78.

27 Daniels, D. and Moos, R. H. (1990) 'Assessing life stressors and social resources among adolescents: applications to depressed youth'. *Journal of Adolescent Research*, **5**(3), 268–89.

28 Brooks-Gunn, J., Petersen, A. C. and Eichorn, D. (1985) 'The study of maturational timing effects in adolescence. Special issue'. *Journal of Youth and Adolescence*, **14**, 3–4.

29 Petersen, A. and Leffert, N. (1995) 'What is special about adolescence?', in M. Rutter and D. J. Smith (eds) *Psychosocial Disturbances in Young People*, pp. 3–36. Chichester: Wiley.

30 Bandura, A. (1981) 'Current research and conceptualizations on stress responsivity', in C. Moore (ed.) *Adolescence and Stress*, pp. 99–103, (DHHS Publication No. ADM 81–1098). Washington, DC: US Government Printing Office (p. 99).

31 Schaffer, D. (1986) 'Developmental factors in child and adolescent suicide', in M. Rutter, C. E. Izard and P. B. Read (eds) *Depression in Young People: Developmental and Clinical Perspectives*, pp. 383–96. New York: The Guilford Press.

32 Frydenberg, E. (1997) *Adolescent Coping: Theoretical and Research Perspectives*. London: Routledge.

33 Ptacek, J. T., Smith, R. E. and Zanas, J. (1992) 'Gender, appraisal and coping: a longitudinal analysis'. *Journal of Personality*, **60**(4), 747–68.

34 Zeidner, M. (1996) 'How do high school and college students cope with test situations'. *British Journal of Educational Psychology*, **66**, 115–28.

35 Plancherel, B. and Bolognini, M. (1995) 'Coping and mental health in early adolescence'. *Journal of Adolescence*, **18**, 459–74.

36 Feldman, S. S., Fisher, L., Ransom, D. C. and Dimiceli, S. (1995) 'Is "what is good for the goose good for the gander?": Sex differences in relations between adolescent coping and adult adaptation'. *Journal of Research on Adolescence*, **5**(3), 333–59.

37 Garmezy, N. (1994) 'Reflections and commentary on risk, resilience and development', in R. Haggerty, L. Sherrod, N. Garmezy and M. Rutter (eds) *Stress, Risk and Resilience in Children and Adolescents*, pp. 1–19. Cambridge: Cambridge University Press.

38 Rutter, M. (1979) 'Protective factors in children's responses to stress and disadvantage', in M. W. Kent and J. E. Rolf (eds) *Primary Prevention of Psychopathology*. Volume 3. *Social Competence in Children*, pp. 49–74. Hanover, NH: University Press of New England.

39 Garmezy, N. (1994) 'Risk, resilience and development: opportunity and danger', in R. Haggerty, L. Sherrod, N. Garmezy and M. Rutter (eds), *Stress, Risk and Resilience in Children and Adolescents*. Cambridge: Cambridge University Press.

40 Heaven, P. C. L. (1996) *Adolescent Health: The Role of Individual Differences*. London: Routledge.

41 Douvan, E. and Adelson, J. (1966) *The Adolescent Experience*. New York: John Wiley.

42 Slater, E. and Haber, J. (1984) 'Adolescent adjustment following divorce as a function of familial conflict'. *Journal of Consulting and Clinical Psychology*, **52**, 920–21.

43 This finding appears not to hold for black American teenage girls, where an association between pregnancy and internal locus of control has been reported (Ralph *et al.*, 1984).

44 Fry, P. and Coe, K. (1980) 'Achievement performance of internally and externally oriented black and white high school students under conditions of competition and co-operation expectancies'. *British Journal of Educational Psychology*, **50**, 162–7.

45 Fombonne, E. (1995) 'Depressive disorders: time trends and possible explanatory mechanisms', in M. Rutter and D. J. Smith (eds) *Psychosocial Disturbances in Young People*. Chichester: Wiley.

46 Munsch, J. and Wampler, R. (1993) 'Ethnic differences in early adolescents' coping with school stress'. *American Journal of Orthopsychiatry*, **63**, 633–46.

47 Millstein, S. G. and Litt, I. F. (1990) 'Adolescent health', in S. Feldman and G. Elliott (eds) *At the Threshold: The Developing Adolescent*, pp. 431–57. Cambridge, MA: Harvard University Press.

48 Hurrelmann, K. and Losel, F. (1990) *Health Hazards in Adolescence*. Berlin: Walter de Gruyter.

49 Heaven, P. C. L. (1996) *Adolescent Health: The Role of Individual Differences*. London: Routledge.

50 Fombonne, E. (1995) 'Depressive disorders: time trends and possible explanatory mechanisms', in M. Rutter and D. J. Smith (eds) *Psychosocial Disturbances in Young People*. Chichester: Wiley.

51 Angold, A. (1988) 'Childhood and adolescent depression I: Epidemiological and aetiological aspects'. *British Journal of Psychiatry* **152**, 601–17.

52 Houlihan, B., Fitzgerald, M. and O'Regan, M. (1994) 'Self-esteem, depression and hostility in Irish adolescents'. Journal of Adolescence, **17**(6), 565–77.

53 Fombonne, E. (1995) 'Eating disorders: time trends and possible explanatory mechanisms', in M. Rutter and D. J. Smith (eds) *Psychosocial Disturbances in Young People*. Chichester: Wiley.

54 Fombonne, E. (1995) 'Depressive disorders: time trends and possible explanatory mechanisms', in M. Rutter and D. J. Smith (eds) *Psychosocial Disturbances in Young People*. Chichester: Wiley.

55 McCauley, E., Kendall, K. and Pavlidis, K. (1995) 'The development of emotional regulation and emotional response', in I. M. Goodyer (ed.) *The Depressed Child and Adolescent: Developmental and Clinical Perspectives*, pp. 53–81. Cambridge: Cambridge University Press; Horowitz, F. D. and O'Brien, M. (1989) 'Children as futures: in the interest of the nation: a reflective essay on the state of our knowledge and the challenges before us'. *American Psychologist*, **44**, 441–5; Heaven, P. C. L. (1996) *Adolescent Health: The Role of Individual Differences*. London: Routledge; Hurrelmann, K. and Losel, F. (1990) *Health Hazards in Adolescence*. Berlin: Walter de Gruyter.

56 Hauser, S. and Bowlds, M. K. (1990) 'Stress, coping and adaptation', in S. Feldman and G. Elliott (eds), *At the Threshold: The Developing Adolescent*, pp. 388–414. Cambridge, MA: Harvard University Press.

57 Millstein, S. G. and Litt, I. F. (1990) 'Adolescent health', in S. Feldman and G. Elliott (eds) *At the Threshold: The Developing Adolescent*, pp. 431–57. Cambridge, MA: Harvard University Press.

58 Colten, M. E. and Gore, S. (1991) *Adolescent Stress: Causes and Consequences*. New York: Aldine de Gruyter.

59 Powers, S. I., Hauser, S. T. and Kilner, L. A. (1989) 'Adolescent mental health'. *American Psychologist*, **44**(2), 200–15.

60 World Health Organization (1992) *A European Alcohol Action Plan*. (unpublished document EURRC42/8/ICP/GDP/11–(6)/7 Rev. 1, 8941B/8942B). Copenhagen: WHO Regional Office for Europe.

61 Institute for the Study of Drug Dependence (1993) *National Audit of Drug Misuse in Britain*, 1992. London: ISDD.

62 Silbereisen, R. K., Robins, L. and Rutter, M. (1995) 'Secular trends in substance use: concepts and data on the impact of social change on alcohol and drug abuse', in M. Rutter and D. J. Smith (eds) *Psychosocial Disturbances in Young People*. Chichester: Wiley.

63 Dolan, B. and Gitzinger, I. (1994) *Why Women? Gender Issues and Eating Disorders*. London: The Athlone Press.

CHAPTER 3

Intervening
to reduce stress

Introduction

The literature reviewed in chapters 1 and 2 indicates the existence of a complex relationship between the experience and appraisal of stressful life events and hassles on the one hand, and negative psychological, behavioural and physical health outcomes on the other. This has led to an increased interest in interventions, both preventive and curative, the primary goal of which is to reduce the symptoms of strain in target populations. This chapter aims to outline the main findings which this research has produced: first, within the adult population (in occupational and clinical psychology), and second within the adolescent population. Societal changes which would help to reduce adolescent stress are discussed in Chapter 10. Factors which contribute to the strength of research designs are discussed, together with a review of the relevant research findings.

The perception of stress as the underlying cause of a wide variety of physical and psychological ailments has led to the development of a variety of diverse stress reduction interventions. In this chapter, the term 'intervention' refers to various cognitive, behavioural and physical strategies for altering existing levels of anxiety, arousal and distress. Research and theoretical contributions to stress interventions have been discussed in chapters 1 and 2. Other influences include George Albee's important work on preventive psychology, which provided a strong rationale and framework for the development of some of this research. Advances in our understanding of the biological components of the stress process stimulated interest in interventions which focused on physical aspects of stress while advances in cognitive psychology led traditional behaviourist approaches to stress management to incorporate more cognitive components.

Stress reduction approaches are varied, and interventions have focused on emotional and physiological regulation through relaxation and guided imagery, psychological distraction and avoidance, cognitive restructuring, meditation, progressive relaxation, exercise, biofeedback, behavioural skills training and social skills training. Biofeedback involves using instruments to detect and amplify specific physical states in order to train people to bring them under their conscious control.

An example of one of the more well-known stress management interventions is Meichenbaum's (1977) stress inoculation training programme, which involves three main steps:

1 A detailed discussion of the stress process to equip participants with an understanding of the conceptual framework and to motivate them to learn new coping skills.

2 Instruction in practice and rehearsal of coping skills.

3 Real or imagined application of newly acquired skills.

This chapter will outline methodological issues common to all of the above, followed by a more detailed discussion on stress management training and meditation as two of the more widely researched and applied stress reduction interventions.

Methodological issues

Much intervention research has been criticized for its over-reliance on self-report measures, the brevity of its follow-ups, lack of control, placebo or comparison groups, its failure to isolate key treatment components and the measurement of stress as a uni-dimensional outcome measure.

In many ways, the treatment of stress has far outweighed systematic attempts to evaluate this treatment.

Treatments which aim to reduce strain may be classified according to three criteria, namely:

• the target of the intervention
• the agent of its delivery
• its focus on prevention or cure

Those planning interventions may choose to target either the individual or the organizational, societal or educational structure of which the individual is a part. Despite continuing claims that a two-pronged approach is required in tackling individual strain, i.e. one which invokes individual and structural change, a majority of interventions concentrate on only one of these potential foci, usually the former. This approach has been heavily criticized for placing the responsibility for change within the individual, even when structural and organizational factors are the major contributors, and the ethics of increasing personal levels of tolerance are continually questioned. In their review of occupational stress programmes, McLeroy *et al.* (1984) reported that virtually all programmes provided instruction on the sources and effects of stress, while none of the studies reviewed attempted to reduce actual work stressors.

The person delivering the intervention may be represented by a member of the organization or a third-party individual, possibly a researcher or a qualified expert. Individuals delivering training from outside the organization, be it a school or a company, may encounter difficulties in that the balance of power is not in their favour. Suggestions and constraints may or may not achieve sanction, and compromises may be necessary with regard to initial research design preferences.

Preventive strategies may be applied at three levels:

- Primary prevention refers to those interventions aimed at normal but 'at-risk' populations (e.g. inoculation programmes)
- Secondary prevention aims to reduce the duration of stress-related problems once they occur.
- Tertiary prevention aims to reduce the severity of these stress-related symptoms. Although usually seen as optimal, preventive approaches may not be regarded as cost-effective in situations with a low proportion of 'at-risk' individuals.

According to Murphy (1987), the literature suggests a negative relationship between experimental rigour and the reported success of evaluated stress reduction treatments. This view is espoused also in a review of research by Newman and Beehr, in which they write:

> Perhaps the most glaring impression we received from the review was the lack of evaluative research in this domain. Most of the strategies reviewed were based on professional opinions and related research. Very few have been evaluated directly with any sort of scientific rigour. In spite of this weak empirical base, many personal and organizational strategies for handling stress have been espoused. Although some of these strategies seem to glow with an aura of face validity, there remains the extremely difficult task of empirically validating their effectiveness. Until

this is done, practitioners have little more than their common sense and visceral instincts to rely on as they attempt to develop badly needed preventive and curative stress management programs. (Newman and Beehr, 1979, p. 35).

The following section outlines the methodological flaws common to past stress intervention research.

General methodological issues

Academic confidence in supporting or disclaiming stress management interventions has been hindered by the notable lack of methodological rigour with which their efficacy has been evaluated. An understanding of the precise effects (if any) of interventions is essential for their inclusion within educational, clinical or occupational settings. Research methods which lend themselves most easily to the examination of stress treatments include both experimental and quasi-experimental designs, and their employment has been relatively rare.

The reluctance of some researchers to adhere to a strong experimental design in intervention research stems from the genuine disparity which occasionally emerges between participant well-being and methodological rigour. Occasionally, design criteria will not be approved by the facilitating organization. In addition, the deliberate (negative) manipulation of independent variables such as actual and perceived stressors may be deemed unethical by researchers. Furthermore, standard research desiderata, such as the inclusion of a random sample of participants, often elude potential researchers, as the use of volunteers implies self-selection of those with certain predisposing factors. Group numbers tend also to be quite small with inadequate controls, lack of follow-up data and inadequate outcome measures.

In a review of nineteen work site stress programmes employing stress management or meditation, McLeroy *et al.* (1984) identified major methodological flaws in a majority of the studies critiqued. Sixteen of the nineteen studies used volunteers rather than random assignment to the experimental group. Nearly all of the studies combined information with skills, making it difficult to ascertain the relative contributions to the outcomes of component parts, and follow-up data were provided for only 8 of the 19 studies. Furthermore, negative findings on dependent measures were mentioned but not discussed. Key points to remember when evaluating stress management programmes are provided at the end of this chapter.

Are all interventions the same?

Given the components common to all psychotherapies, interventions and stress management programmes, it is not surprising that similar research outcomes have emerged from a range of diverse treatments. This phenomenon has been labelled the 'equivalence paradox' and refers specifically to the lack of differential effectiveness contrasted with obvious technical diversity in treatment approaches. Several possible explanations have been put forward, including inadequate reviewing procedures and measures, lack of sensitivity to brief events within sessions and the common generic core elements listed in the table on p. 73.

In a review of comparative outcome studies, Smith and Glass (1977) reported that 'the results of research demonstrate negligible differences in the effects produced by different therapy types' (p. 760). Many researchers have failed to combat this phenomenon. For example, despite the superior efficacy claimed by behaviour therapists for behavioural therapy, a review by Klein and colleagues (1983) found support for this claim in only two of the thirteen comparative studies they reviewed.

The development of more sophisticated analysis procedures, such as meta-analysis (where the results of many studies are analysed together), has continued to report this paradoxical finding. Despite the existence of hundreds of different therapies and interventions, comparative studies continue to yield similar results. Steps have been taken by interventionists to improve accuracy and reduce the likelihood of equivalent results, for example, by manualizing and dismantling treatments. Manualization refers to the preparation of a detailed manual together with an assessment of the agent's adherence to this. Dismantling of treatments was developed to identify the active elements within complicated treatment procedures. The pursuit of greater differentiation of outcome measures is also aimed at enhancing sensitivity with regard to evaluating programme efficacy. This entails broadening assessments so as to represent multiple vantage points, i.e. participant, observer, therapist/interventionist, significant other and so on.

Enhancing self-confidence and self-efficacy have emerged as general and essential intervention components. These have been referred to as 'non-specific effects', and may account for the apparent shared benefits to be found in intervention and control groups. As mentioned below, these include taking 'time out', sitting in a relaxing position, attending to a new perspective, the perception of being valued, and a desire to please the interventionist. The general relaxation response has proved to be particularly central to effective outcomes. Common to most relaxation methods are muscular relaxation, frequent practice, use during everyday stressful situations and cognitive strategies for mental calming.

In contrast to the studies described above which report largely equivalent results arising from comparative studies, Lehrer *et al.* (1994) have argued strongly for specific effects for various stress management strategies. They report that cognitively oriented methods have specific cognitive effects, autonomically oriented methods have specific effects on the nervous system and muscularly oriented methods have particular muscular effects. In their review, a generic relaxation response was reported together with the specific effects mentioned above. An overlap may be observed in that those disorders which rely on self-report and symptomatic interpretation (such as anxiety, insomnia and anger) may benefit from cognitive interventions.

SUMMARY

The following are common to most effective stress management interventions.

1 Common therapeutic core elements such as:

- taking 'time-out'
- attending a new perspective
- the perception of being valued
- a desire to please the interventionist
- enhanced self-confidence and self-efficacy

2 General relaxation response

- sitting in a relaxing position
- muscular relaxation
- frequent practice
- use during everyday stressful situations
- cognitive strategies for mental calming.

Stress management training and meditation are discussed below, first in relation to adults and then to young people. These interventions have demonstrated substantial empirical support, acceptability to participating organizations, and are easily administered.

Stress management training

Adequate scientific validation in support of the efficacy of stress management training has proved difficult to attain. The transition of stress management training from strictly clinical and occupational settings into the more experimental, evaluative arena was greeted with some scepticism. The term itself has proved to be problematic, given the diversity of techniques included under the general auspices of stress management training, thus limiting the potential for comparative studies. Continued research has, however, been stimulated by a growth in the perceived need for interventions of this nature, and positive findings from well-designed studies have emerged.

What is stress management training?

Stress management training usually includes some or all of the following elements; education about the causes and consequences of stress, training in methods to reduce psychological and physical arousal, instruction in relaxation, biofeedback and cognitive reappraisal exercises, and information on nutrition, exercise and social skills. Stress management is described by Roskies (1991) as 'a general treatment approach to a broad category of adaptational and health problems' (p. 412). A large number of possible techniques may be included in any particular stress management course, and Chapters 4 to 9 include details of many of these. Current practice is very much in keeping with the belief that 'having a particular weapon in one's arsenal is less important than having a variety of weapons'. However, there is a recognized danger in presenting the participant with an overwhelming and potentially confusing array of techniques.

Does stress management training work?

> There is unequivocal, clinical experimental evidence for a wide range of interventions that can successfully alleviate stress-related disabilities. (Pelletier and Lutz, 1991, p. 485)

Interventions which have been shown to be effective in reducing stress-related symptoms include meditation, biofeedback and progressive relaxation. There is strong evidence to suggest that it is the command of the relaxation response central to these techniques which provides a highly effective buffer against stress-related outcomes, such as tension headaches, insomnia, chronic anxiety and essential hypertension.

Following a review of studies aimed at alleviating occupational stress, Murphy (1984) concludes that 'stress management programmes are feasible and that a variety of techniques can be effective in helping workers reduce physiological arousal levels and psychological manifestations of stress' (p. 11). He does, however, lament the dearth of studies aimed at alleviating structural sources of stress through organizational change, job redesign and restructuring. The same is true for educational structures. Empirical support for the subjective nature of stress and the role of appraisal as a strong moderator in the stress-strain model does not, according to Murphy, undermine the primary influence of objective sources of stress in an individual's environment. That said, he concedes that secondary approaches to the problem of stress, as represented by stress management programmes, constitute a valuable endeavour, and favours their inclusion in a more all-encompassing approach to occupational stress.

Comparative studies

As mentioned above, intervention research is frequently criticized for failing to isolate treatment components with a view to ascertaining the specific aspects of the treatment which make it effective. Several studies have emerged which seek to redress this omission. A study by Yorde and Witmer (1980) divided volunteers into two stress management groups. The first of these took a lecture-discussion format, whereby information on appraisal and relaxation was presented to participants over four weeks. The second group received biofeedback training to decrease frontal EMG activity. The outcome measures showed large reductions in anxiety and subjective stress for the first group only.

In another study by Thayer *et al.* (1994), exercise was found to be the most singularly effective mood-regulating behaviour. In their study, tension·reduction was achieved most effectively by a combination of relaxation, cognitive and exercise techniques. Smith and Nye (1989) compared strategies which seek to manipulate mood with those where participants rehearse their responses to events to acquire stress management coping skills. Although both training conditions produced significant reductions in test anxiety, the former exerted a stronger influence on this measure, while the latter produced more generalized effects on trait anxiety.

The psychophysiological effects of several stress management techniques were examined by Forbes and Pekala (1993). In their study, the effects of hypnosis, progressive relaxation and deep abdominal breathing on skin temperature and pulse rate were compared. The former two strategies demonstrated significant effects in raising skin temperature and decreasing pulse rate (which shows a reduction in arousal), while deep abdominal breathing affected only skin temperature.

When choosing and comparing interventions, the most appropriate and important criteria, according to Murphy (1984), include cost, simplicity, instructional period, usefulness, feasibility and duration of the course. In an extensive review of stress management interventions for the workplace, meditation was reported to be the most cost effective and easily administered intervention, scoring highest on the above criteria. The following section examines the role of meditation as a stress management tool.

Meditation
What is meditation?
Although traditionally embedded within many religious traditions, meditation has more recently been successfully employed in a context-free, reductionist manner as a clinical and cognitive-behavioural tool. A growing mass of Westerners have learned and practised meditation in the past three decades to relieve distress and improve psychological well-being.

Shapiro (1987) has distinguished between three types of meditation, each depicting different forms of attentional strategy. The first is mindfulness meditation which infers a focus of awareness on one's whole attentional field. The second is labelled concentrative meditation due to its focus on one specific object (e.g. breathing, a candle, a mantra). The third type is integrated meditation which assumes a shifting back and forth between the two. Shapiro provides a camera analogy whereby the first strategy is likened to a wide-angled lens, the second to a zoom-lens and the third to alternating between the two.

Meditation has been defined as *'an attempt to focus attention in a non-analytical way and not to dwell on discursive, ruminating thought'*[1] and

> a family of practices that train attention in order to heighten awareness and bring mental processes under greater voluntary control. The ultimate aims of these practices are the development of deep insight into mental processes.[2]

Does meditation work?
Meditation is a 'scientist's nightmare' due to its ineffable outcomes and the innumerable confounding variables at work during its process. However, despite the methodological difficulties involved in attempting to measure the effects of meditation, a considerable amount

of research has accumulated regarding its process and outcomes. A large corpus of evidence now exists associating meditation with the promotion of psychological and physical health. Its efficacy has been demonstrated: in producing the following increased resistance to stress, anxiety reduction, expansion of consciousness, amelioration of cognitive resources, heightened perception, improvement in inter-personal relations, personality development, and the general promotion of mental and physical well-being.[3]

Herbert Benson and his colleagues (1975) have argued that various relaxation techniques elicit a general relaxation response involving all physiological systems in concert. Benson demonstrated that following meditation, heartbeat and respiration rates slow down, oxygen consumption falls by 20 per cent, blood lactate levels drop, galvanic skin response falls, and EEG ratings of alpha brain wave patterns increase.

Meditation has also been shown to reduce anxiety. However, these findings have been produced with equal success by comparable interventions such as muscular relaxation, mental imagery, hypnosis and muscular biofeedback. This has led some authors to conclude that any relaxation procedure which incorporates certain minimal components will result in a unitary relaxation response. These components include closed eyes, low muscle tone, a 'mental device', a passive attitude and a quiet atmosphere. The central differentiating factor appears to exist in self-report measures which show superior rates of reduction in scores following meditation.

The successful use of meditation has been chronicled by Carrington (1978, 1987) for the treatment of high blood pressure, heart disease, strokes, migraines, diabetes, arthritis, obsessive thinking, anxiety, depression and hostility. This author has provided clinical and statistical data for the success of her form of non-cultic meditation (clinically standardized meditation). These supported existing findings for the following: reduction in tension anxiety, improvement in stress-related illness, increased productivity, reduced self-blame, anti-addictive effects, mood elevation, increase in emotion, increased sense of identity and lowered irritability. Following the success of a pilot study conducted by Carrington (1980), a programme was launched at the New York Telephone Company with training in meditation given to 3,500 employees. Results show significant reductions in physiological complaints and symptoms of stress.

In summary, meditation has been demonstrated as effective in the reduction of stress-related symptoms. Findings also show heightened immune defence and disease resistance. This has been attributed to the exertion of strong pressure on the lower abdomen through the acquisition of deep breathing skills. Findings such as these have led to the National Institute for Health's (1984) consensus report which recommended meditation above prescription drugs for the treatment of mild hypertension.

Interventions for young people

The latter half of this chapter will focus on intervention programmes which aim to help young people to cope with stress, beginning with general programmes and then concentrating on stress management training and meditation. Although an attempt is made to distinguish between stress management training and other forms of intervention, techniques are frequently common to more than one programme.

Do we need interventions for young people?

Chapter 2 dealt in depth with the issue of stress in young people, and presented research which indicates an increase in perceived stress and its manifestation in adolescent mental and physical health. Despite the growing body of literature reflecting concern at these rising statistics, there remains a paucity of interventions for children and adolescents compared to those targeting the adult population. However, there exist an increasing number of adolescent intervention studies which indicate a heightened awareness among practitioners, researchers and policy-makers of growing adolescent vulnerability to stress-related outcomes.

Risk and resilience

Research into risk and resilience in adolescence has done much to stimulate interest in possible intervention strategies which might act as a buffer for young people against stressful environments. The personal characteristics of resilient adolescents have been explored as well as their social milieux. Research of this nature provides a theoretical background to the development of programmes, as do advances in the adult stress literature. It is argued that in order to prevent a disorder, efforts must be made to reduce, eliminate or mitigate the effects of factors that put people at risk of disorder.

Productive coping strategies, social skills, health-promoting behaviour, problem-solving ability, self-efficacy, ability to access social support and sustained competence under stress have emerged as protective factors in individuals. These skills have been incorporated into many stress management and intervention programmes. It is believed by many 'risk and resilience' researchers that competencies once obtained can serve as powerful protective factors.

Preventive programmes

Compas (1993) has highlighted the importance of delivering and evaluating preventive programmes during adolescence, arguing that 'the multiple stresses associated with adolescence, especially early adolescence, make the attainment of effective coping skills an important development task during this period' (p. 160). Compas outlines three possible levels at which adolescent interventions may be targeted.

Adolescent interventions can comprise:

1 programmes aimed at ameliorating coping skills
2 programmes aimed at developing a healthy social environment
3 programmes aimed at promoting mental health through public policy

It is argued that the first of these should be delivered as part of the school curriculum and should aim to foster a sense of self-efficacy and positive feelings towards the self as well as general coping and social skills.

Specifically, according to Compas, stress management for adolescents should teach youth to identify sources of stress in their lives, recognize the physical and emotional consequences of stress and implement adaptive coping responses.

A systems approach to effective prevention should:

• integrate adolescent interventions with those aimed at children and adults
• sequence general and problem-specific interventions correctly
• initiate social change
• generate and disseminate adequate data for thorough evaluation of the programme

Preventive interventions have been supported by Hurrelmann (1990), one of the leading researchers in this field. In an analysis of youth problem behaviour including substance use, risk-taking driving and aggressive behaviour, Hurrelmann describes these as 'signals of stress' (p. 231) and prescribes two forms of intervention: 'preventive' and 'corrective'. These depend on the stage of problem behaviour development at which the intervention occurs. Preventive interventions attempt to reduce the likelihood of potential disorders in health or personality development from taking place, while protective interventions aim to reduce or remove disorders already manifest. Furthermore, interventions may be targeted at personal or social resources.

Stress management training for adolescents falls into the first of these two categories. It is a preventive strategy aimed at ameliorating the personal resources of adolescents. Six key skills are advocated by Hurrelmann as essential components of such a programme. These skills are largely derived from research on resiliency.

RECOMMENDED COMPONENTS IN PREVENTIVE INTERVENTIONS FOR YOUNG PEOPLE

- general problem-solving and decision-making skills
- general cognitive skills
- skills for increasing self-control and self-esteem
- adaptive coping strategies for relieving stress and anxiety
- interpersonal skills
- assertive skills

Putting prevention into practice

Despite the acknowledged level of support for prevention as a goal in adolescent psychology, its application to administered and evaluated programmes remains too infrequent. In some leading textbooks on child and adolescent psychiatry, there are often no chapters devoted to prevention and the term is not listed in the index. There appears to be a reluctance in researchers to commit themselves to the exploration of prevention in real-life settings rather than as a vague ideal within the profession. The number of publications devoted to the topic still far outweighs well-established findings. The difficulty in gaining maximum support from schools and funding bodies has contributed to this lack of research, leading researchers such as Weissberg and Elias (1993) to call for 'policy makers and funding agencies to support long-term collaborations among educators and scientists to develop and evaluate comprehensive social competence and health education programmes' (p. 179).

Furthermore, as with occupational stress management, interventions which target structural sources of stress, such as school organization, are rare, and there have been calls for more systematic approaches to adolescent stress. It is obvious that by alleviating parental, teacher and care worker stress, adolescents will receive more support and learn to cope better with their own stress. Unfortunately, practitioners and action researchers rarely secure funding to enable promising and comprehensive frameworks such as this to take place.

In summary, the relationship between stressful life events and physical and psychological maladjustment is well documented for young people. Equipping adolescents with coping skills which are 'durable and generalizable methods for avoiding psychological, academic, and social problems linked with stress' is seen by many researchers on adolescent mental health as imperative if current levels of suicide, depression and maladaptive behaviour are to be curtailed or reduced.

The school as a forum for interventions

> *The object of education is to prepare the young*
> *to educate themselves throughout their lives.*
> Robert M. Hutchins.

In addition to the curriculum and design issues detailed above, adolescent interventions require appropriate forums for delivery. Many researchers have emphasized the school as the optimum forum for the administration of preventive and interventive programmes for adolescents.[4] Indeed, the assertion has been made that equipping young people with adequate coping skills is an essential component of education and should be incorporated within the national curriculum.[5] Hamburg writes:

> We can no longer take for granted the life skills training and social support systems that were built into human experience over millions of years. Now increased attention is being given to formal education to provide or at least supplement life skills training (including social skills) that historically were built into the formal processes of family and kin relations. (Hamburg, 1990, p. iv)

Together with access to adolescents and their parents on a regular and consistent basis, schools exert a real influence on young people's development and behaviour. They provide daily opportunities for the assimilation and rehearsal of acquired skills. Schools also provide a professional staff and a structured framework. Major goals of the school are usually compatible with the aims of the intervention, that is optimizing student adjustment and improving their quality of life. Schools also usually provide a supportive group environment which may facilitate discussions regarding problems, anxieties and concerns through which shared insights can be fostered.

Providing stress reduction interventions may also serve to enhance teacher morale in that the positive effects are usually quickly visible, and teacher–student relations may also see improvements. The school environment may itself be a source of stress for adolescents as outlined in Chapter 2, and stress reduction interventions within the school structure may successfully target these specific stressors and address pertinent issues which arise from discussions therein.

Certain criteria should be consulted prior to choice of a school for an intervention course. It is often the influence of organizational-systematic and community factors that result in the success or failure of comparable social skills programmes. In order for interventions to receive as much support as possible, efforts should be made to ascertain the degree of teacher and pupil commitment to the project, the availability of trained personnel (particularly counsellors), adequate links to services for identified high-risk participants, compatibility of school norms for responding to misbehaviour and rule-breaking with programme norms and level of organizational readiness (e.g. teacher morale, staff health, decision-making procedures, reward structures and shared school goals).

Types of intervention
Interventions for young people may comprise general or focused skills training, but are usually aimed at improving coping and reducing symptoms of distress. Examples include physical exercise training, coping skills training, relaxation training, family-based stress management, cognitive-behavioural prevention programmes, problem-solving training, social competence training, social skills training, psycho-educational programmes, stress inoculation training and life discussion groups.

There is some disagreement regarding how specific these interventions should be when teaching coping skills. According to Seiffge-Krenke (1995), 'intervention programs that focus on the development of global coping behavior intended to be applied according to a variety of stressor types may be less effective than programs that are specific to a particular stressor' (p. 236). Seiffge-Krenke urges programme planners to facilitate developmental needs by incorporating a wide range of coping strategies within courses and communicating the importance of flexibility in responding to stressful situations.

Particularly important for young people are learning the ability to see different facets of the situation, generating a variety of solutions and the opportunity to explore different strategies. Compas and his colleagues (1993) concur and further recommend general intervention programmes for adolescents followed by more focused courses for 'at risk' adolescents. The latter may be facilitated by a more precise understanding of what has been described as 'environment–development relations'. Hauser and Bowlds point to the need to become more aware of appropriate intervention timing, and reiterate the necessity for strong designs in evaluating intervention programmes. They write:

> We will need prospective longitudinal designs that incorporate rigorous sampling (control groups, comparison groups), consistent observational procedures, and appropriate timing of observations (baseline, during the intervention, and at near and distant points following interventions). (Hauser and Bowlds, 1990, p. 412)

The choice of interventions available to adolescents has also been criticized. Rutter (1994) describes the availability as inadequate, and argues that 'there is a need for the exploration and testing of a wider range of interventions' (p. 374). The following is a review of the findings regarding the demonstrated efficacy of the above interventions.

Do interventions for young people work?

Physical activity and exercise training have been shown to exert positive effects on psychological strain and well-being in young people. Studies show that high-intensity aerobic exercise significantly reduces feelings of perceived stress, anxiety and depression in 13- to 17-year-old students. This corresponds with the finding that the relationship between stressful events and physical and emotional health in adolescents is heavily moderated by physical exercise.

Problem-solving training has been reported to be the most effective intervention in improving adolescent coping skills and reducing distress. Black and Frauenknecht (1990) have developed a problem-solving programme aimed at young people who they believe are 'often ill-equipped to manage excessive stress because of inexperience, poorly developed or non-existent adaptive coping skills, and an emotionally non-supportive environment'. They argue that 'programs that may be applied as primary prevention strategies are sorely needed to increase the resilience of adolescents to stress and its consequences' (p. 90).

Based on Lazarus and Folkman's transactional model of stress (1984), this model conceptualizes stress as combinations of stressors and personal factors with an emphasis placed on the importance of evaluation within the stress process. Their programme consists of ten steps focusing on the evaluative stage and decisions made therein. These are: (1) problem orientation, (2) general problem identification, (3) specific problem identification, (4) selecting a problem to manage,

(5) listing alternatives, (6) weighing the consequences, (7) choosing one or more alternatives, (8) putting the plan into action, (9) evaluating progress, and (10) reorganizing and beginning again if the problem is not resolved. These researchers argue that problem-solving training provides the most effective form of stress management training for adolescents, as it provides flexible techniques which are relevant to a variety of stressful situations.

Social skills training has received much attention in adolescent intervention research, particularly with regard to 'at risk', minority or disadvantaged young people. Social skills training has been used successfully with diabetic adolescents.[6] Improvements were observed in their ability to cope with stressful social situations, and participants were seen to feel less embarrassed when discussing their illness with peers.

The 'life discussion' group has also been put forward as an appropriate preventive strategy to help young people, particularly those in their final year of secondary school. It aims to confront, discuss and potentially resolve issues related to preparing to leave school, finding a job or gaining college entry, as well as more unfocused fears and anxieties.[7] Subjective reports and observation have shown that participants became less likely to stereotype peers and adults, became increasingly aware of the communality of concerns and conflicts, gained self-confidence in expressing views, and gained a heightened sense of identity. It appears that the life discussion group is useful for individuals who are going through similar experiences.

A final example of the successful use of an intervention targeting the adolescent population is to be found in the psychoeducational intervention designed by Rice *et al.* (1993). Although appropriate for use with asymptomatic adolescents to help cope with the general challenges of puberty, this intervention was designed with the aim of teaching preventive skills to offset adolescent depression. This programme was based on skill-streaming training and group treatment for adolescent depression. Each of the sixteen sessions concentrates on a specific social skill, coping strategy or problem, incorporating discussion, role-playing or modelling exercises, and rehearsal and integration of skills. Significant increases have been reported in coping repertoire, heightened perceptions of control, and improved peer and family relations for participants in the follow-up.

Stress management training for young people

Stress management training programmes usually incorporate physical exercise information, problem-solving training and social skills training, as well as information on the sources and consequences of stress, cognitive-behavioural exercises, relaxation exercises and specific skills training. Extensive literature reviews have revealed a paucity of stress management training courses designed for adolescents. Stress management training is most frequently evaluated within occupational and clinical settings. Its use as a preventive programme with asymptomatic youths is rare, despite continual references to the importance of prevention particularly at vulnerable transitions such as adolescence. The remainder of this section details the results of research into stress reduction programmes for young people.

Cognitive interventions

Beneficial effects have been found for a cognitive stress reduction intervention programme for young people.[8] In this intervention programme, adolescent thinking patterns and cognitive strategies employed in coping with various situations were discussed. Participants were also taught how to recognize and control stress-promoting cognitions while producing more adaptive cognitions and practising newly acquired skills. The authors report significant reductions in anxiety and anger levels. They also recorded significant improvements in self-esteem and positive cognitions in the experimental group compared to the control group. These gains were maintained at a ten-week follow-up. These results have been replicated with much success.

Social competence training

Another approach to adolescent intervention programmes consists of social competence training. Proponents argue that social competence is central to adolescent well-being, performance and behavioural adjustment. Social competence has been described as the capacity to integrate cognition, affect and behaviour to achieve specified social tasks and positive developmental outcomes. Caplan *et al.* (1992) have developed a programme labelled the 'Positive Youth Development Program', which consists of six units (twenty sessions) designed to promote social competence. These focus on stress management, self-esteem, problem-solving, substances and health, assertiveness and social networks. In a study examining the effects of this programme, which combined broad-based skills training with specific instruction on substance abuse, findings indicated major improvements in interpersonal and problem-solving skills, and reductions in anxiety and self-reported substance use.

Cognitive-behavioural interventions

A cognitive-behavioural, school-based prevention programme was designed by Klingman and Hochdorf (1993) aimed at reducing adolescent distress and self-destructive behaviours. In particular, the programme was designed to target cognitive processes such as suicidal ideation, loneliness, hopelessness and coping strategies associated with maladaptive behavioural tendencies. This programme was based heavily on Meichenbaum's (1977) three-stage intervention model, comprising educational-conceptual, exercise-training and implementation-application phases. Using this model as its underlying framework, the programme used a cognitive-oriented approach to introduce the following topics: adolescence and distress, learned helplessness, hopelessness and depression, self-destructive behaviours and youth suicide, learned resourcefulness, empathy training, help-seeking behaviour and peer support, stress inoculation and prevention.

The first phase of this programme communicated the theoretical background to these concepts, while the second phase concentrated on role-playing and exercises designed to aid skills acquisition. The final phase of the programme consisted of out-of-class assignments and feedback discussions aimed at consolidating and reinforcing newly acquired skills. Despite some methodological inadequacies, the results indicate improvements on a number of outcome measures. Suicidal predilection appeared reduced, particularly for young men, and there were increases in empathy scores, particularly for young women. The study failed to show a decrease in loneliness scores but subjective reports rated the programme as 'very beneficial'.

Information and problem-solving

Their research on adolescent stress and coping led Schinke *et al.* (1987) to design a stress management course for adolescents who they saw as poorly equipped to cope with stress. According to these authors, stress-related problems such as school failure, emotional disorder and antisocial behaviour emerged due to ineffective 'trial-and-error' coping. Their intervention comprised information on school requirements and prospective academic challenges, problem-solving with regard to assessing the 'cognitive, interpersonal, and environmental cues that signalled anxiety and stress' (p. 17), learning to use self-instruction to monitor and alter their thinking, and communication skills to aid interpersonal relations. Students who took part in this eight-week course showed significant improvement compared to the control group on six outcome measures, including generation of options, direct refusals, ability to handle stress, ability to deal with peer pressure and general readiness for change. The authors, together with other researchers, point out that stress management interventions often yield benefits for participants' friendships and family relationships.[9]

Specific interventions

An example of a more specific stress management training course is that designed for young people with diabetes by Boardway *et al.* (1993). As stress can exacerbate diabetes, stress management training was seen as a useful intervention for this group. In particular, it was hoped that training in coping skills would improve metabolic control, which in turn influences the course of the disease. Previous studies have failed to improve metabolic control with different stress management methods. These include relaxation training and biofeedback in adults, and anxiety management and social skills training with adolescents. Boardway *et al.* designed a stress management course based on accurate assessment behaviours, cognitive restructuring, coping skills, assertiveness training, and dietary and insulin administration skills. While no important effects were found for metabolic variables, there was a significant reduction in diabetes-specific stress. General life stress measures remained unchanged.

The authors conclude that their limited findings suggest that a stress management training course which combines cognitive restructuring (changing the way we think about stress) and assertiveness training with relaxation training may produce more significant effects on outcome measures. The findings of Boardway *et al.* are similar to those of Gross *et al.* (1983), who reported significant reductions in disease-related distress following a social skills training course, while failing to affect metabolic control in these youths.

Other vulnerable groups of young people have also been targeted for stress management training courses which combine general stress management skills with more specific skills relevant to the particular group. Examples of these groups are pregnant adolescents, adolescents who abuse drugs, adolescents with clinical depression, suicidal adolescents, adolescents with anorexia nervosa, and hospitalized adolescents.

Meditation and relaxation training for young people

Research on the effects of meditation on young people is scant, but some studies have emerged which suggest that meditation and relaxation training may have beneficial effects for this age group. As with other interventions, practice would appear to have pre-empted empirical validation, and meditation and relaxation techniques are reported to have been used with success in youth counselling and therapy.[10] Transcendental meditation (TM) has been used successfully in lowering blood pressure in young people.[11] Smith and Womack (1987) reported the successful use of meditation on young people with symptoms of a high psychophysiological component (including headaches, chest pain, abdominal pain and dizziness). These authors present a case study of a 17-year-old male with mild hypertension, which was successfully normalized using meditation (the relaxation response). According to Compas and Hammen (1994), depressed youths may also benefit from relaxation training, although such interventions have yet to receive empirical evaluation.

The new Code of Practice included in the 1993 Education Act (UK) gives advice about stress reduction for teenagers.[12] Relaxation training together with general stress management and study skills training are recommended. Nath and Warren (1995) report significant reductions in anxiety following the delivery of this course to pupils aged between 14 and 15. Similar reductions have been demonstrated in young people following relaxation training programmes.[13] Impressive results were reported by Field (1992) whereby significant reductions in anxiety and depressed mood, motor activity, anxious and fidgety behaviour, heart rate and cortisol levels were recorded in anxious adolescents following relaxation training. Meditation techniques were included in an anxiety control training course designed by Snaith *et al.* (1992). Considerable reductions in generalized and phobic anxiety were reported for those who took part.

Resources for designing stress management programmes for young people

This section provides an overview of helpful resources for tackling stress in schools, working with groups of young people, and adolescent counselling. Given the dearth of agencies that provide stress reduction services for adolescent groups, it is often necessary for practitioners to design and deliver stress reduction interventions. Part 2 provides advice, skills and information around talking to young people about stress. It is useful to evaluate these courses for future fine tuning and development. This is consistent with the 'action research' approach discussed in much stress reduction literature.

Tackling stress in schools

In response to a growing recognition by researchers, healthcare workers, counsellors, teachers, parents and others that levels of adolescent distress appear to be increasing (for example, as evidenced by the

quadrupling of suicide rates in young males in the last two decades[14]),
several publications have appeared which aim to provide advice for
teachers and parents on helping young people cope with stress.

I have designed a course entitled *Stress Management Programme for
Secondary School Students* (2000). This course is unique in providing
a comprehensive and structured stress management course for
teenagers. It is firmly based on research on resiliency and coping, and
will allow teachers and practitioners to teach essential coping skills to
young people. The course was designed to inform adolescents about
ways in which they could reduce actual and perceived sources of stress
in their lives, as well as ways of improving their coping skills, adopting
a healthier lifestyle, learning new skills and handling the effects of
distress in a more constructive manner. A high emphasis is placed on
discussion as a central learning tool and opportunity for peer support.

The importance of discussion has been stressed by many researchers,
including Weinberger and Reuter (1980), who argue that group
discussions 'allow the participants to realize both the uniqueness and
commonalities of their lives as they deal with the same developmental
issues' (p. 6). Furthermore, there is evidence to suggest that the 'lecture-
discussion' format is more effective in teaching stress management
than skills-based programmes alone.

The programme has been evaluated over a twelve-month period,
and has produced highly significant improvements in adolescent mental
health and academic performance. Those students who took part in
the programme reported less frequent stressful events, less negative
mood, anxiety and strain. Unlike many resources available today, it has
been evaluated using control and comparison interventions which
support its efficacy in reducing stress in young people.

The resource pack contains many advantages including:

- Verbatim notes for teachers, thus removing the necessity for
  teachers to receive training in delivering the pack. It has been
  standardized for maximum efficacy.
- Useful handouts to help students to absorb the material
  outside of class time.
- Contact details for relevant organizations to help with specific
  problems.
- Useful book lists to enable students to follow up areas of
  interest.
- The sessions are timed for the teachers.
- A learning-friendly format, with group participation, role-play
  and other helpful learning tools.

- Opportunity for peer support, through group discussions.
- Teachers will learn a lot from delivering the pack. General guidelines for managing stress in adulthood and adolescence share many essential components, including relaxation, breathing, nutrition, exercise, relationships, rest and recreation.

The material used in the pack was originally gathered as a result of extensive research and experience with adolescents as well as a comprehensive overview of relevant and useful literature on adolescent mental health and stress management techniques.

There are six (fifty minute) sessions which cover the following topics: understanding stress and its symptoms, mental coping strategies, physical coping strategies, study skills and time management, communication skills, boosting self-esteem and self-confidence, and coping with depression and anxiety.

The sessions include short talks, general and small group discussions, exercises, role-plays and homework exercises. These represent different modes of learning or communication. The timing of the sessions is tight and structured. Talks given by the facilitator *follow* discussions on the same topic so as not to bias the discussion. Students tend to learn more and find the answers more meaningful and relevant when they generate the answers themselves. Homework exercises are designed to enable students to think ahead of time about subsequent topics of discussion. These involve diary work, through which a greater awareness of their feelings and behaviour can emerge. It is intended that the atmosphere in each session is one of relaxation, fun, exploration and learning.

Other useful publications include *Tackling Stress in Schools: A Practical Guide* (Health Education Authority, 1990), *Stress in Schools* (Wright and Frederickson, 1992), *Helping Children to Cope with Stress* (Markham, 1990), *The Life Skills Training Manual* (Ellis and Burns, 1987), *Lively Ideas for Life Skills Teachers* (Wilson, 1988), *Relax and be Happy: Techniques for 5–18 Year Olds* (Madders, 1987), and *Young People under Stress: A Parent's Guide* (Burningham, 1994). These are summarized below.

The first of these publications gives information regarding national bodies in the UK which specialize in providing workshops on teacher and student stress and in training teachers to give stress workshops to students. These include the Centre for Research in Teaching (CRIT), the Health Skills Project Network, and the Look After Yourself (LAY) Project. Unfortunately, although listed as active at the time of publication (1990), on seeking information from these bodies, I was informed that they were no longer providing these services.

The second of these publications, *Stress in Schools* gives advice on how to set about designing courses within the school framework and suggests topics and skills for inclusion within these courses. Wright and Frederickson advise that SRIs begin with a consensus by all participants that stress is affecting their lives and is an issue which they would like to learn more about. Participants should feel that they are active from the outset in the development of the course and believe that the topics included on the course are relevant to them. Participants should feel that the content of the course is closely aligned with their experiences and that the skills they will learn will build on these experiences. Finally, the course should aim to help participants to solve real problems which they are encountering at that time. Other ground rules include an agreement that all topics discussed in the sessions would remain confidential, that no activities would be compulsory, that solutions were offered as alternative options rather than prescriptive advice and that the aim of the courses was primarily preventive rather than therapeutic.

Wright and Frederickson suggest that all participants are advised of counselling facilities available to them prior to the commencement of the intervention. Following completion of the programme, they also advise that students are asked if they felt better able to manage stress, if their behaviour had changed, and what aspects of the course and its materials were most helpful (to aid evaluation). Many of these suggestions are consistent with occupational and clinical literature on stress management training. Most of these courses begin with a lecture/discussion on the causes of stress, moving on to a discussion of a variety of coping strategies and their relative usefulness. These sessions (or units) are followed by more focused skills training, including assertiveness and interpersonal skills, cognitive and problem-solving skills, time management and relaxation skills.

These units are recommended by Wright and Frederickson for teachers and pupils alike. The last section in the publication, however, concentrates solely on adolescent stress management and suggests the following as important for inclusion within a course aimed at this age group: social skills training, assertiveness training, problem-solving skills, self-esteem raising, social network building, social competence training and teaching adolescents positive ways of expressing emotion. To reduce the effects of student stress, the authors encourage teachers to:

> work preventatively with their pupils to eliminate the causes of unnecessary stress in school, empower them to deal effectively with life changes, develop in pupils those skills that protect them

from the damaging effects of stress and provide students with some strategies for dealing with unavoidable stress. (p. 255)

The proposed stress reduction course devised by Markham (1990) in *Helping Children Cope with Stress* is divided into three sections: (1) identifying stress, (2) discussing the causes of stress, and (3) 'stress-proofing'. Again, the course structure shares many of its elements with contemporary stress management courses for adults. It is aimed primarily at children. The first section informs participants of the symptoms and signals of distress, such as changes in behaviours, attitudes and emotions. The causes of stress discussed in the second section are specific to young adolescents and include coping with divorce or separation, child abuse, and coping with exam stress. The final section explains the rationale behind prevention, and discusses the importance of nutrition, exercise, sleep and relaxation. Markham is a strong advocate of learning relaxation skills at an early age and believes that 'learning a method of relaxation young can provide a beneficial tool through life' (p. 118). The benefits of positive thinking together with effective communication skills are also included in this suggested course outline.

The Life Skills Training Manual is broader than most stress management courses. It highlights techniques and topics for use with adolescents. This manual is also useful in providing interesting ideas on how to impart information to young people in a lively and enjoyable way. This is essential to maintain participant commitment. Suggested methods and techniques include action research projects, role-plays, small and large group discussions, elected spokespeople, films, team projects, games, videotapes and so on. Certain handouts from this manual are recommended including those on effective listening, describing one's feelings, expressing hurt, and giving and receiving feedback.

Wilson (1988) provides ideas for activities for introducing different topics to young people. Handouts from this publication are useful in prompting discussions on issues such as identity, perceptions of others, sleep and exercise, thought processes, unhealthy behaviours and the stress process. Wilson's use of animation, puzzles and worksheets also provides stimulating ideas for the design of courses.

In *Relax and be Happy: Techniques for 5–18 Year Olds*, Madders (1987) begins with a rationale for teaching relaxation skills to children and adolescents. Young people are particularly in need of learning such skills, as they are 'immature, have limited experience, are passing through periods of rapid change and are particularly vulnerable'. Unlike adults, young people have yet to form habits of 'over-reacting, over-arousal and prolonged muscle tension'. Introducing relaxation skills to this age group will, Madders asserts, 'encourage positive attitudes to mental and physical health and will become a skill of value throughout life'. In keeping with the manuals described above, this text begins with an overview of the stress process, with an emphasis on the centrality of attitudes in that process.

Young People under Stress: A Parent's Guide is also useful during initial stages of course design, as it provides advice on how to discuss non-normative as well as normative stress with young people. It is helpful for course deliverers to be aware of a wide range of potential stressors and their effects on young people, together with advice on channels of help available to them. This book provides advice as to how to provide appropriate responses to a variety of potential problems. These include coping with: adoption, bereavement, bullying, disabilities and special needs, family problems, foster care, friendship and peer groups, sexual orientation, illness or accidents, race, pregnancy, parental separation and divorce, sex and relationships, sexual abuse, step-families, substance misuse, unemployment, anorexia, bulimia, depression, anxiety and suicidal feelings. The book also provides a useful reference guide of organizations and professional services in the UK for young people experiencing these difficulties, as well as facts regarding young people and the law, of which professionals working with young people must be well informed.

Working with groups of young people

There are also more general publications which give advice on facilitating groups of adolescents and which prepare facilitators for specific group dynamics that may emerge. Careful attention to detail in designing the structure and format of the course is as important as the content, and these texts are useful in highlighting potential areas of difficulty and suggesting ways in which they can be prevented. These recommendations are especially important for facilitators with no previous experience of working with groups of adolescents.

Recommended texts include: *Learning Together: A Health Resource Pack for Working with Groups* (Billingham, 1990), *Working with Young Women: Adolescent Project Training Papers* (Flanagan *et al.*, 1987) and *Group Exercises for Adolescents: A Manual for Therapists* (Carrell, 1993). Other relevant publications include: *Working with Troubled Adolescents: A Handbook* (Coleman, 1987), *Groupwork with Children and Adolescents* (Dwivedi, 1994), *Child and Adolescent Therapy: A Handbook* (Lane and Miller, 1992), and *Greater Expectations: A Source*

Book for Working with Girls and Young Women (Szirom and Dyson, 1990).

The first of these publications, *Learning Together* provides detailed recommendations on the timing of programme sessions, choosing venues, resource possibilities, methods of communication, techniques for increasing the relevance of course topics and evaluation techniques. Billingham demonstrates an intimate knowledge of adolescent group dynamics and many of these recommendations are made on account of personal experiences with such groups. The publication emphasizes choice of venue as a core factor in programme success. Venues should be welcoming and represent a different environment from participants' normal arenas of interaction. In this context, sports halls, dance studios and small school theatres are preferable to classrooms. The timing of sessions should reflect known facts about adolescent attention spans and should not force concentration above these points. Sessions should be broken up into small chunks which differ in form from each other. A break in the middle of the session is also recommended.

Billingham suggests that the core aims of the programme are discussed upon commencing the course so as to maximize student perceptions of control and participation. Additional resources such as flip charts, pens and paper and the provision of refreshments are recommended. She advocates sessions which interchange between talks, discussion, exercises and recaps. The advice given in the current text concurs with much of this with regard to introductory exercises, brainstorming, checklists, whole group discussions, small group discussions, case studies, quizzes and questionnaires, role-play and practical activities. 'Contingency plans' are also discussed in the event of people leaving the group in large numbers or group dynamics indicating that certain people dominate the group.

Counselling for young people

Although stress reduction programmes are usually delivered in group settings and have a preventative rather than a therapeutic orientation, it is desirable that those giving stress management workshops to young people should have a basic understanding of counselling issues prior to the commencement of the courses. However, given that this is not always possible, it is recommended that course facilitators are familiar with the referral agencies available to participants. They should provide participants with details of counselling facilities, together with support for specific difficulties such as abuse, eating disorders, alcohol and substance addiction and so on. This is necessary as many issues will be raised, possibly for the first time, during the course.

Useful resources

Many questions may be addressed to the facilitator. It is therefore useful to have an understanding of pertinent youth issues and appropriate responses to such questions. This section provides an overview of some of the main issues. Some useful texts include *Counselling for Young People* (Mabey and Sorensen, 1995), *Surviving Adolescence: A Handbook for Adolescents and their Parents* (Bruggen and O'Brien, 1986), *Adolescent Health Care: A Practical Guide* (Neinstein, 1991), *Bullying: A Practical Handbook for Schools* (Elliott, 1991), *The Adolescent Years: The Ups and Downs of Growing Up* (Buckler, 1987), and *The Teenage Years: Understanding 18–20 Year Olds* (Copley and Williams, 1995).

Issues facing contemporary youth

Mabey and Sorensen (1995) discuss issues facing contemporary youth, together with effective counselling procedures with which to help young people confront difficulties. They believe that, contrary to the popular belief that 'young people do not encounter serious difficulties, merely experiencing minor problems with peers, young people have identical concerns to adults, often further intensified by having less power than adults' (p. 67). They cite abuse, bullying and depression as frequent adolescent problems. Peer group counselling is often put forward as a useful and beneficial mode for offering counselling to school students. Part 2 of this book describes how small group discussions and facilitated peer counselling can help students discuss problems and allow them to offer advice and suggestions to each other as to how to counter these difficulties. Mosely (1993), a strong advocate of peer group counselling, writes:

> We live in troubled times; schools often seem irrelevant places and the problems and the tasks of childhood and adolescence are exacerbated even further. It is crucial we can offer counselling as a positive force in pupils' lives; not as a 'safety net' nor as an unwitting form of social control but as a means of helping young people think for themselves, make their own decisions, value their own integrity. (p. 105)

As suggested by Mabey and Sorensen, and in keeping with the authors' experiences of working with young people, 'to survive it one needs resilience, endless patience and a lively sense of humour' (p. 74). In addition to these attributes, special considerations must be made when offering advice to adolescents as their autonomy is limited. Often they have no control over the way their family lives and the options they can call upon in challenging times. It may not be in their power to alter difficult situations, rather they may be forced to accept such situations as the only way of relieving distress. When designing, introducing and delivering courses, these observations should be noted.

Participant commitment

Furthermore, several counselling techniques for maximizing participant commitment are recommended. These include contract setting, whereby the participants note their expectations for programme outcomes. This is a useful intervention or counselling strategy, as, by listing their goals, participants feel more in control of the progress made and accept more responsibility for this. They are also more convinced of the benefits of taking part, as they have outlined the goals themselves. In addition to contract setting, the design of these courses should include an introductory session whereby all students are asked for their primary motive for participation. This serves to elucidate group goals and to clarify for each participant their individual goals within the course programme. It can also prove useful in that from an early stage in the course, shared vulnerabilities and concerns are voiced which brings a sense of reassurance and peer support.

Timing of programmes

The timing of programmes, whether they are counselling or group intervention programmes, is highly important. Both the adolescent and adult literature on stress management training courses recommend courses which last between six and eight weeks. Meditation and relaxation courses are usually approximately this length. Counselling courses with school students are also usually structured around six-week programmes. Attention should be paid to absenteeism, and how it may be used by this age group to express ambivalence or direct criticism at the way in which sessions are unfolding.

Power sharing

The issue of power within counselling relationships and in the relationship between a course facilitator and group members is important. Sensitivity to power dynamics in designing and delivering interventions is crucial. Delivering advice in an individual or group setting involves vulnerability and disclosure in 'clients', and assumed knowledge and evaluation in the counsellor or course facilitator. Failure to prepare for this perceived power differential could lead to heightened feelings of exposure and consequent resentment in the client/participant. It is therefore recommended that sufficient attention is given to the prevailing tone in each session, particularly the first.

Mabey and Sorensen recommend some self-disclosure from the course facilitator or counsellor at various stages of the programme to at least partially address this differential. Above all, it must be communicated overtly to the participants that their views are valued and respected, and there are several counselling techniques which enable the course facilitator to achieve this. Young people may distrust the apparent air of acceptance and set out to shock the facilitator or test his or her limits. Alternatively, young people may behave in a surly or uninterested manner in order to express their suspicions and doubts regarding the course administrator or course rationale. Course facilitators need to be aware of the likelihood of these behavioural tendencies emerging, and to have prepared appropriate and constructive ways of proceeding should they arise. In other words, it is important to 'walk the thin line between real acceptance of their clients while avoiding collusion or condescension, both of which will usually be picked up in seconds by the young client' (p. 60). An initial reluctance to participate in group discussions for some groups can be ameliorated by introducing more levity and humour into the situation.

Supervision
Regular supervision has become standard practice in counselling for young people (see Bond, 1993). To reiterate, although these precedents are not always observed in interventionist settings, they are ethically important to try to implement as thoroughly as possible. Preferably, a trained school counsellor should attend to provide supervision and support and to give useful feedback to the course facilitator after each session. It can also be arranged that those students who (1) feel that issues had been raised which would benefit from extra discussion or (2) miss a session and need to pick up the appropriate handouts and homework are encouraged by the counsellor after each session to make an individual appointment.

Contingency plans
The Mabey and Sorensen text is helpful in preparing for a range of other possible situations likely to emerge. These include dealing with long silences, levels of appropriate depth at which discussions should be pitched (degrees of intrusiveness), unusual behaviour, discussion breakdowns and alternative modes of communication (e.g. drawing), and childlike behaviour (often facilitated by authoritarian reactions). Other suggestions, such as conducting a needs analysis, choosing appropriate settings, using referral protocols and assessment procedures are useful. Other texts such as that by Copley and Williams (1995)

provide a good insight into adolescent sources of stress and ways of coping. Approaching the subject from a phenomenological perspective, this text fosters an empathic understanding of adolescent difficulties, which aids one's skill as a course facilitator.

Every attempt should be made during the design and delivery of courses to adhere as closely as possible to the guidelines set out by the above literature on adolescent counselling, working with groups of adolescents and tackling stress in schools.

Evaluating programmes

If you decide to design and deliver a stress management programme, you may wish to evaluate the effects of the programme. This will enable you to (1) see if it can be improved, and (2) demonstrate its success in reducing stress to ensure its future delivery or to secure funding. Methodological and measurement issues are important at this stage. You may choose to interview students and ask them to write in their own way about their experiences of stress during and after the programme, and invite them to comment on core course components.

Alternatively, you may wish to evaluate the programme in a more quantitative fashion. To measure stress levels in students it is recommended that you measure as many as possible of the following in order to capture the stress process adequately: number of life events and daily hassles, perceived strain or symptoms, coping styles, self-esteem, levels of social support, perceptions of control, personality factors and appraisal of stress. If you can only measure one of the above, symptom measurement by a questionnaire such as the General Health Questionnaire (Goldberg, 1988) is recommended.

Make sure when choosing measures that these:

- have published norms for comparison purposes
- have been assessed, and have demonstrated adequate reliability and validity
- are not too long or complex
- are culturally appropriate
- are developmentally appropriate
- are within your budget

Try to ensure that you receive permission in using the measures if they are copyrighted. Your budget may determine whether you choose questionnaires that are expensive or ones that are free to photocopy.

When designing a study, the following are recommended:

- measure stress before, during, one week after, one month after and six months after the intervention
- measure the stress levels in a control group (i.e. a group of comparable young people who do not take part in an intervention)
- measure the stress levels in a comparison group (i.e. a group of comparable young people who take part in a different type of intervention)
- ask the young people themselves, their teachers, parents and friends to complete questionnaires on their stress levels and behaviour
- use other sources of information, such as changes in levels of absenteeism or grades
- assess whether changing the selection procedure, location, facilitator or timing of the intervention impacts on the programme's success

CONCLUSION

The studies described above illustrate the adaptability of this age group to personal change and development and indicate that current adolescent stress levels may be successfully combated with effective interventions. These interventions, though diverse, share the common goal of alleviating distress and providing adolescents with enduring skills with which to confront ongoing and prospective situations in their lives.

Many researchers believe that there is an acute need for the evaluation and implementation of more interventions in order to meet the growing needs of today's adolescents. They have referred to the desperate need for education/prevention programmes that offer adolescents alternatives to unhealthy responses to excessive stress.

This is similarly expressed by Curran, who writes:

> It seems rather ludicrous in light of the high levels of stress faced by adolescents, their often self-destructive ways of handling it, and the relative ease of instituting programs aimed at stress reduction and teaching coping skills, that more has not been done. (Curran, 1987, p. 186)

The remainder of this book is aimed at providing those working with young people with the skills, knowledge and expertise required to teach young people how to manage stress in their lives.

Notes

1   Kwee, M. (1990) 'Cognitive and behavioral approaches to meditation', in M. Kwee (ed.) *Proceedings of the first International Conference on Psychotherapy, Meditation and Health at Noordwikerhout*, The Netherlands, pp. 36–54. London: East-West, p. 70.

2   Walsh, R. N. (1983) 'Meditation practice and research'. *Journal of Humanistic Psychology*, **23**, 18–50 (p. 19).

3   See for review: West, M. A. (1980) 'Meditation, personality and arousal'. *Personality and Individual Differences*, **1**, 135–42.

4   Black, D. R. and Frauenknecht, M. (1990) 'A primary prevention problem-solving program for adolescent stress management', in *Human Stress, Current Selected Research*, **4**, pp. 89–109. New York: AMS Press; Graham, P. (1994) 'Prevention', in M. Rutter, E. A. Taylor and L. Hersov (eds) *Child and Adolescent Psychiatry: Modern Approaches*, pp. 815–29. Oxford: Blackwell Scientific Publications.

5   Curran, D. K. (1987) *Adolescent Suicidal Behavior*. Washington, DC: Hemisphere; Compas, B. E. (1993) 'Promoting positive mental health during adolescence', in S. G. Millstein, E. O. Nightingale and A. C. Petersen, *Promoting the Health of Adolescents: New Directions for the Twenty-first Century*. Oxford: Oxford University Press; Phillips, B. N. (1993) *Educational and Psychological Perspectives on Stress in Students, Teachers, and Parents*. Brandon: Clinical Psychology Publishing.

6   Gross, A. M., Heimann, L., Shapiro, R. and Schultz, R. M. (1983) 'Children with diabetes: social skills training and hemoglobin A1C levels'. *Behavior Modification*, **7**(2), 151–64.

7   Weinberger, G. and Reuter, M. (1980) 'The "life discussion" group as a means of facilitating personal growth and development in late adolescence'. *Journal of Clinical Child Psychology*, **Spring**, 6–12.

8   Hains, A. A. and Szyjakowski, M. (1990) 'A cognitive stress-reduction intervention program for adolescents'. *Journal of Counseling Psychology*, **37**(1), 79–84.

9   See also Haggerty, R. J. (1980) 'Life stress, illness and social supports'. *Developmental and Medical Child Neurology*, **22**, 391–400.

10   See for summary, Chang, J. (1991) 'Using relaxation strategies in child and youth care practice'. *Child and Youth Care Forum*, **20**(3), 155–69.

11   Aracki, S. (1986) 'Transcendental meditation as a relaxation method in the treatment of essential hypertension'. *Psihijatrija Danas*, **18**(4), 409–19.

12   See Nath, S. and Warren, J. (1995) 'Hypnosis and examination stress in adolescence'. *Contemporary Hypnosis*, **12**(2), 119–24.

13   See Culbertson, F. M. and Hatch, A. (1990) 'Relaxation strategies with an anxious school-aged child. 96th Annual Convention of the American Psychological Association: Hypnotherapy with children and adolescents'. *Psychotherapy in Private Practice*, **8**(3), 33–40.

14   Fombonne, E. (1995) 'Depressive disorders: time trends and possible explanatory mechanisms', in M. Rutter and D. J. Smith (eds) *Psychosocial Disturbances in Young People*. Chichester: Wiley.

PART TWO

What Can We Do?

Practical Suggestions on How to Help Young People to Cope more Effectively with Stress

Part 1 aimed to provide an overview regarding the meaning of adolescence and adolescent stress. Research has shown an alarming increase in the number of stressful events which adolescents encounter, a decline in support for young people and a growth in maladaptive ways of coping with stress. This research has highlighted coping skills which exert a strong protective role for young people.

Part 2 aims to help you communicate these skills to young people. This part of the book moves away from research findings and represents a more practical application of this knowledge. Its tone is deliberately more informal. It provides advice, information and techniques on mental and physical ways of coping with stress, study skills and time management, communication skills, and coping with depression and anxiety. It begins by suggesting how to frame initial conversations with young people on the meaning of stress and recognizing stress.

CHAPTER 4

Talking to young people about stress and coping

The aim of Chapter 4 is to help young people identify the source of stress in their lives and the impact this has on their thoughts, feelings, health and behaviour. Having done this, you can move on to mental and physical ways of coping with stress.

The chapter aims to help you to introduce the area of stress and to get young people thinking and talking about the sources and symptoms of stress in their own lives. It will help you to discuss what they mean when they say they are stressed, how they respond when they feel stressed, when a challenging situation leads to poor coping and why they respond in this way. It discusses the benefits of learning to cope more effectively with stress, and examines the relationship between stress and performance.

Issues to consider before starting your discussion on stress

Setting the right tone

The aim of this book is to provide a guide for preventing the manifestation of stress-related symptoms in adolescents. Therefore, since these discussions are being held as a purely preventive, mental and physical health-promoting context, the tone should be one of relaxation and exploration. Young people should be encouraged to relax, to be themselves and to see this as 'time out' to explore and develop in a non-judgemental and caring environment.

Allowing young people to set the agenda

When talking to young people about stress, it is often helpful to ask them their opinion before seeking to inform them. This encourages the young person to explore issues and look back at their own experiences. It also shows young people that their views and experiences are just as important as what you have to say. Asking them to think about the issues first is also important so as not to bias the discussion, and to allow topics and issues to emerge which may not otherwise have been discussed.

As with adults, when a young person initiates a discussion it may be difficult to ascertain the root causes behind this desire to talk. Giving them the space to raise issues, asking them for their opinion, and giving them a chance to reflect on these questions before sitting down to talk properly will establish democracy within the conversation and will help to facilitate a respectful attitude from both parties. Young people are keenly aware of being 'talked down to' or 'talked at', and while this book seeks to equip you to deal with questions and help you to guide the young person, this should always be done in a consultative way with ears open at all times. These discussions should obviously be conducted with the utmost sensitivity.

Role shifting

If you are a teacher, it is worth remembering that these conversations involve a shifting of roles both for you and the young person. They require a different type of cooperation. They may require you, as the interventionist, and the young person to adapt to the new situation, particularly if they are taking place in a formal setting, such as a school. It may be worthwhile discussing this with the participants. There are no longer any right or wrong answers, and the aim of the conversation is to explore issues and experiment with new ways of looking at things.

Confidentiality

It is of fundamental importance that the issue of confidentiality is discussed with the young person. It is usually recommended that you make it clear to the young person at the outset the information which will remain confidential at all times, and the information which you may be obliged to share with appropriate others. Mandatory reporting mechanisms vary from country to country and it is important to know the law in relation to your own position. In the case of the young person disclosing that they have been the victim of sexual abuse, you may wish to inform them from the outset that you may wish to pass this information on to the relevant services. However, you can assure the young person that the decision will be made in consultation with them.

If you are conducting these discussions in a group format it is equally important that a clear discussion on confidentiality is held before the group is asked to disclose anything of a personal nature. Group members may be asked to draw up and sign a contract of confidentiality which will be of benefit to all of them in that their disclosures will be secure. The participants in the group should be encouraged not to discuss issues or incidents raised which they feel might be sensitive for other students.

Giving the ideas a chance
Having discussed confidentiality, the young people should be encouraged to be honest and open in discussions or at least to make an effort to be honest with themselves in their private reflections. This latter point is not as easy as it seems for anyone, teenagers notwithstanding.

Follow-through
You might suggest that any students or participants who wish to discuss any matters that have arisen as a result of these discussions can approach you or the school counsellor in private. Psychological back-up should be in place in conjunction with the course, with the school's permission.

Why learn more about stress?
When talking to young people about stress, it is useful to be in a position to point out the benefits of coping with stress. You can ask them to try to think of these first. Why would they want to learn more coping skills? Perhaps they feel that learning stress management or coping skills is boring, uncool or not relevant to them. You can point out that once they have learned more coping skills they will have more energy, study better and be able to relax more easily, their relationships should improve, they will have fewer headaches, better quality of sleep, feel more in control, experience improved health and probably enjoy life more.

Breathing and stretching
A good introduction to breathing and stretching exercises is provided by Whelan (1993). At the risk of being thought eccentric or a hippy from a bygone age, it is hugely helpful if you succeed in doing these exercises with the young person prior to and after any discussions on stress and coping. It will break down barriers, make them feel more relaxed, help them to realize this is 'time-out' and allow them to feel that they don't have to be in control of what they say and do, but rather can be open, relaxed and honest. It will also help them to experience the relaxing effects these exercises can have.

Engaging young men and women

With young women often tending to focus more on interpersonal and emotional stress, relationships with peers and the opposite sex are frequently cited as sources of stress. It is often more difficult to discuss stress with male students, as they are more reticent about raising these issues and can act as if nothing were wrong. These observations are consistent with the results of much research whereby males report less psychological distress. Despite the difficulties, it is crucial that we continue our efforts to engage young males by persuading them to discuss issues that are a cause of concern for them.

However, although young men sometimes look bored or act in a derisive way, it is worth holding conversations they can listen to, even if they choose not to participate. They may be behaving in a macho way while actually absorbing a good deal of the information. They often respond to very practical advice, problem-solving and humour.

Try asking them whether the issues under discussion prevent them from achieving what they want from life. If they are feeling tired, under pressure, depressed, lonely, inadequate, unable to cope, or angry without being able to express this, they are less likely to fulfil their potential and lead happy, healthy lives. Challenge them to be brave enough to give these ideas a chance. You could try experimenting with single-sex or mixed-sex discussion groups to see whether this impedes or aids the ease with which topics are discussed. Provide them with real-life experiments if they are cynical about suggestions. Assure them that young men often feel overwhelmed by the future.

Engaging younger and older adolescents

Younger adolescents are often seen to be coping with many developmental and pubertal processes and are more prone to peer conflicts and bullying. They often enjoy role-playing, games and visual representations of the ideas you are trying to communicate. Look out for cartoons or funny advertisements. Younger adolescents are often, however, very good at taking part in discussions around different issues.

Older adolescents tend to experience a higher number of conflicts with parents, and become increasingly concerned with final exams and college/employment opportunities. They may have responsibilities which include looking after younger siblings or a part-time job. Older adolescents often appreciate more mature approaches and may feel patronized by game-playing. It is important to allow them ownership of the group, to use humour and levity to oil the wheels, to be sensitive to issues which are difficult for them, and to avoid appearing over-earnest, as this can be perceived as naivety. Older students often appreciate discussions about forthcoming events. They are curious and anxious about leaving school and the challenges that lie ahead.

Engaging adolescents from different backgrounds
Sources of stress may vary depending on socioeconomic status. Financial worries may be more salient in schools in less advantaged areas, together with the vicarious stress at seeing parents unsuccessfully attempt to find employment. Pressure on students to take drugs and their side-effects can also be a source of stress. Students may witness different coping styles at home. Some research suggests that students from disadvantaged backgrounds may be less used to using problem-focused coping styles.

Students in more advantaged areas are more likely to mention exam stress and parental and internal pressure to achieve as sources of stress. Loneliness and bullying are also huge problems in boarding-schools.

Sources of stress
The following questions will help you to begin your discussion on stress and coping. If you are conducting this discussion with a large group, students should be divided into groups of four with perhaps one person allocated to feeding back the answers. Encourage them to generate answers which are meaningful and real to them, not necessarily the ones you would expect or the ones that appear in this book. In summary, before moving on to defining stress and its effects, it is recommended that young people be asked about the following.

SOURCES OF STRESS

- To generate the sources of stress in their own lives, past and present.

- To compile a list of things which have made them stressed, both in general and specific terms.

- Are the big events or the little things that happen more frequently more stressful?

- What kinds of hassles do they experience on a daily basis?

- Is stress easier when it is predictable or unexpected?

- Can stress be a positive thing?

- Can stress come from within you, as a person, as well from the outside?

The stress process
Stress is part of life
If you have been conducting this conversation in a group setting, it will become clear to the young people that everyone has experienced stress at some time, and it is normal for people to feel that they are losing control and under pressure from time to time. It is often reassuring for young people to learn that they are not alone in experiencing stress or pressure, indeed that stress is an ordinary part of life. You could even say that if you never felt stressed in your life it might mean that there was nothing in your life of value or importance to you. This means that by feeling unhappy about things like their relationships or workload, people feel a certain degree of commitment to these aspects of their lives.

The fact is that stress in young people is so common that many people are now arguing that all teenagers should be given the opportunity to learn about stress and coping at school as part of their normal curriculum. Once you have established that everyone undergoes stress from time to time, you can then proceed to unravel what this means and where this stress comes from.

Internal stresses
It is likely that when you asked for sources of stress, these consisted of external or outside stresses, like being given too much homework, being nagged by parents or being picked on by others at school. However, one of the most important lessons for young people to learn is that stress can come not only from outside but also from inside themselves. This type of stress includes their own way of looking at life and the things that happen to them and other people, their attitude to stress, coping and relaxation, and their wants, needs and feelings.

Outside stresses
Outside stresses include the pressures or burdens young people may feel they are carrying. Sources of stress that come from inside are often harder to think of for both adults and young people. Wanting to do well in school, to succeed, to be liked and to make other people happy all put pressure on the young person.

As discussed in Chapter 2, sources of stress for young people may include carrying out necessary developmental tasks, undergoing major pubertal changes, making transitions, dealing with difficult family and peer relationships, family conflicts, academic difficulties, coping with the school environment, fear of failing exams, dealing with emerging sexuality, coping with parental separation, introduction of step-parents or parental boy/girlfriends, bullying, having nothing to do, feeling left out of a group, feeling anxious about after-school prospects, experiencing poverty or racial prejudice, parental pressure, having negative feelings about one's appearance or personal health, financial worries, losing the motivation to work, too many school and home obligations, illness or death in people they know, lacking confidence, and relationships ending.

In addition, when we get little exercise and our diet is poor, this can place stress on our bodies which may make us less able to cope and enjoy life to the full. It is normal for young people (and adults) to acknowledge only the social stresses in life. It is important to realize the contribution that the environment and physiology also make to our perceived stress levels. Once we become aware of these, we can learn to reduce them or their impact on us.

Resources

Just as stress can come from the inside as well as the outside, so too can the solutions. We often talk about two types of resources which we have to deal with stress. These are personal resources and external resources or sources of support.

You can try asking young people to think of the personal resources they have to deal with stress. Examples of resources from outside oneself include support from friends and family. Young people in their mid- to late teens are likely to ask for advice from friends as often as from family or other adults. Inside resources also come from the way the young person sees the stressful situation. This includes believing they can handle stress, the way they view themselves as a person, the way they respond or anticipate change, religious beliefs, self-esteem, self-confidence, sense of humour and health.

The balance

What one person finds stressful, another may find an exciting challenge. Sometimes internal sources of stress combine with external sources to produce too much stress. When this happens, we can reduce the stress by (1) reducing the external stress, (2) reducing internal stress (for example, by changing attitudes), or (3) changing both. When we appraise a situation as demanding or frustrating, it causes a mental, emotional, physical and behavioural response. The strength and duration of this response is highly variable. If young people perceive the demands on them as too many and they feel they have inadequate resources, they will feel stressed and unable to cope. In other words, stress can be seen as a perception of demands as greater than resources.

You can help the young person to visualize this process by imagining demands on one side and resources on the other, like weighing scales.

What is stress?

It is always worth exploring what we mean by stress, as this is so fundamental to the way we go on to deal with it. Ask young people to define stress. Make sure you give them enough time to think their answer through. Perhaps you could ask them whether they think stress is what happens in them, the way they feel or whether it is both of these things.

These are the three most common ways of looking at stress. Perhaps stress is all three things at different times, but usually stress is both what is happening in your life and the personal attributes and social resources you bring to the situation. This can be both an exhilarating and a scary idea to take on board, as it means that we have more control over the situation than we might otherwise have thought. However, it is worth bearing in mind that young people have less control over their environments than adults and so they should balance this sense of control with an understanding that it is sometimes up to them to adjust to their situation as they may not always be able to change it. This book should help to distinguish between these different types of situations. Teaching young people that they can control how they perceive a situation does not mean that they must adjust to situations as they are. It means that they can generate more solutions. This can often involve the help of others.

Identity and appraisal

> Don't laugh at a youth for his affectations; he is only
> trying on one face after another to find his own.
> Logan Pearsall Smith.

It follows that the way young people interpret and define their experiences and what they see as the likely consequences will either relax and reassure them or make them feel stressed. If the young person interprets irritability from their parents as a sign of rejection it is likely to make them feel anxious. If they interpret the same thing as their parent feeling tired or just thinking about their own problems it will not be as worrying. Young people are often under the impression that they are the focus of other people's thoughts or concerns. This is because they are going through an important process of shaping and forming a new identity for themselves and they are heavily concerned with all aspects of this identity. They sometimes feel that others are equally concerned. It is very interesting to discuss this with groups of young people or to do role-plays which demonstrate that everyone has their own concerns.

Helping young people to understand that their interpretation of events does not always equate with reality is advice of enormous importance. Try asking them to recall events which you may have witnessed and see if you agree on all or any points. Ask them to discuss their perceptions of events honestly with their peers to see how frequently the same events are perceived differently by different people. Once they understand the role that their psychology plays, they can begin to learn coping skills that will stay with them for life.

Change can be stressful

Stress is a natural part of life. All changes which require adaptation, even when they are positive changes, can cause some stress as the young person tries to navigate a way through uncharted waters and to adapt to the new demands made by the change. Moving to a nicer house, changing to a new school class or starting a new relationship, though exciting, will all require adjustment and new things to cope with. This draws on our energy reserves and can even make us vulnerable to illness, as our resistance is lowered. This is particularly true when changes happen together or in quick succession. In many ways, adolescence is a time when both negative and positive extremes of emotion are experienced. This is one of the joys of being a teenager. In other words, whether the stress they experience is the result of major life changes such as experiencing their parents separating or moving house, or the buildup of smaller daily worries, it is how the young person responds and copes with these experiences that is important in determining the impact on their lives.

As already mentioned, teenagers are often naturally adept at staggering changes so that they don't have to deal with them all at once. This, however, is not always possible. When two or more changes occur at once, the strain on the young person may prove more difficult to cope with than if the changes had unfolded one by one. The onset of puberty may coincide, for instance, with the transition from primary to secondary school, or moving home may coincide with the young person's first relationship with a member of the opposite sex. These and other combinations can sometimes be difficult for the young person to get through. Support from those around them will help.

Unexpected events in life and situations which we have no control over are often particularly stressful. What we find stressful depends on personality, attitude, health, the circumstances surrounding the event, social support and the way our body reacts.

Positive stress

Earlier, it was suggested that you ask the young person for examples of positive stress. Although it often takes longer to think of these, remembering times when we were adrenalized is useful, as it can help us to realize what life would be like if we did not react and respond strongly to its challenges. These can be exciting and important learning experiences for us that eventuate in personal achievements we can be proud of. These include exams which, although not always seen as positive stress, can result in a real sense of reward and achievement if we are helped to cope with preparing for them. Other examples are participating in sports and falling in love.

Daily hassles

As mentioned above, daily hassles may include forgetting homework, being late, interruptions, distractions and minor conflicts. If we realize that these hassles have made us feel strained, we are less likely to lose our awareness. This can make us take it out on others and blame the wrong things for our stress.

To help them understand the centrality of appraisal and changing vulnerability, try asking young people to think of a situation when:

1   they reacted strongly to a minor hassle
2   they were calm when something major happened.

This usually helps us to realize that when we are feeling strong and in control, when things are well spaced out and we appraise them as unthreatening, we do not respond with a stress response. Sometimes we get through situations without problems and it is only later that we feel drained and tired from our coping efforts.

Stress-related symptoms

Try asking the following questions to help young people to recognize their own reactions to stress.

RECOGNIZING STRESS

- How does it feel when they're stressed?
- How would they and others know they're stressed?

- What sorts of thoughts do they have?
- How does it affect their behaviour?
- How do they relate to others at these times?
- How do other people behave towards them?
- How would they recognize stress in themselves?
- How would they recognize it in others?
- Do they know anyone who is stressed?

The aim of this section is to help young people to recognize their own symptoms of stress. This is an essential first step to coping with stress. It requires an understanding and awareness of our own well-being. Once you have helped them to recognize these symptoms, you can move on to providing them with the skills they need to alleviate or eliminate many of them.

Everyone reacts differently to increasing levels of stress. Some people become cranky while others become passive and withdrawn. Sometimes it can be difficult for adults to recognize symptoms of stress in young people or to distinguish them from mild forms of depression. This is because the symptoms of depression and stress can differ between adults and adolescents. When adolescents are feeling depressed they often appear moody, irritable and intolerant. Adults are more likely to feel numb, sad or cry a lot.

It is important for young people to be familiar with their own signs and symptoms, as this will help them to cope better with stressful situations. It is often useful to ask them to think about times in the past when they felt under pressure. If they can remember these times, they can then try to recall the symptoms they experienced. When they learn to recognize these symptoms early on they can take action before the stress gets out of hand. The following are common symptoms of stress. Ask the young people to think about which ways stress affects them. Does it depend on the situation? What types of situation affect them in these ways?

Ask the young people to think of situations when they have experienced any of these symptoms. It is important to reassure them that these things can happen more or less often when just dealing with everyday ups and downs. They may also have symptoms which are not listed here.

RECOGNIZING STRESS

Mental symptoms

They may find themselves suffering poor concentration, having difficulty remembering things, being in a hurry all the time, acting indecisively, having no confidence, over-reacting to things, feeling really tired, feeling confused, making mistakes, always putting things off, not being able to plan far ahead, always imagining the worst, worrying rather than trying to solve problems, and becoming stubborn and controlling.

Physical symptoms

They may experience muscular pains, tension headaches, aching neck, shoulders and back, stomach pains, feeling sick, choking feeling in throat, twitch in eye or lips, shakiness, clenched teeth or fists, raised heartbeat, palpitations, sweating palms, poor circulation, dry mouth, frequent urination, dizzy spells, irregular breathing, diarrhoea or constipation and allergies, asthma or skin problems becoming worse.

Emotional symptoms

They may feel irritable, aggressive, withdrawn, unable to relate as normal, lowered self-esteem, moody, cynical, guilty, anxious or feelings of panic, depressed, oversensitive to criticism, edgy, angry, hopeless, worried, miserable, feel like crying and have irrational fears.

Behavioural symptoms

They may notice that they are worse at managing time and at organizing themselves, rushing around without getting much done, sleeping or eating a lot more or less than usual, doing things in a hurry, losing touch with friends, blaming others for the problem, taking it out on others, needing a drink, turning to drugs, over-reacting, fidgeting, smoking and drinking more, behaving obsessively, or missing school a lot.

Why do we respond in this way to stress?
The 'fight-or-flight' response
Much of the way that our body responds to stress can be attributed to the fact that we have inherited a way of responding to stress through evolution called the 'fight-or-flight' response. This was discussed in Chapter 1. These reactions are there to help us to cope with the threat. If we do something and the conflict is resolved, the body returns to its original state. However, if no relief comes the body may remain physically strained, which can result in long-term damage to our health. It is meant to be a temporary reaction and so cannot be maintained. When we feel threatened we release a stress hormone called cortisol. This makes us think quickly (but not very well), forget things, feel irritable and angry, and behave aggressively.

We may become vulnerable to illness after periods of stress. This is because our immune system cannot fight infection so well at these times. When we appraise situations as threatening, our body actually stops making natural killer cells and antibodies which fight against invading foreign cells.

Stress and performance
The young people you are talking to may feel that stress helps them to perform well at school or in their job. Although some stress is healthy and makes us feel challenged, young people should note the results of many studies which suggest that there is an optimum level of stress at which we feel alert and challenged. We perform well when we appraise situations as a challenge and are not confronted with overwhelming levels of stress. Having no stress can lead to us doing nothing, feeling bored and lacking energy. Too much stress will eventually burn us out and lead to us feeling totally exhausted. If maximum stress is given ten points and minimal stress is given one point, they should aim to stick to a level of around five or six points.

Conclusion
We have learned that stress is a process which starts with stressful events and minor hassles. If we perceive these as threatening they will have short- and long-term effects on our behaviour, mood, relationships and health. The intensity and duration of these effects are in part determined by many factors including social resources, personal attributes, genetic make-up and health.

KEY POINTS

In initiating your discussions with young people about stress, the key points to remember are to:

- ensure that the discussions take place in a neutral forum
- ensure that the atmosphere is relaxed and informal
- prepare them for the change of roles – there are no right or wrong answers
- discuss confidentiality
- ensure that they know who they can talk to in private about specific issues
- allow them to set the agenda in terms of the issues which are causing stress
- discuss the benefits of learning to cope more effectively with stress
- divide large groups into smaller groups of four
- experiment with single-sex and mixed-sex groups
- help to identify specific sources of stress
- encourage a discussion on internal as well as external sources of stress (attitudes, wants and assumptions)
- explore gender, age and social factors in contributing to stress and ways of coping
- ask them to think about their resources
- explore the stress of change
- discuss the symptoms of stress
- discuss how stress affects performance

In Chapter 5 we will be learning about ways that young people can cope effectively with stress. If you intend to discuss some of these issues with young people, it is often helpful to ask them to fill out a stress diary for one week. This means recording when they felt stressed, what the preceding event was and what thoughts and feelings followed. This can help young people to be more informed about the sorts of things in their lives that are causing them stress so you can get straight to discussing ways in which they can cope better. If they would rather not share this diary (understandably), you might suggest that they jot down a summary or some thoughts on the way that stress made them feel during the course of one week.

CHAPTER 5

Mental strategies
for coping with stress

Having identified the main sources of stress for young people, this chapter aims to help you discuss coping strategies for dealing with stress together with preventive strategies which will reduce the likelihood of feelings of strain. It is useful to initiate these discussions using stress diaries to explore the events and mental precursors to feelings of tension. If you are discussing these issues in a group setting, it is important that young people know they are not required to discuss specific events or thoughts in detail (unless they want to), but rather to think about the patterns. What you are really trying to establish is the link between events, thoughts and feelings. If you are discussing this with young people in a group setting, it is a good idea to divide the larger group into groups of four for the discussion and then ask them to report back to the group as a whole. As with all discussions around stress and coping, it is a good idea to begin and end with a breathing and stretching exercise.

In your discussion you might like to ask the young people the following questions:

- What kinds of things did they find stressful from their stress diary?
- What kinds of thoughts did they have when they were stressed?
- What kinds of feelings did they experience when they were stressed?
- Which came first, the stressful *thought* or the *feelings* of stress?
- Do they notice negative thoughts saying negative things to them again and again?
- Did they notice any patterns?

Learning to control our thoughts

As we already learned in Chapter 4, appraisal is a central component in the stress process and learning how to control the way we appraise or think about things is an important key to stress management. It does not mean that we always have to change ourselves rather than the situation. It does mean that we can generate more solutions because we have a better perspective on the event. In young people, an inability to generate alternative solutions in light of highly stressful events can have serious consequences. They can feel trapped and frustrated and often try to cope with this by themselves. Suicide has been linked to a failure to generate solutions and to seeing 'no way out'.

Learning to control your thinking is a very powerful stress management tool. It allows young people to control the way situations affect them, how and if other people affect them and gives them more power to decide how they are going to live their lives.

Recognizing stress

Recognizing the problem is the first step. Awareness is the key to learning to manage stress successfully. Young people can learn to recognize signs of stress in their body, their moods or their cognitions. Unfortunately, young people may feel conditioned to hide signs of stress from others. In doing so, they are often not acknowledging it to themselves. Many young men, in particular, may feel uncomfortable about admitting to themselves and others that they feel vulnerable, strained or unhappy.

As with adults, young people will feel more vulnerable at certain times. This is influenced, for example, by their personality, the number of life changes they have experienced which require adaptation (especially recent ones), the absence or presence of social support, their general health, their nutritional status, their physical fitness, their age, previous training in learning to cope with stress or, in the case of girls, just before or during a period.

At certain times, these factors may combine to make young people feel vulnerable. Everything they have to deal with during these times when resistance is low can seem like a major obstacle. They can feel irritable and react strongly to minor hassles. At other times, young people can display enough confidence and energy to rise to any challenge.

Being aware that they are under stress and the reasons behind this is highly important for young people. If they do not recognize that they are under pressure or have insights into what may be causing the strain, it is more difficult for them to try to address this constructively and to solve the problem. The symptoms of stress were described in

Chapter 4, so you can help young people to recognize their own individual response to stress as a first step towards taking action.

Encourage young people to get into the habit of mentally noting daily stressors and their effects. If they suffer badly from stress-related symptoms you could suggest that they keep a stress diary in which, every hour, they write down what they are doing and if they have any stress symptoms, whether physical, emotional, mental or behavioural. This has already been suggested as a way of discovering more about stress for the purposes of these discussions. However, diaries can be regularly used as a stress awareness tool.

Their stress diaries will assist young people in tracing feelings of stress to events or thoughts which they may not realize came first. For example, they may have noticed that they began to feel physically tense when playing video games or watching television. They can then retrace this physical discomfort to their thoughts and feelings. Perhaps they felt guilty about not studying. Similarly, if they felt tense talking to certain people, this will relate back to their thinking in some way. Did they feel low in confidence, angry about an event in the past or dislike aspects of the interaction?

As we have seen in Chapter 4, some stress is challenging and can improve performance, so you are not trying to teach young people to remove all stress from their lives. Having nothing to do can be stressful too. The important thing is for young people to learn their limits and to recognize signs of overloading, like fatigue and crankiness, and see these as signals for a break. Unfortunately, with the huge emphasis in contemporary society on academic achievement at an earlier age, we are often so busy telling young people to work harder that we forget that in order to be happy and productive they must be healthy and relaxed too!

'Here's one I prepared earlier' – predicting stress and being prepared

We cannot stop young people making mistakes, and these are important learning tools. However, we can help them to prepare for challenging situations. It's all about seeing things as a threat or a challenge. If they feel afraid when approaching an event, their body will respond as if they are really in a threatening situation. This usually means butterflies in their stomachs, headaches and so on. If they believe they can handle the situation they will remain relaxed, both mentally and physically. This in turn sends feedback to the brain that there is nothing to worry about and they will feel more in control again. Research has shown that the effect of stress on the individual is seriously influenced by the degree of predictability and control they feel they have over it. Visualizing the event will help them to predict their responses.

Some stressful events are predictable, such as sitting exams. Other situations can make us feel uncomfortable without knowing why. A stress diary will help young people to see patterns in stressful situations. Once they know the problem, they can plan productively how to cope with it.

It is commonly known that worrying about a forthcoming event is an energy drain and achieves little. However, proper preparation for events which we know are going to happen can be a fantastic stress management tool. For young people, these can include school tests, confrontations with peers, dates and difficult discussions about the future.

LEARNING HOW TO PLAN AHEAD

Suggest that young people think of a stressful situation they are presently dealing with or know is coming up. Then suggest that they:

- *Imagine* it in detail, particularly how they are likely to feel. Rehearse this while doing breathing and stretching exercises.

- Start *preparing* – if it is their reaction to aggressive comments which is likely to be stressful, they should prepare for ways of dealing with these comments without feeling upset. If it is not being able to answer a particular question on an exam paper, they could get extra help with that subject, talk to other students about it or try doing a bit more reading on it.

- Be familiar with *likely possibilities* and decide that they will be calm and relaxed.

- Make *contingency* plans – these will make it seem less threatening; for example, if they are asking someone along to something that they really want to go to, they should have someone else in mind who they can ask if their first choice can't make it.

- Do some *relaxation* before the situation. Going for a run or doing some breathing and stretching exercises should help.

- Plan *relaxation* time as well as a *reward* for after the stressful event.

Preparing for regular events

As with adults, for young people much of their stress will come from regular situations such as having to talk to people they don't like, being behind with homework, or witnessing conflicts. If they can learn to see these situations coming and prepare for them they will be less likely to get upset, because they will feel more in control. Again, their stress diary will be useful to help them to identify the types of stress that come up frequently or regularly. You can suggest the following as some ideas for dealing with regular stressful events.

DEALING WITH STRESSFUL EVENTS

1 *Get out* of the situation when appropriate (e.g. by not mixing with peers who make them feel uncomfortable).

2 *Prepare* (e.g. get their homework done early).

3 *Meet* the situation head-on (e.g. go and talk to a source of stress).

4 *Decide* what is best at keeping stress levels down – ask them to think about the way they normally handle a situation and if this is working for them. If not, then it is time to *re-evaluate their strategy*. For instance, if ignoring a friend every time they upset them or arguing with parents over homework results in them getting upset, perhaps they need to think of other ways of handling these situations.

Sometimes young people feel that anticipation is not necessary or natural, but for us to cope successfully we need to anticipate problems so that we can plan to take the most appropriate actions which will lead to the best outcomes for us. After we have been engaged in positive anticipation for a while, we can then re-evaluate the situation by asking the following questions: Have we been successful in achieving our *goal?* Can we *improve* our strategy? Would changing our strategy be more *beneficial?* (e.g. talking to someone directly rather than showing our annoyance by ignoring them).

When discussing these issues with young people, it is always helpful to relate them to real experiences and examples produced by the young people themselves.

Keeping things in perspective

Again, the simple three-way relationship between events, thoughts and feelings can help young people to understand that their feelings, whether they are ones of anxiety, depression or worry, have been produced by their thought processes and this is where they need to intervene in order to restore their emotional balance. This can then help them to change their objective circumstances by making them feel more in control.

When they feel upset or under pressure, young people are likely to:

- view everything in black and white

- generalize

- attach disproportionate significance to a particular aspect of an event

- think in a very extreme way

- exaggerate the consequences of the situation

- look only at the bad things

- take things personally

- blame themselves or other people in an irrational way

- jump to conclusions which are often unfounded.

This will lead to much more anxiety as, unfortunately, the body will react according to the way the mind has *interpreted* the situation, and thus stress can often continue or be made worse. This is because the mind is insisting on telling the body that we are in some kind of danger. If young people can learn to replace these extreme thoughts with more realistic and helpful ones they can learn to tone down their stress response. You can suggest that instead of using words such as 'always', 'never', 'must' and 'should', they can use 'often', 'rarely' and ' might'.

The following are common examples: 'I *never* do anything right', '*Nothing* is going right for me', '*Nothing* good is ever going to happen', 'I can *never* adapt to this' and 'There is *no one* who loves me'.

Much research has shown that those people who reinterpret a stressful situation more positively experience less intense physiological response and take less time to recover.

You can suggest an experiment: the next time the young people feel tense or stressed, they can try following their thoughts and challenge them. They can practice re-labelling the situation by trying to be more moderate and positive. If they do this, they will notice how much more quickly they return to feeling relaxed.

Replacing the negative with the positive

Man is not disturbed by events, but by the view he takes of them.
Epictetus.

Everybody has private conversations with themselves every day. We all have a critical inner voice that can hound us, making us feel strained, inadequate and low in confidence. These conversations can take the form of negative statements about ourselves. Young people in particular can experience doubts about themselves and what they can achieve. It is a vulnerable time when they compare themselves to peers and often receive criticism and conflicting messages from all around them. These internal conversations can bring self-doubt about their abilities to, for example, do well in school, cope with tense family relationships, start a career or form a relationship. It can make them come down on themselves, for example, when they tell themselves that 'I always mess things up', 'I look horrible', 'I have nothing to offer anyone', 'I don't fit in', or 'I'll never make a success of anything'.

Praise youth and it will prosper.
Irish proverb.

It is important to discuss these types of internal conversations with young people as they are constantly chipping away at their feelings of *self-worth* and emphasizing their weak points in an irrational way. Young people need to be encouraged, praised and supported. We often tend to forget that they are their own worst critics.

You can ask young people to think of things they say to themselves about themselves which may not be true. These may contain references to themselves that are so taken for granted that they are not even aware of the immediate increases in stress which follow and the resulting feelings. Unless they feel very comfortable in a group, it is unlikely they will want to share these thoughts as they relate to their most intimate images of ourselves.

They can look for clues as to what these statements to ourselves sound like. For instance, when we find ourselves over-using the word 'should'; for example, 'I should always be fun to be with or I'll lose my friends', 'I should always look confident and in control' or 'I shouldn't need any help from others'.

We are all inclined to think in an extreme way about our personal life; for example, if we don't have a partner we might feel it's the end of the world, or if people fail to ring us we feel utterly rejected. Young people can learn to be more moderate and realistic in the way they choose to interpret situations.

In summary, the way young people feel is not just about the actual events. In between the event and the feelings lie internal conversations which may be realistic or unrealistic. It is this 'self-talk' that produces the emotions. The way we think, directed and controlled by ourselves, is what creates negative feelings of anxiety, hostility and unhappiness.

A typical example of how this can affect young people is the negative self-talk which follows when they feel they have been excluded by their peers. Learning to reinterpret people's behaviour so that their self-esteem does not suffer is important. For example, they can learn that when friends don't call, it is often to do with other circumstances than their own popularity. If we can only impress upon young people that there are several ways of seeing things, we have introduced an element of doubt into this chain that can weaken it, even if they are not totally convinced!

The emotional outcomes of irrational self-talk are anxiety, depression, anger, guilt and low self-esteem. These internal conversations represent the way we view the world. If the self-talk is accurate and in touch with reality, we function well. If it is irrational and untrue, we experience stress and emotional distress.

Albert Ellis (1984) developed a system to attack irrational ideas or beliefs and replace them with realistic statements about the world. He believed that we *do* have a choice in how we train ourselves to view the things we experience. Negative training will lead to stress, while positive training will act as an antidote in times of stress. The following are common negative self-talks and the alternative positive statements. You can give this as an exercise for young people to fill out to practise seeing things from a different perspective.[1] Here are some of the possible ways that these can be answered.

- *Negative*: I can't help it if people or events stress me out.
- *Positive:* It's my decision whether I let these things get to me.
- *Negative*: I can't control the way I feel or how long I feel this way.
- *Positive:* I can actually control how long I feel like this and how much it hurts.

- *Negative*: It runs in the family. My father was just like me.
- *Positive:* This doesn't mean I have to be. I can change this behaviour.
- *Negative*: I need everything to work out well.
- *Positive:* That's life, not everything works out. I have to learn to take the rough with the smooth.
- *Negative*: How can anyone behave like this towards me when I've been so good to them?
- *Positive:* In an ideal world things like this wouldn't happen, but there is probably a reason for this person's behaviour.
- *Negative*: This is unbearable.
- *Positive:* I have the strength to deal with this and there are others who can help me. I have to keep things in perspective.
- *Negative*: I'm no good at anything.
- *Positive:* I have to focus on what I'm good at.
- *Negative*: Things will never get better for me.
- *Positive:* I have to be positive. Things will work out.
- *Negative*: I always ruin everything.
- *Positive:* Sometimes things don't work out as planned, but it happens to everyone and I try my best.

Thought stopping

'Thought stopping' is a technique that can help people to overcome thoughts which cause stress and worry and which prevent them from being able to relax. It was originally introduced as a therapy aid for people suffering from obsessive, nagging worry and doubt, and has since been used in the treatment of depression, anxiety, phobias and panic attacks. It can help in day-to-day life.

Many young people experience recurring thoughts which cause them anxiety. Typical ones include feeling unattractive, unpopular, unintelligent or incompetent. Persistent thoughts may take the form of self-doubt; for example, feeling that they will never succeed at school, or have a relationship. They may also take the form of anxiety; for example, worrying about their parents splitting up or things not working out.

Thoughts like these can understandably cause a lot of stress. Thought stopping is a simple but surprisingly effective technique. First of all young people must know the sorts of thoughts they are likely to have and then to switch off and empty their mind. They can either simply say 'STOP' to themselves, or they can get into the habit of replacing these thoughts with reassuring and more constructive, rational statements such as 'I won't fail if I work a little harder, it'll be fine'. These are the sorts of reassurances that young people seek from others, but unfortunately adults and friends may not know on which points they need reassurance. While reassurance from others is important, it is also important to be able to treat oneself with the compassion and support we seek from others.

If you are conducting a conversation with young people about recurring thoughts, you can try asking them to 'take a reality check' on these thoughts they may have learned to live with by asking themselves the questions in the box on pp. 128–9. The process of challenging their rationale is in itself a useful one. For instance, adolescents who harm themselves have often become so used to telling themselves that they are useless, unattractive or unloved that they never challenge these thoughts. While this method of stress management cannot uproot the possible negative messages which young people have absorbed, it can alleviate the symptoms and protect young people from suffering unduly. Issues around self-esteem are discussed in Chapter 9.

Ask them to think of a negative thought about themselves which they have often. Then ask them to think about the following questions. If they feel comfortable enough they could discuss them with you or a friend: Does the thought seem rational or irrational? Is it useful or useless in helping them get on in life? Do they find it difficult or easy to stop thinking these thoughts? Where might these thoughts have come from?

This type of coping skill undoubtedly requires discipline, but it is something that we can train ourselves to do. Ask the young person to choose one recurring thought and decide that it is unrealistic, unnecessary and an obstacle to their happiness.

Ironically, thoughts like these can cause so much anxiety that they stop people from doing what they need to do to ensure that they don't come true! Many teachers and parents have witnessed this in relation to teenagers who worry so much about their exams that it impedes their ability to study effectively. Thought stopping involves concentrating on the unwanted thoughts and, after a short time, suddenly stopping and emptying your mind.

Steps for tackling stressful thoughts

You can ask the young people to try the following exercise which involves identifying persistent stress-producing thoughts and rating them on a scale of one to five for the discomfort (how painful and intrusive they are to them, regardless of how big or small they would appear to others) and interference they cause. Any thought with a rating of over three for discomfort and over two for interference may warrant thought-stopping procedures.

The following is a list of stressful thoughts experienced by most people from time to time. If they begin to cause the young person undue distress as they cannot take their mind off them and they begin to intrude on their lives, they may want to try thought stopping as a way of reducing the stress that they cause. Some worries are there for a reason, and there are obviously things that young people are concerned about which might happen. In this case young people should obviously be encouraged to take appropriate action. Deciding what recurrent thoughts are necessary and what are just energy drains that make us feel anxious is discussed further in Chapter 9.

EXAMPLES OF STRESSFUL THOUGHTS

Do they find themselves:

- worrying about their physical or mental health?
- feeling guilty all the time?
- worrying all the time about having said the wrong thing?
- having unpleasant or frightening thoughts or words going over and over in their mind?
- being troubled by certain thoughts of harming themselves or others?
- going over and over a job that's finished, thinking that they could have done it better?
- being unable to make even simple decisions?
- having constant doubts about everything?
- having an irrational fear about doing certain things?
- always thinking things will get worse?
- feeling engrossed in anger when people don't do things the way they would like?
- thinking about details all the time?
- having ongoing feelings of jealousy, or fear of being rejected?

- preoccupied with desire for things they cannot have?
- preoccupied with negative aspects of their appearance?
- thinking again and again about their failures?
- thinking a lot about things they are ashamed of?
- worrying frequently about what the opposite sex thinks of them?
- worrying constantly about failing their exams?

In summary, thought stopping involves (1) imagining the thought, (2) saying 'Stop!' every time you start saying this to yourself, (3) thinking of a positive, assertive statement that will make you feel the way you want to feel. For example, if you are nervous about asking someone out and always say to yourself 'I'm too unattractive', say instead 'I've got a lot to offer!' This procedure may sound simple, but when practised regularly with discipline it has helped many people overcome thoughts which recur and cause stress and pain.

Coping skills training[2]

Like thought stopping and changing irrational thinking, coping skills training is about replacing stress-inducing thoughts with more constructive thinking, this time using relaxation techniques. This technique is also called 'stress inoculation' and was developed by Meichenbaum (1977) (see Chapter 3). Coping skills training teaches people to relax away anxiety and stress reactions. It gives us more self-control in the particular situation that we find anxiety-provoking.

As is the case with adults, some young people are better at coping in certain situations than others. Coping skills training centres around learning to relax using progressive muscle relaxation, so that when we encounter stress we find it easy to release the tension.

The first step is to construct a list of *stressful situations* and arrange the list from the least threatening to the most threatening situation. Using their imagination, young people can call up each of those situations and learn to relax away any stress they feel. They can then learn to create their own personal list of stress-coping remarks which they can say to themselves at times of stress, rather than the usual comments we say to ourselves, such as: 'I can't do this . . . I'm not good enough . . .', 'Everyone else is more on top of things than me . . .'.

Making a stressful events hierarchy

Making a list of all our current life situations which trigger anxiety is important if we are to start tackling these with coping skills training. When writing this list, young people should include any stressful event they are likely to encounter in the relatively near future (e.g. finding it hard to study, worry about exams, problems with family or friends, boy/girlfriend problems). They should get as close to twenty items on their list as possible. These can run from mild discomfort to their most dreaded experiences.

This list can be turned into a hierarchy by ranking the stressful experiences in order, from the least to the most anxiety-provoking. Each item on the list should represent an increase in stress over the last item, and the increases should be approximately equal. To do this, Wolpe (a leading researcher on coping skills) has recommended that we rate each situation as *Stressful Units of Distress* (SUDS). Being fully relaxed is zero SUDS, while the most stressful situation in their hierarchy should be rated at 100 SUDS. All the other situations are between one and 100.

There are huge individual differences in what people find stressful. Discussing this with young people can be interesting in itself and reassuring to realize that things which may be unproblematic to some cause major anxiety to others. This can help boost confidence.

EXAMPLE OF A STRESSFUL EVENTS HIERARCHY

Rank	Item	SUDS
1	Rushing to get to school on time	10
2	Parents hassling me about housework	15
3	Having to attend a class in which I don't like the teacher	20
4	Having problems settling down to homework	25
5	Bad mark in essay	30
6	Friends falling out with each other	35
7	Not being allowed to go to a club with my friends	40
8	Parents arguing in front of me	45
9	Anxious over exams	50

10	Feeling sick	55
11	Trying to make conversation with someone I fancy	60
12	Being pressured to take drugs	65
13	....	......
14	....	......
15	....	......
16	....	......
17	....	......
18	....	......
19	....	......
20	Worried about pregnancy/girlfriend pregnant	100

. . . and so on.

Using relaxation with the hierarchy

This list can be used to help learn how to relax while experiencing stress. Young people can begin with the first situation (lowest SUDS) and build a clear picture of the situation in their imagination. They can try to hold on to the image for about half a minute. They should notice the beginning of any tension in their body and any sense of anxiety. This sensation of tension should be used as a signal for deep muscle relaxation and deep breathing. Tightening in our body is like an early warning system of what later will be real emotional discomfort. It is possible to relax away this tension, even as we imagine the stressful situations.

When they have imagined a particular scene twice without feeling tense or anxious, the young people can go on to the next situation in their list. Over the next few days they can move through their entire hierarchy of stressful situations following the same steps, going from the least to the most stressful. At the end, they will have a deeper awareness of how and where tension builds in their bodies. They can learn to welcome early signs of tension as their signal to relax. Mastering the situations with the highest SUDS provides a degree of confidence that stress reduction is possible, even in the most threatening situations.

To learn this relaxation skill, each scene must be clear and realistic. This means making a real effort to conjure up all aspects of the situation including the way things sound, smell, look and feel. The more they practise, the easier it will be to feel as if they're really there.

When they begin practising relaxation this way, young people should not push beyond three or four scenes. When they're ready, usually after four or five days, they should have made it through their list. They should then feel a great deal more confident about dealing with these situations in real life.

Learning to relax

Progressive muscle relaxation is often used for this exercise. This involves lying down and focusing on one muscle at a time, starting from your toes and moving up your body. You tense each muscle for a few seconds and then relax that muscle. They can try this at home alone or with a group in school or other group setting. Suggestions for physical ways of coping with stress together with the directions for progressive relaxation are provided in Chapter 6.

Learning to breathe from your abdomen is the key to relaxation. This is called deep breathing. Suggest that students put their hands on their abdomen and breathe in so that they feel the air expanding their tummy and pushing out their hands. They should then breathe deeply and try to reach a comfortable rhythm, feeling the air push their hands. They should breathe out with a sigh, and visualize the tension flowing out of their body as they let go of each breath.

Students can practise and prepare for these situations by imagining them in detail. When they are imagining them, they will begin to notice tension in their body, their muscles will start to tense, or they will have feelings of upset, anger or anxiety. When they feel these, they will know that they need to begin relaxing their body. When this happens they need to take some deep breaths, making sure they are breathing from their stomach, and to begin by tensing up each muscle from their toes to their neck and then releasing the tension.

Stress-coping thoughts

Once they are comfortable using these relaxation skills, young people are ready to create their own repertoire of stress-coping self-statements. To understand how they work, it is useful to consider the four components of an emotional response.

1 *Event*: Their teacher gives them a lecture about not doing enough work.

2 *Physical response*: Their automatic nervous system produces symptoms such as feeling tense, their muscles get tighter. . . .

3 *Action*: They attempt to deal with the situation by apologizing or becoming defensive and getting away as quickly as possible.

4 *Thoughts*: Their appraisal of the situation, predictions and self-evaluations are what creates emotion. If at this point they say to themselves, 'I can't stand this. . . . It's too much for me. . . .', then the emotional response will be fear. If their self-statements are 'I've had enough of him/her telling me what to do all the time, God, I hate that teacher . . . ', then their emotional response is likely to be one of anger.

Their *interpretations* of the incident, how they imagine it will affect the future and what they say to themselves about their own worth are the ways they select and intensify the emotions they will feel.

Using coping skills training while going through a stressful situation, young people can begin using calming statements such as 'Relax. . . . Breathe deeply. . . . You've been through this before. . . . Stay calm. . . . He can't really affect me'.

The final stage in this technique, after they have gone through their hierarchy of stressful situations in their *imagination*, is to learn to apply coping skills to *real-life situations*. When they feel stress, they use their body tension as a cue to relax. They can also use the stress-coping thoughts they have learned to reassure, relax and congratulate themselves when the event is over.

The more attention they give to their coping statements, the quicker will come relief from physiological arousal and over-reaction. They will feel much better. Suggest that they make their own list of stress-coping thoughts and learn them, as these will be the most useful.

Young people can then prepare things they say to themselves at each stage while confronting the stressful situation. While preparing, they can tell themselves, *'there's nothing to worry about'*, *'I've done this before'*, *'I'll just start and it will get easier'*. While dealing with the situation they can tell themselves *'I can only do my best'*, *'I just need to focus'*, *'I can get help if I need it'*. If they feel anxious, they can say to themselves, *'If I feel tense, I know now how to relax'*, *'I need to breathe deeply'*, *'I can handle this'*. After the situation they need to reward their efforts and congratulate themselves for getting through it, and they can tell themselves, *'I went through it, and coped'*, *'Next time it won't be so bad'*.

Encourage them to learn some statements for each stage of coping: preparing, facing the event, feeling anxious and congratulating themselves for getting through it. They should put the list somewhere convenient, such as on their desks or in their bedrooms, and get used to seeing it regularly.

In summary, coping skills training provides rehearsal in imagination for the real-life events that young people may find distressing. They can learn to relax in the imagined scenes and are thereafter prepared to relax away tension when under fire, when facing deadlines for homework, when in an argument, when in exams and so on. Eventually, self-relaxation procedures and stress-coping thoughts become automatic in any stressful situation. Coping skills training has been shown to be effective in the reduction of general anxiety as well as exam anxiety.

Problem-solving skills[3]

A good deal of research has shown that problem-solving ability in young people represents a resiliency factor which makes them less likely to experience maladaptive outcomes both in adolescence and in adulthood. Problem-solving is a skill which can be applied in many situations and, once learned, can stay with us for life. As mentioned above, failure to acquire problem-solving skills or undervaluing the role of problem-solving has been linked to suicidal attempts in male and female teenagers.

Problem-solving as a technique

Many of us consider problem-solving to be such a simple and effective technique that we underestimate what an important stress management tool it is. We cannot assume, however, that the young people with whom we are engaged will have experienced a strong culture of problem-solving. Some parents are more inclined to react with emotion or sanction in the event of problems relating to their teenage children and so it may be that young people have yet to witness the positive benefits which effective problem-solving can bestow.

The use of problem-solving is associated with better adaptation. The important thing is to be methodical in the way we approach problems. Again, as with the other mental strategies for coping with stress, it is always helpful to ask young people to think of a real example before engaging them in this exercise.

Stage 1. What's the problem?

This is the most obvious and yet the most difficult part of the process. The problem must be clearly identified and defined. Often when we feel stressed or upset we have vague feelings of strain, sadness, irritability or fatigue. These are much harder to combat than clearly defined problems.

All the work they have done on awareness of stress and tracing these feelings back to thoughts and events will be a huge bonus to young people at this stage. However, it can still remain difficult to identify what the exact problem is. For example, a teenager might complain that he or she feels 'stressed out' because their mother's new partner is leaving the house in a mess or invading their privacy. The real problem may lie somewhere else altogether and may focus around unresolved conflicts with this new person. Perhaps there has been no attempt to include them in decisions around the new arrangement.

If young people are finding it hard to specify what their problems are, they might try speaking to someone they respect and trust and who knows them well, taking time out to allow them to gain a clearer perspective, and asking themselves questions such as do they feel worse during the day or at night, at home or school, with friends or family, working or relaxing.

Sometimes we find it difficult to be clear and honest about where difficulties lie. This may be because the problem is a deep-seated one and one that is painful to explore. Even in these cases, acknowledging the problem is the first step towards solving it. Counsellors are highly skilled in helping people move on from here.

Stage 2. Brainstorm
Generating solutions to problems is an innate skill for some, but the rest of us have to work hard at it. We can promote this skill by learning how to discuss things with different people, not shooting down solutions too early, trying to see things from different perspectives or making a list.

You could ask young people to choose one of the problems they have already identified at Stage 1, and do a brainstorming exercise to think of as many solutions as they can. They can ask a friend to help them and write down each of the possible solutions. They can use the ideas suggested by the friend as a springboard to help reactivate their own problem-solving. The important point is not to reject a solution at an early stage however stupid or way out it sounds, but to write it down and go on thinking about other possible solutions. Brainstorming is now becoming fashionable in practically every setting, not just for war strategies. Businessmen are increasingly using it to generate new ideas and escape old ways of thinking. It can be just as dynamic when used to solve our own personal problems.

In summary, this stage involves (1) defining the problem, (2) suggesting whatever solutions come to mind, (3) not censoring these regardless of how much sense they make at first, and (4) noting these ideas and continuing.

Stage 3. Give it a go!
The young people should then:

- Look through their list of solutions and *choose* which one looks the most encouraging and helpful. It may help to discuss this with someone whose opinions they value and trust.
- *Have a go*. They should then work out exactly what it would involve, and take the necessary steps.
- *Assess the outcome*. The solution they have selected may or may not work. If it works, they need to remember this so that they can do it again if they need to, or persist if it looks as if it has put them on the right track. If it doesn't work, it is even more important that they know, so that they can go back to their list of solutions and try something else. Many solutions are helpful but do not provide the complete answer. They need to know this also so that they can work out whether to persist with the chosen solution or to look for further solutions. Whatever happens, they need to evaluate it.
- *Keep going* until they feel better. Their assessment might show that they are on the right track but have not gone far enough. Problems are often not solved overnight. Some persistence is usually necessary.

PROBLEM-SOLVING: FOUR MORE THINGS TO REMEMBER

1 *Move on*. If the problem cannot be solved, move on and forget about it. There is no point wasting time 'flogging a dead horse'.

2 *One thing at a time*. Sometimes young people can feel inundated with pressures, which all seem to come at once. Effective problem-solving can often mean solving one problem at a time.

3 *You can only change yourself*. If the problem is a social one, there is a chance that, when you ask young people what needs to happen, they will recommend that someone else needs to change their behaviour. For problem-solving to be successful, young people have to rely on changes they can make in

themselves. They need to take responsibility for their role in the problem. This is discussed further in Chapter 8.

4 *Accepting is acceptable*. Sometimes they may have to accept that the best thing to do is to do nothing. Accepting a problem and deciding to cope with it is sometimes a valid solution.

The laughing cure!

As someone who has worked or intends to work with young people, you will know the difference that humour can make to our relationships with young people. If you tell a joke or a young person jokes, this can bring much needed levity and good feelings into what would otherwise be tense, uncomfortable or simply joyless situations. We all remember teachers at school whose sense of humour brought them respect and affection. Being humorous, without sarcasm, in appropriate situations when talking to young people is also a good lesson in keeping perspective.

The knowledge that laughter is the best medicine is part of folklore and, like any folk remedy, we are usually sceptical about it, unless there is scientific evidence to back the claim or we have had personal experience of its benefit. There are, however, scientifically proven benefits to having a good laugh. It releases serotonin and endorphins, which are natural tranquillizers and immediately improve our mood. In addition, when we laugh we are more likely to breathe from our bellies which helps us relax, we take in more oxygen which is invigorating, our facial expressions feed back to our brain and tell us that we are happy. Humour makes us look at things in a different, lighter and less threatening way.

Coping

Chapters 1 and 2 discussed different ways of coping and their effects on outcomes. Studies show that the more coping skills one has, the better, i.e. using humour, problem-solving, detaching, relationships, recreation, confrontation and so on. We often talk about approach or problem-solving coping as opposed to avoidance or emotion-based coping.

- *Approach coping* sometimes means seeing your stress as a problem and taking steps towards solving it.
- *Avoidance coping* can mean ignoring the problem or trying to find ways to distract yourself.

For young people, using approach coping is probably most helpful in situations in which they have a degree of control. Avoidance coping may help when there is nothing they can do except accept the situation or tune out.

A SUMMARY OF STRESS MANAGEMENT

In the remainder of this book many more ways of dealing with stress are discussed. In summary, in order to keep their stress levels down, young people need to:

1 Look around

Gauge the pressure – Realize how much they have on their plate at any one time. They need to include daily hassles and recent changes that required adaptation; even if the changes aren't in themselves negative, they may represent energy drains.

2 Look inwards

- They need to be familiar with their own symptoms – Do they get irritable or sad? Do they think negatively or tend to overgeneralize, do they become inactive or try to do too much?

- Are they aware of changes in themselves that might be due to a buildup in stress? They should think about the way they think, act and feel.

3 Look ahead

They should always try to think about whether the solutions they choose will help them in the long run as well as the short term.

4 Look back

Think about the patterns in their relationships or the way they have dealt with similar situations in the past and try to learn from them whether they were helpful or unhelpful, rational or irrational. Think about where these patterns might have come from.

5 Look after themselves

- Take breaks when the pressure gets too much.

- Do one thing at a time. Eat, rest, exercise and socialize without doing other things at the same time.

- Make lists to aid memory and help with planning and time management.

- Remember to BREATHE – that means watching breathing, relaxation, exercise, reducing alcohol and tea and coffee, and healthy eating.

- Learn not to procrastinate: putting off doing things makes us feel stressed, guilty and tired. Get down to it and then relax.

- Be nice to themselves. Treat themselves the way they would like others to treat them, with care and respect. Learn to lose all those undermining attitudes which bring them down.

- Make sure they relax, have fun and nurture their relationships.

CONCLUSION

To help young people improve their mental strategies for coping with stress:

1 Discuss the link between events, thoughts and feelings.

2 Encourage them to see this pattern in everyday situations.

3 Suggest they keep a stress diary.

4 Familiarize them with the symptoms of stress – emphasize the importance of recognizing stress.

5 Explain the key role of appraisal in the stress process.

6 Encourage them to be aware of the effects of sources and symptoms of stress.

7 Present advice on:

- learning how to plan ahead

- preparing for negative events

- keeping things in perspective

- thought stopping

- coping skills training

- learning how to relax
- problem-solving
- laughing
- coping

You should suggest that people keep an exercise, sleep and diet diary for one week, as Chapter 6 discusses the effects these have on stress and coping. They could record what they eat and drink and how much exercise and sleep they get each day, and their levels of stress this and the following day.

Notes

1 See Patel, C. (1989) *The Complete Guide to Stress Management*. London: Vermillion.

2 Davis, M., Eshelman, E. and McKay, M. (1995) *The Relaxation and Stress Reduction Workbook* (4th edition). Oakland, CA: New Harbinger Publications.

3 Butler, G. and Hope, T. (1995) *The Mental Fitness Guide: Manage Your Mind*. Oxford: Oxford University Press.

CHAPTER 6

Physical ways of coping with stress

This chapter looks at physical ways in which we can help to combat stress. This includes looking after nutrition, sleep and exercise in order to keep our immune system strong and our energy levels high. We will also learn more about relaxation and premenstrual tension.

Feeling healthy and fit can prevent young people from feeling undue strain when they encounter stressful events in their lives. It may even prevent some of these events from occurring in the first place. For instance, if young people are exercising, eating and sleeping well, they may study better and so limit exam stress, they may relate better and so limit relationship stress and so on. Persistent stress can also lead to many physical complaints, including tension headaches, migraine, backache, palpitations and chest discomfort, allergies, coughs and colds, asthma, high blood pressure, angina (chest pain), anxiety, chronic fatigue, irritable bowel syndrome and ulcers.

The following questions will help you to begin your discussion with young people on areas of health which are important for stress prevention. If you have asked them to keep the diaries suggested in Chapter 5, you can use these as a basis for your discussions. These are useful in that they allow discussions to begin in an informed and realistic way based on accurate estimates of sleep, exercise and nutrition as well as how young people felt during the week.

Before beginning a discussion on physical well-being, it is a good idea to simply ask young people what they feel would enhance their physical well-being. These days, young people are provided with a good deal of information about health. If you begin by assuming they do not already have this knowledge, you risk patronising them and wasting time. If they appear to already possess a good understanding of the basic tenets, move on to how they have applied these in their own lives. Chances are you can be helpful in discussing the obstacles to applying these principles.

Nutrition and eating habits[1]

You can begin this discussion by asking young people to look at their food diaries. If they haven't kept a diary, you can have a general discussion based on the same questions.

HEALTHY EATING

- Do they feel their diet is healthy?
- How do they feel after eating certain foods?
- Do they feel energetic in general?
- Do they often feel tired?
- Do they have trouble concentrating?
- Do they skip meals?
- How much caffeine do they drink?
- How much water do they drink?
- Do they eat breakfast?

Eating well is crucial to good health, and being healthy will help young people cope better with life's stresses. It is a useful skill to recognize the foods which make us feel energetic and positive and those which can make us feel fatigued and negative. Nutrition plays a vital role in warding off headaches, sluggishness, irritability and even premenstrual syndrome. It boosts the immune system, thus keeping us healthy and able to cope.

Despite the fads which come and go, there are basic general principles to healthy eating. These are to reduce saturated fats, sugar, salt, caffeine and alcohol and to increase fibre and starches, fruit and vegetables. Diets should also contain a variety of foods, individuals should try to maintain their ideal weight, and use exercise to regulate appetite and weight.

It is also recommended that we eat calm, frequent meals and take a multi-vitamin tablet daily if we are feeling run down. Nutrition must be understood as a whole system; in other words there are no good and bad foods, only good and bad diets. Eating the odd bar of chocolate and fast food meal is only important in the way it fits into the overall diet, i.e. how regular it is and what other foods we are eating.

Starches are also referred to as complex carbohydrates and should form the main source of energy in our diet. They exert such a positive effect on mood that they have been referred to as natural tranquillizers. This is because they cause the release of serotonin which improves mood. It is recommended that the bulk of our calorific intake comes from starches. Examples include potatoes, rice, pasta, bread, porridge, breakfast cereal and muesli. Young people are often worried that these foods are fattening. However, you can reassure them by informing them that contrary to this belief they can actually keep weight down by controlling the appetite and preventing the sudden drops in blood glucose levels which cause snacking. It is best to eat wholegrain varieties – wholemeal bread or pasta, brown rice – because they contain more fibre, vitamins and minerals and are also more filling.

Protein is required for growth and repair of body tissues. Starches, fruit and vegetables should be eaten in much greater quantities than protein.

Young people should get all the *vitamins and minerals* they need from eating a well-balanced diet and particularly from fresh fruit and vegetables. However, if they are not eating well, they may feel tired and run down. In these cases, you should recommend that they take a multi-vitamin course. If they feel their diet contains insufficient nutrients, they should discuss this with their parents.

On average we require at least one litre of *water* a day. If they are eating a lot of fast food, young people may need more water as it contains a lot of salt. Those who take regular exercise will also need to drink more. It is worth telling them that many soft drinks actually dehydrate the body.

Caffeine is contained in coffee, tea, chocolate and some carbonated drinks. Because it is a stimulant, caffeine can contribute to irritability, tiredness, and sleep problems. It is often a surprise for people to work out exactly how much caffeine they actually consume. You can help young people to estimate how much their daily caffeine intake is by referring to Table 6.1 on p. 144. The recommended amount of caffeine per day is 200 mg, which is about one cup of brewed coffee.

Alcohol

Alcohol is high in calories and can therefore lead to weight gain. A gram of alcohol contains seven calories, which is nearly twice as much as sugar. In addition, alcohol reduces our body's ability to break down fat because it slows down the body's metabolism, and the liver processes the alcohol rather than burning fat.

Table 6.1 *Caffeine content in drinks*

Type of drink	Serving	Caffeine
Brewed coffee	10 oz	170–200 mg
Decaffeinated coffee	10 oz	10 mg
Instant coffee	10 oz	90–140 mg
Tea	10 oz	60–100 mg
Coke	2 oz	40–60 mg
Milk chocolate	1 oz	6 mg
Dark chocolate	1 oz	20 mg

Females get drunk faster than males, not only because of their smaller size but also because they have only about half as much of the enzyme 'alcohol dehydrogenase' that breaks down alcohol in the stomach before it enters the bloodstream. This enzyme helps prevent us from getting really drunk and damaging our livers. In other words, the way one drink affects a female is the same as the way two drinks affect a male. Men drinking a pint while women drink a half therefore makes a lot of sense. Females also remain drunk for longer than males.

Many young people are surprised to learn that alcohol is a depressant. If they are feeling low and have a few drinks there is a risk that they will feel even worse the next day. Alcohol also depresses your brain's activity, so as well as making us feel unhappy and depressed it can seriously affect our ability to concentrate. This can have a highly deleterious effect on young people's school work. Alcohol also depletes Vitamin B levels, alters blood sugar and raises blood pressure. All of these things can make us feel under strain. Mixing drink with drugs is extremely dangerous and potentially lethal. The combination can make people vomit in their sleep and cause suffocation.

SUMMARY

Drinking too much can cause many problems, including mood swings and even relationship problems. Drinking also

- is a physically addictive drug producing withdrawal symptoms which can be fatal

- can lead to violent behaviour

- reduces inhibitions, and can lead to risk taking behaviour, which has long-term consequences for the young person

- can kill by alcohol poisoning

- kills brain cells; research in the US has shown that a large number of teenagers drink enough to affect their school performance

- multiplies the cancer-causing effects of smoking.

It is important to help young people feel confident to make their own decisions about drinking and not to drink just to fit in with the crowd. They should feel they are not missing out on anything, that by not drinking they may have more energy to enjoy themselves and will look better too.

To help young people to tell when their drinking is becoming a problem you can ask the following questions:

- Do they drink because they have a problem or to help them face up to stressful situations?
- Do they drink when they get angry with others?
- Do they prefer to drink alone rather than with other people?
- Is their drinking affecting their work?
- Do they get into trouble when they are drinking?
- Do they often get drunk when they drink, even though they don't mean to?

These questions will help form the basis for frank discussions around the role of drinking in the young person's life.

Fat

The reason why women often have more *body fat* than males is because, in prehistoric times when there was not a lot of food available, they needed to have extra energy stored to feed themselves and their babies. A woman must also be a healthy weight to menstruate and give birth. Men had more muscle and less fat due to the activity involved in searching for food. This is one reason why dieting often does not work, as when you cut your food intake dramatically, your body responds as if there were a threat of starvation. It slows down your metabolism (the rate at which the body burns up calories), and stores as much spare fat as possible. A moderate intake of fat is necessary for lots of things including skin and hair maintenance, body temperature maintenance and cell functioning. Many people's diets contain too much fat.

How to reduce fat in the diet

Fat in the diet can be easily reduced by choosing low fat products, switching from saturated fats like butter to polyunsaturated fats, such as olive or sunflower oil, and cutting down on fried foods, and grilling or boiling instead.

When the level of glucose in your blood is low, you tend to feel hungry. *Snack foods* that contain refined carbohydrates and sugars are quickly digested. However, the brief boost in blood glucose is quickly followed by a fall in blood glucose levels so that we feel hungry again very soon after. This may lead to more snacking, is an easy habit to fall into, and can lead to weight gain. If your meal is balanced, that is, contains other nutritional elements as well as carbohydrates, the food is more slowly digested and absorbed and it should be some time before you feel ready for the next meal.

Dieting and eating disorders

Dieting and eating disorders are on the increase for both young males and females. To tackle these, we first need to understand the reasons behind their onset. For some young people, these reasons may be deep-seated and need a good deal of therapeutic intervention to come to terms with. Other young people may benefit from open discussions around cultural assumptions of weight and success.

You can ask young people whether they are happy with their body shape, whether they believe that thin women have more friends, are happier and more successful, and what sources of reference they use when thinking about their ideal body weight (e.g. magazines, friends, television, family), and what causes people to diet or develop unhealthy eating patterns.

Age 14 to 16 is the most vulnerable period for the onset of eating disorders, although they can start as early as 9 years old. Anorexia peaks between 14 and 18 years. The mortality rate for anorexia is 10%. Theories explaining its onset vary. Low self-esteem has been linked to eating disorders together with having an external locus of control, whereby one tends to feel out of control, helpless and depressed. Family climate may be an indicator where families are seen as rigid, enmeshed, with no appropriate conflict resolution, and where self-reliance and self-sufficiency are not encouraged.

The figures for eating disorders and dieting in adolescent girls has risen sharply in the past few years. There are strong cross-cultural differences; for example, the international mean rate of anorexia is one in 100,000; however, a recent study of white, middle-class girls' schools in Britain found the rate to be one in 1,000. The medical effects of bulimia include loss of tooth enamel, menstrual irregularity, oesophogeal tears, gastric rupture and cardiac arrythmias. Only 10% of anorexics are male. Medical consequences include amenorrhoea (cessation of periods), reduced cognitive function, cortical atrophy, non-normal production of neuro-transmitters, hypotension, possibility of heart failure, constipation and osteoporosis.

Weight and body shape

Many young people today, particularly young women, express dissatisfaction with their appearance and body shape. This appears to be affecting girls at a younger age than ever before. Many female role models are thin, and the desire to be thin has made dieting in adolescence a common occurrence. The diet industry is worth approximately £21 billion a year and has a lot to gain from projecting images of slim models having a happy and successful lifestyle. Women's magazines, television, cinema and the music industry are all involved in selling the myth that happiness and being thin go hand in hand.

It is a good idea to open a discussion with young people on the subject of weight by exploring these basic assumptions. Ask young people to bring along some of the magazines they read, or a picture of their favourite pop artists or actors. You will recognize that almost every girl photographed is very slim with a beautiful face. They never show photographs of a plain, unhappy, thin girl, so we tend to associate thinness with attractiveness and happiness.

Discuss the effect that these pictures have on the young people. Do they make them want to buy the product? Do they automatically believe that these people are happy? If so, these pictures have done their job in manipulating insecurities and stimulating desires. Acknowledging that this is the sole purpose of these images is the first stage in undermining their truth or realism.

There is a growing concern about the effect that all these magazines, pop and television images are having on the health of women. Girls as young as 9 are now going on diets in order to be as skinny as these 'role models'. This is dangerous, as it will interfere with normal growth and development, both physically and psychologically. Diets also affect metabolism and can ultimately lead to weight gain. It is estimated that 95% of people who go on a diet end up the same weight or even put on weight within a year. Young girls and teenagers who diet may prevent their bones from growing normally and can impede the production of oestrogen (which makes skin soft and hair shiny). Dieting can also lead to depression.

It is estimated that at present, a quarter of all women are on a diet. Approximately nine out of ten women express dissatisfaction with their body shape. This is obviously having an impact on teenage girls. There has been a large increase in the number of people with serious eating disorders. If dieting begins in young girls, it is eight times more likely to lead to anorexia or bulimia, which can be fatal. There have been calls from researchers, medics and professionals working with young people to persuade the media to display more realistic images of female bodies.

Does being slim bring happiness?
It is worthwhile exploring with young people if they really believe that slim women are happier. The truth is that many slim girls are unhappy.

Are slim girls more attractive?
It is now a well-known fact that when men and women are asked to choose a figure they find most attractive in women, women always choose a thinner figure than men. If you are holding this discussion with a mixed group, you could ask the male members of the group to talk about a girlfriend, or someone they find attractive, and ask them to say why. Usually, a woman's personality, smile, eyes, sense of humour, hair, intelligence, voice, posture, interests and confidence will be just as important as her figure.

If a girl is always dieting she can become less attractive to her peers. She may appear vain and self-obsessed, she might not be much fun to be around, or seem very interested in other people. If she appears dissatisfied with her appearance, boys may be influenced by this and also think less of her. Dieting removes the shine from girls' eyes, hair and skin, giving a lack-lustre appearance. Dieting can take energy away, thus making a girl lose her sense of humour and self-confidence. She may become depressed.

Our relationship with food
It is often the case that while boys simply eat food, girls have a relationship with food. Many young women feel guilty if they think they've eaten too much. Food can become something they want to control, or an enemy that they must battle against. Appetite can be affected by emotions. Feeling depressed or stressed can cause us to eat less or more than usual.

Eating disorders may be a way of avoiding other issues by focusing on food, a way of coping when life becomes too difficult, or a way of feeling more in control. They may be caused by family issues, dieting, emotional problems, adolescence, societal pressure to be slim, genetic factors or sexual abuse.

Eating disorders can have serious consequences including:

- Depression, due to chemical changes in the brain.
- Difficulty in concentrating or thinking clearly as brain cells do not have enough nutrition to function normally.
- Brittle bones which can dissolve and break easily.
- Broken sleep.
- Risk of attempting suicide.
- Vomiting produces acid which can burn away tooth enamel. The salivary glands in the neck can become swollen, leading to puffiness in the face.
- Laxatives can produce constant stomach pains, swollen fingers and constipation.

The effects of dieting

Dieting messes up our metabolism and, when young people decide to eat normally again, they may find they gain weight quickly. It can lead to bingeing as it confuses their natural appetite and will make them crave fattening foods. Severe weight loss leads to hormonal imbalances which can cause facial hair growth in girls. Girls who are obsessed with food will miss out on so many other important aspects of life and often feel tired, irritable and under pressure.

The best way to lose weight

Try to encourage young people to maintain a well-balanced, low fat, high fibre diet and also to eat breakfast. This speeds up the metabolism and will give them energy throughout the day. It also reduces the need to eat snacks which are high in fat later on.

When eating becomes a problem

Try asking young people: Is their weight below normal? Have they ever tried dieting to lose weight? Have they stopped menstruating? Have people commented that they look thin? Do they think about avoiding food all the time? Do they feel a little obsessive about their intake of calories? Do they binge and make themselves vomit, or use laxatives to lose weight? Are they secretive about eating? If they answer 'yes' to any of these questions, they may have an eating problem. You should suggest that they talk to their parents about this. Possible options will include counselling for them or with their family, joining a support group, or seeing their GP.

Exercise[2]

To begin this discussion, start by asking young people the following questions. They can comment on their exercise diaries or on an average week. How much exercise did they take this week? How much exercise do they usually take? What types of exercise do they enjoy? Do they feel they get enough exercise? How do they feel after they have exercised? How do they feel when they don't exercise? What do they feel are the benefits? What are the obstacles? What would make it easier?

What is exercise?

Exercise should not be seen just as a PE class or having to go through the pain of an aerobics class. Exercise should be seen as physical activity which should be a natural part of living life to the full. Dancing, walking, running, swimming, cycling, soccer, tennis and rollerblading are examples of aerobic exercises.

Why exercise?

There are so many reasons for advising young people to take plenty of exercise. Mentally, it will reduce stress, improve their performance at school, improve concentration and memory, lift depression, improve self-confidence and even enhance creativity. Physically, it improves self-image, boosts energy levels, lowers body fat, improves general health, boosts the immune system, improves quality of sleep, and reduces physical tension. It affects behaviour by reducing hostility and irritability.

WHY DOES EXERCISE MAKE YOU FEEL GOOD?

- Exercise causes the brain and spinal cord to produce their own powerful opium-related drugs called endorphins. These enhance mood because they have a chemical make-up similar to opium-based drugs, and explain why people feel a 'high' after exercise, particularly aerobic-type exercise, like running, dancing, aerobics, soccer and so on. This is why people enjoy dancing until they're tired and sweaty – lots of aerobic movement and a hard, steady beat.

- Exercising will make young people feel more attractive as it improves their *self-image* of their body.

- It reduces and prevents *depression* by lifting mood. Participating in sports can also give young people a sense of team spirit and achievement. It allows them to forget about their worries and focus on the moment.

- *Stress* and nervousness are dramatically reduced by the chemical effects of exercise. Physical activity neutralizes the stress hormones that make you jittery and leaves you feeling more balanced. Physical activity relaxes your muscles which also allows you to feel more calm. Going for a run before a stressful event, like an exam, can relieve much nervousness and stress.

- Research has shown that *mental performance* on IQ tests improves greatly following just twenty minutes of aerobic exercise. Physical activity improves alertness and the speed at which we think.

Why is exercise good for you?

As well as keeping us healthy and slim, exercise helps to build up muscles, increase energy, prevent heart disease and increase longevity. It improves our immune system because running is interpreted by the body as a sign that we may be in danger. The body therefore goes about boosting the immune system and creating more natural killer cells. This is why those who are physically active suffer less from colds.

When exercising, young people should

- Do at least twenty minutes of aerobic activity at least three times a week. This means increasing your heart rate and breathing.
- Keep active! Walk or cycle to school or a friend's house instead of taking the bus, help out with housework, go dancing.
- Exercise should not become a new, more acceptable form of diet addiction; its aim is to make people healthier and a side-effect will be a better body shape.
- When you are aerobically fit you have more 'fat-burning compartments' inside your muscles. This keeps you burning fat a lot of the time and means that if you continue to eat normally, you will burn more calories than you take in. Exercise controls your appetite and makes you less likely to crave unhealthy foods.

- Muscle is a 'hungry' tissue: 450 grams of muscle burns thirty to fifty calories a day just doing nothing, while the same weight of body fat burns only two. So the more muscles you have the more calories and fat you burn, even when you're just sitting down.

Why not exercise?

It is easy to come up with excuses for not exercising, even when we are aware of all the benefits. Excuses which should sound familiar are feeling too tired, not having enough time, being too busy, feeling self-conscious, feeling too fat (or too slim, so don't need it), or that it's boring.

Making exercise a part of life

Young people should be encouraged to think of *physical activity* rather than 'exercise'. They should try to incorporate it into their routine. They should choose different types of exercise for different days, keep active during the day, and make sure they choose convenient times and places to exercise. It's a good idea to make exercise sociable (e.g. by joining team sports). This creates incentives as young people can meet up with others, and they will feel they are letting others down if they don't show up. If they are not enjoying PE, you could suggest that they talk to their PE teacher about more fun ways to exercise.

Sleep

Sleeping well is central to coping with life, managing stress and having positive feelings of well-being. Sometimes it is difficult to know whether we have a sleep problem, as everyone needs different amounts of sleep. Ask young people how they slept during the last week. Do they feel they get enough sleep? Do they regularly feel tired throughout the day? Does sleepiness interfere with their daily activities?

Experiencing poor sleep quality can make us feel miserable, irritable and unable to cope. It is therefore an important stress management tool for young people to learn how much sleep they need, and to try to get this. There are three main kinds of problem: difficulty falling asleep, wakefulness during the night, and waking too early in the morning. Many people think they have a sleeping problem, when they are actually underestimating how much sleep they get.

Although sleep needs vary greatly, most young people need about nine hours' sleep a night. They may need more around exam time. If they miss one night's sleep, this should not affect them too much. A change in sleep routine will take a few weeks to get used to. Losing even one hour's sleep in a night can affect concentration the next day. Feeling depressed, lacking exercise, eating poorly and worrying can affect sleep quality. Taking sleeping tablets is a major cause of insomnia and should be discouraged in young people.

The part of your body that requires sleep the most is your brain. The rest of you can get by without it as long as you get enough rest and food. There are two main types of sleep: 'deep' sleep and 'light' (REM) sleep. The first of these revitalizes your brain and the second is when dreams occur. If young people are not getting enough sleep you can suggest the following tips.

IMPROVING SLEEP QUALITY

- Accept that whatever sleep you do get will be of benefit, enjoyable and restful, and do not fret about how much sleep you're getting.
- Try to go to bed at the same time every night and always set an alarm when you need to wake up at a certain time; otherwise sleep can be disturbed as you worry about waking.
- Do not indulge in weekend sleep binges that disturb this routine.
- Try relaxation exercises about an hour before bed.
- Take regular exercise.
- Do not eat heavy meals or take drinks containing caffeine before bed.
- Try taking warm milk or warm malt drinks before bed.
- Avoid taking sleeping tablets as these ultimately exacerbate sleep difficulties.

Other tips include making sure the bed and bedroom are comfortable, urinating before going to sleep, and avoiding alcohol.

Having a relaxing evening routine can help people with sleeping difficulties. Doing something calm, like watching television, reading or having a bath, allows the mind to settle and relax. Warm milk contains a mild sedative that some people find helpful. Exercising, studying, playing very active video games or watching anything disturbing on television might contribute to difficulty in getting to sleep.

Getting up earlier in the morning can sometimes do the trick in making people tired enough to fall asleep in the evening. If young people report difficulty in getting to sleep, suggest they stick to the same routine every day and forgo weekend sleep-ins, as these confuse the body clock. For most teenagers these are a normal part of catching up on sleep. If they regularly wake early, you could also suggest that they do something productive or enjoyable during this time (like reading or making plans). This will stop them getting frustrated and dreading this time.

If young people are having difficulty in sleeping, encourage them to learn relaxation skills. They can try being stern when worries enter their head, and refusing to follow these thoughts. They can also try progressive relaxation exercises, counting sheep, counting breaths or visualizing relaxing places. The main thing for them to remember is that few problems are solved in the early hours of the morning. A good idea is to write down the things that are bothering them, and decide to look at this list again in the morning.

Learning how to relax

Try asking the young people the following questions: Do they find it hard to relax? What things do they do to help them to relax? Do they suffer from muscle tension? What is the hardest thing about becoming relaxed? Do they feel stressed because they are too relaxed? How would they advise others to relax? Are there any unhealthy ways of relaxing? What would be the biggest benefits of learning to relax? Have they become more skilled in identifying their own personal stress response? Do they use a stress diary?

Living life in a relaxed way is a philosophy, a habit, a skill and a way of life. First, it has to be an outlook on life; being calm and laid back. It is also a skill that can be learned, i.e. being aware of our body; knowing when our muscles are tensed up, and learning to let the tension go through mental and physical exercises. It is also a routine, i.e. getting into the habit of sustaining a calm lifestyle and learning to react to stress in a particular way. It is a way of caring for yourself by replacing energy resources that are being used up all the time. Developing relaxed attitudes and habits is the best way to prevent stress in your life. Quite simply, relaxation is all about letting go.

Why should young people learn how to relax?

Perhaps young people don't want to relax. They may find the idea boring or think it means leading a less exciting or fulfilling life. A useful exercise is to ask young people to tense up their body and their face really tight and to think of a list of things they need to do. Then ask them to stand up and shake out all the tension and to take some deep breaths. Then ask them to make a list. Ask them which way was easier. This exercise usually dispels the belief that being tense makes us think more efficiently.

The important thing to convey is that learning coping skills and how to take things in our stride will actually allow us to lead an even fuller life with more energy to enjoy it. For some people, relaxing is an automatic skill. Others need to learn techniques. These all centre around being aware of the way we react to situations both physically and mentally and learning to stay relaxed. Being aware of muscle tension and following through with breathing and stretching exercises is often a first step. It is often interesting to suggest that young people relax their shoulders. They may not have realized that their shoulders were tense.

Tension brings pain and discomfort, often in the neck, back and shoulders. It can also lead to tension headaches. Having tense muscles can make us feel even more stressed, and can lead to anxiety about the aches and pains. Getting into the habit of relaxing or 'dropping' our shoulders is a fast relaxation strategy. Young people will be surprised how often they need to relax them. Having tense muscles can also make us tired (as tense muscles are working muscles) and irritable (as your body is feeding back to your mind that you are under stress). This is a waste of energy that could be used better. Muscular tension can be found in people with specific attitudes. For example, a female student who believes that no matter how hard she studies she is bound to fail her exams may experience chronic neck tension and pain, while a male student experiencing a lot of anxiety about the future may develop chronic stomach problems.

Learning to relax involves keeping an eye on posture, not rushing around, making time to do relaxing and enjoyable things, creating options so that we don't worry too much about things not working out, taking breaks, and finding a quiet time everyday. Young people could also try listening to a relaxation tape, taking a hot bath, burning some scented candles, having someone rub their feet or back or going for a walk. Sleep, exercise, rest, eating properly, humour, pleasure, relationships and time management can also help us relax.

Breathing

There are two types of breathing: chest breathing and abdominal or stomach breathing. Suggest that young people place a hand on their stomach and a hand on their chest to find out which way they are breathing at any one point in time.

Chest breathing

This type of breathing is useful when we are undergoing vigorous exercise but is inappropriate for ordinary, everyday activity. It is part of the 'fight-or-flight' response and consists of shallow, jerky, unsteady breaths. When we are feeling stressed or anxious, the mind interprets this as a threat and activates this response to enable you to run. However, today, many people experience ongoing levels of anxiety and stress and so are in a constant state of chest breathing, although they are unaware of this. The effect of this, paradoxically is to maintain feelings of anxiety in a vicious circle. Until chest breathing is replaced by deep, even and steady diaphragmatic breathing, all efforts to relax the body, nerves and mind will be ineffective.

Abdominal breathing

This is the most efficient way of breathing in terms of the amount of oxygen you take in. If we actively practise breathing from our stomach, together with mental and physical relaxation, we can bring down our blood pressure and reduce feelings of stress leaving us feeling more calm, composed and able to cope. The advantages of abdominal breathing are that it gives the body enough oxygen, it expels carbon dioxide adequately (unlike chest breathing), it relaxes the body and mind and it improves circulation to abdominal organs (which aids digestion and protects against ulcers).

PROGRESSIVE RELAXATION

This exercise is a popular relaxation method and can be done during the day or evening to relax, or to aid sleep.

- Sit upright and comfortably in a chair. Close your eyes without squeezing them tightly.

- When you are comfortable, curl and clench your toes and tense your feet as hard as feels comfortable. Hold this for a few moments and then breathe out and let the tension go. Stretch out your feet and feel them relax.

- Now breathe in and tense your legs and thighs as hard as feels comfortable. Hold it for a few seconds and as you breathe out feel the tension being released.

- Breathe in again and as you do tense your stomach by pushing it out – hold this tension for a few seconds then breathe out and relax.

- Move to your chest, and as you breathe in feel your chest expand – hold this expanded position for a few minutes and then relax and breathe out.

- As you breathe in, tense your back, particularly in between your shoulder blades. Hold the tension for a few seconds and then release it as you breathe out.

- Now tense the whole upper half of your body – feel the tension – breathe out and let go of the tension and relax.

- Tense your shoulders by lifting them up towards your ears as you breathe in – hold for a few seconds and relax, and drop the shoulders as you breathe out.

- Clench your fists as tightly as possible and experience the tension in your hands and arms. Hold the tension. Now let it go and shake out the arms and hands.

- Move your attention to your head and face. Scrunch up your face, tightening up all your facial muscles – hold the tension – then release it, relax and let go as you breathe out. Breathe in and yawn with open mouth and raised eyebrows. Hold for a second and release and let go.

- Stay seated for a few minutes and focus your attention on your breathing, allowing the breath to become slow, deep and even.

Pre-menstrual syndrome

The Professor of Human Metabolism at the University of London describes premenstrual syndrome (PMS) as the world's most common disease, yet there is still no agreement among doctors about the best way to treat it. There are over 150 different symptoms, and it affects teenagers as well as older women. Symptoms include irritability, anxiety, depression and fatigue. Even as early as the ancient Greeks, Hippocrates noted the symptoms of agitation and lethargy associated with blood trying to escape from the body. There are several reasons why PMS may be affecting more women today than in the past: these include fewer pregnancies, stress, diet and the contraceptive pill. It is also likely that we are more aware of this condition nowadays.

The organization of reproduction in women is carried out at the *menstrual controlling centre* in the hypothalamus at the base of the brain. This is a part of the brain which also contains the controlling centres for day/night rhythm, weight and mood control. Although we are still not sure what the exact causes of PMS are, we do know what helps to alleviate it.

Coping with PMS

- *Diet* has been argued to be the most important way of reducing PMS. Young people should be advised to avoid sugar at this time, as it can cause a sharp drop in sugar levels after a while, making them feel cranky or tired and crave sweet things. In addition, if they find that caffeine makes them feel tense, agitated, anxious or interferes with their sleep, they would be well advised to cut down on caffeine before and during their premenstrual time. According to Dr Katharina Dalton, a leading researcher in the field, the strongest influence on PMS is low blood sugar levels, caused by an inadequate diet. She claims that during this period, the timing between meals or snacks is extremely important – i.e. there should never be a gap of more than three hours (except when we are asleep). She recommends eating a starchy snack every three hours. Finally, we still don't know whether the bloating associated with PMS is due to excess salt, but some researchers recommend cutting down on salt during this time. Dr Dalton believes that it is lack of regular starch and not salt that results in bloatedness.
- *Coping skills*: By charting their good and bad days on a menstrual chart, young women can learn when their most vulnerable times are. They can then take extra care of themselves at these times, for example, by resting more, using relaxation, or taking mild exercise, like walking.
- *Avoidance tactics*: Young people should try to be aware of when their symptoms are at their worst and not plan anything difficult for this time. Factors which make PMS worse include tiredness, hunger, stress, alcohol and smoking, so they should be advised to avoid these if they can.
- *Stress* is not the direct cause of PMS, but it does make it worse and we may be least able to cope at this time. Stress and PMS naturally aggravate each other.
- They should avoid working very late at night. The controlling centre for the day/night rhythm is situated in the hypothalamus, at the base of the brain adjacent to the

menstrual controlling centre, so any disturbance to the day/night rhythm centre upsets the menstrual hormones. The effect is very like jet lag, when our biological clock is disturbed.

- They should make sure they get enough *rest*. If they suffer from PMS they will need a full eight hours' rest in bed. Lack of rest results in irritability and tiredness. If they can't sleep, lying resting in bed is just as effective.
- *Exercise*: There is a world of difference between everyday physical exertion and beneficial exercise. To be beneficial, exercise must be sufficiently prolonged to increase the pulse rate for some minutes after exercise has stopped. This could be twenty minutes of aerobic activity, like brisk walking, jogging, cycling or tennis. Exercise is invigorating, increasing the circulation of blood and oxygen consumption, which helps to release tension, and premenstrual aggression.
- They should cut down on *alcohol*. Even small amounts of alcohol make PMS worse. When alcohol is taken it interferes with the normal action of progesterone in brain chemistry, which may exacerbate any feelings of depression they are already experiencing. PMS sufferers will also find that they are not able to take nearly as much alcohol as at other times without becoming intoxicated.
- For some women, the contraceptive pill can alleviate the symptoms of premenstrual tension.
- Other forms of treatment include relaxation skills, assertiveness training (see Chapter 8) and evening primrose oil (although the evidence is very controversial on this).

CONCLUSION

This aim of this chapter is to help you to pinpoint the important relationship between physical health and feelings of strain. To do this, it is recommended that you:

- discuss normal eating, sleeping, exercise and drinking routines

- explore the way these habits affect thoughts, feelings and behaviour

- explain the role that nutrients, sleep quality and physical activity play in mental health

- discuss the problems that excessive drinking can cause
- explore the myth that slim equals happy
- explain the health hazards of dieting
- discuss the benefits of exercising and potential obstacles
- discuss the importance of relaxation, breathing and stretching
- suggest ways of coping with premenstrual syndrome

As Chapter 7 deals with homework and study, you could try asking young people in advance to make a list of what the biggest problems are for them as regards studying and what they find helps them to work better.

Notes

1 Sigman, A. (1992) *Getting Physical – A Teenage Health Guide*. London: BBC Books.
2 Ibid.

CHAPTER 7

Study skills and
time management

Stress appears to be hitting people at increasingly younger ages because of the more complicated and competing demands being placed upon them. Our society, more than ever, is pushing the importance of success, achievement and winning. While teenagers may feel they have more opportunities than their parents, they may also feel they must take these opportunities and succeed more than ever. We're made to believe that the more successful job you have the happier you will be. A postman is more unhappy than a brain surgeon or a pop star, which of course is not the case.

It can be difficult to help young people to put their exams into the right perspective. On the one hand, as an adult with their best interests at heart, you will want to encourage young people to achieve the best they can and you will know the consequences of not achieving well at school. On the other hand, exam stress and pressures at school have been shown to contribute significantly to adolescent stress, sometimes to such a degree as to adversely affect the young person's ability to do well. There are also more opportunities available today to people who want to repeat exams, try alternative educational careers or pursue options which are not solely dependent on academic results.

The key is to help young people achieve their best at school while at the same time nurturing their self-esteem, self-confidence and mental health, and acknowledging that the teen years are difficult enough without young people feeling undue pressure and stress. To do this, you need to be able to help them develop essential study skills, time management and relaxation skills. This will help them to work efficiently, to 'switch off' when they're not working and to keep things in perspective. Informing them of the range of options available to them in their future career is essential so that they do not panic if the option they're pursuing doesn't work out.

Sessions on study skills and exam preparation have always proved highly popular. The advice and tips are usually of immediate benefit to secondary school students as well as young people pursuing other courses that require application. While it is important to relay these guidelines, it is also important for students to be able to give each other advice on what works for them, and this can be encouraged within the discussion time. Although this chapter, more than any of the others, is related to school and may involve you if you're a teacher, the same effort should be made to sustain a relaxed atmosphere, or 'time out' from normal classes. This will encourage students to raise issues and to feel that the discussion is as much to do with their well-being as their exam performance.

Talking to young people about studying

It is usually a good idea to ask students in a group setting to suggest what, for them, are the main obstacles and problems with studying. It is helpful for most young people to realize that others share their concerns and difficulties. Students should be asked whether there are further issues they would like to discuss, as the obstacles to studying can vary. If these issues haven't been adequately addressed by the end of the discussion, invite students to bring this to your attention so that they can be explored and potential solutions discussed.

Divide the students into groups of four, and elect a spokesperson for each group. Ask them for feedback to the overall group.

- What are the main problems regarding homework, studying and keeping up with course work?
- What feelings and obstacles arise regarding study habits?
- What do they feel is the most difficult part of studying?

Study skills[1]

Studying for exams is one of the most stressful and difficult challenges young people have to face. Some people seem to be better able to manage their time, and cope with homework and revision demands. It is more than likely that rather than being 'more intelligent', these people have simply learned to use effective study skills to help them to get the work done without becoming too bogged down in it and feeling helpless and depressed. This chapter aims to provide ideas and techniques to help young people to improve their study routines and to make the time in which they do study more productive. Many of these tips are relevant for any activity that requires them putting their mind to something, like learning a new skill, a musical instrument or writing fiction.

- *Input:output*: The most important study technique is to invest time in study. No amount of study tips will allow them to escape the fact that the more time they spend working, the more they will learn and achieve.
- *Getting started*: Many find it hard to get down to study. In fact, a lot of people say that this is the most difficult part. You can ask your students whether this is true for them. Identifying that this is the hardest part of study is important, as they can then focus their efforts on this aspect.

Being able to get down to work is the true divider between those who get a lot out of study and those who don't. When people find they can't get down to work they don't get as much done and produce stress for themselves. They are neither relaxed nor working. This achieves nothing. Students should make starting work as pleasant as possible. Once they begin they'll usually discover that the work is less awful than they imagined it would be!

Making it easy

1 Where they study
Wherever the student studies should be made as attractive and comfortable as possible. They should try to work in the one place each time (e.g. their room). This will help them to keep things organized. Keeping their desk tidy and free of unnecessary clutter is also a good idea, as it will help them to feel in control and focused and will not turn them off studying.

2 How they study
Listing what they have to do is essential for efficient studying. Students should always write down what they want to get out of their study session before they start. It is a good idea to prepare a schedule for the amount of time and incorporate breaks into this. This is also a good idea, as a common excuse is that we don't know what to do or where to start as we have so much to do. Not knowing what to do can make it easy to not do anything. In addition, ticking things off a list will give them a sense of progress as they work through the items.

3 *Why they study*

Everyone loses motivation sometimes when they are working towards something. A good idea for students is to write down their reasons for working and what they hope to achieve in the short and long term.

Making it enjoyable
Body clocks

It may not be possible for young people to choose the time of day when they study. Equally, they may not feel that this is important. However, research has shown that some people concentrate better at certain times of the day, i.e. mornings, afternoons or evenings. If they notice a difference in how productive their work is at different times, it is a good idea to work around this. This may be relevant at weekends when they have more control over when they work. They should use the time to study when their concentration is at its best and then not to feel guilty relaxing at other times. However, it is important to remember that exams don't take place at night, and developing a habit of working late may not help them to perform on the day.

Taking breaks

If we felt when we sat down to study that we had to stay there for hours, it would be a huge disincentive to even begin. Having realistic chunks of study planned before they sit down will help students to get down to work. Concentration is best when we stick to chunks of about forty-five minutes with ten- to fifteen-minute breaks in between. If breaks are timetabled in, students won't feel guilty about taking them and will stick to their schedule.

A change is as good as a rest

It is usually easier to study when we choose several different subjects to look at in one session. In addition, large projects broken down into smaller chunks are far less intimidating and enjoyable to work on.

Finishing the study period
A tidy desk is a tidy mind

Taking a couple of minutes to store and file study materials at the end of each session is important. It makes it easier to begin the next session and cuts down on time-wasting while looking for notes. It is often an unconscious excuse to potter around the room without getting down to study. Convince students that time spent at their desk should be time spent working, which will leave more time for guilt-free relaxation and recreation afterwards.

Use a carrot!

The oldest trick in the book is rewarding ourselves for doing things we'd prefer not to do. This is especially true for studying. If we associate studying with treats, we will find it easier the next time. Ask students to think of ways they can reward themselves for studying. For example, if they spend their Saturday afternoon studying, they might decide to treat themselves to a night out. Even after completing small chunks of work, it is a good idea to give themselves a small reward. This could be watching their favourite television programme, going for a walk, making a phone call, eating something they like or a soak in the bath, but only if they get everything done that they had planned.

Students should be imaginative in what treats they use and not stick to the old favourites of chocolate and television. This way, they are giving themselves something to look forward to *and* getting the work done! Treats must come after the work is done. Students can try asking parents or teachers to provide some rewards based on the amount of study they do. Ask students to think about things they would really like to do, such as music lessons, driving lessons or simply having a friend over. These can be used as incentives.

Make it social

As this book hopes to show, discussing issues aids learning and the absorption of information. For students, this can be an effective study tool if it helps them to work through the material and explain it in their own words. This is an excellent memory device. If they can talk to a friend about the work, it means they are more likely to remember it. Working with others also makes studying more enjoyable. Suggest that they choose a topic to revise with a friend (on their own) and then get together to talk about it. Some of us find it impossible to work when we have good company around, however, and if this is the case it is advised that they try to work efficiently on their own and arrange to meet their friend later.

Spread the word

Ask students to ask their friends what tips they might have for making study easier.

Health and studying[2]
Body clocks and sleep

The concentration required by studying requires that our body clocks are not disturbed. This means going to bed at the same time every night, getting up at the same time every morning and getting enough daylight. If we confuse our body clock we feel sluggish, sleepy and our concentration is poor. We are unlikely to do productive work. We also find it difficult to remember the material we read at these times. Young people, as a rule, require more sleep than adults, up to nine hours or more, particularly coming up to or during exam time. Regular sleep patterns, and plenty of daylight and fresh air are therefore recommended. Suggest that students study near a window and take lots of breaks outside. It is also worthwhile reminding young people that if they get into the habit of working late at night, they are (1) less likely to take in the material, (2) at risk of making going to sleep difficult, and (3) less likely to remember the material during the exam which will take place during the day.

Physical activity

Students who are fairly fit tend to do better at their schoolwork. Recent research has also proved that doing twenty minutes of aerobic exercise will have an immediate positive effect on performance in IQ tests, feelings of stress and anxiety, alertness and concentration, accurate and quick thought processes, memory and learning, and creative thinking.

Aerobic exercise is any exercise which makes our heart beat faster and our breathing rate increase. This means any activity using the large groups of muscles, particularly in the legs, for example: jogging, fast walking, cycling, swimming or dancing. The key is to increase your heart rate and rate of breathing and to keep it there for at least twenty minutes. When you do this, your brain releases endorphins which influence the way you think and feel. The endorphin 'high' you get from this will immediately improve your brain's capacity to think creatively and make decisions.

Advise students to do some aerobic exercise three times a week, especially coming up to an exam, and to do a little aerobic exercise immediately before the exam. They can also try walking rather than taking a lift, or go for a twenty-minute jog. This is particularly useful before an afternoon exam, where they might otherwise feel a little drowsy after lunch.

Nutrition

Blood sugar

Our ability to concentrate is very quickly influenced by the level of glucose or blood sugar in our bloodstream. If this falls we feel less alert, find it hard to make decisions, concentrate or remember things. We can also feel tired, low, irritable and sometimes hostile. Try asking young people to suggest possible causes for dips in blood sugar levels.

Blood sugar levels dip when young people go on diets or skip meals, particularly breakfast. Levels also fall, paradoxically when we eat or drink things with too much sugar. This is because normal foods provide enough sugar for the body, and so when we consume foods and drinks which contain too much processed sugar, the body reacts by lowering the level of sugar circulating in the bloodstream. We often end up feeling tired and sluggish which can make us crave sweet things, so a vicious circle ensues. Sugar produces serotonin, which can cause fatigue.

Getting into the habit of eating breakfast, particularly before an exam, and eating regular healthy snacks and meals will help keep blood sugar levels stable. Eating breakfast will also stop them getting hungry mid-morning and going for a sugary, unhealthy snack. While eating complex carbohydrates is healthy, eating a lot at lunch-time can lead to sluggishness.

Glucose sports drinks, glucose tablets and sweets also lead ultimately to drops in blood sugar levels which can inhibit concentration and make us feel tired.

Caffeine

Try asking young people, if they drink coffee when doing homework or studying, how many cups of coffee they usually drink, if they feel that coffee is a good way to help them concentrate and what drinks or food contain caffeine.

Caffeinated drinks are often used to help provide stimulation coming up to an exam and to keep students awake. However, going for a walk, having a shower or taking a break are far more effective. Caffeine though providing short-term stimulation, actually lowers blood sugar levels after a short time, producing tiredness. It is well known to lead to edginess, and can make young people feel more nervous and stressed out about their exams.

Alcohol

Alcohol, antihistamines and cannabis all affect alertness, so students should be advised to avoid these before studying and the night before an exam if they want to be at their best. Alcohol kills brain cells. In addition, if they need to take medication (for instance, if they have hay fever, or a cold or flu) some medications (including some night-time cold remedies) contain alcohol or antihistamines which can cause drowsiness the following day.

Television and music
These can affect concentration, and students should be encouraged to avoid them while studying or to choose undemanding programmes that do not vie for their attention.

Organizing the study area
Advise young people to study in the same place and to ensure that this is a bright, tidy, quiet and organized place.

Reading material

Advise students to:

- *Prepare*. Look through the text to get a sense of the main subject areas, the way the material is broken down, interesting pieces, how it fits in with what they already know.

- *Get an overview*. Students should read any summaries or conclusions in the material. This will help them to reread the chapter or book and be clear about what they are looking for in terms of its main messages.

- *More detailed reading*. Students should be encouraged not to give up if they cannot follow the text. They should read on to see if the following chapters will help them to understand it. Students should be encouraged to raise difficulties with the teacher, and be assured that everyone finds some texts difficult. This may be the fault of the author or the intrinsic difficulty of the material.

- *Review*. It is always a good idea for students to consolidate what they have learned by going back and organizing the material. Students could set up their own categories or simply reflect on how the material is presented. A good approach is to study for thirty-five minutes and then review what they have read.

- *Test*. Nothing will help students remember what they have read more than testing themselves. Jotting down a few questions, taking a break and coming back to see what they remember is an excellent memory strategy.

Taking notes
The most important thing for students to remember when they are taking notes is that, for the notes to be useful and aid memory, they

must be actively processed by the student. They should not just be passive recordings of the original. Students should digest and organize the material in their own individual way, i.e. in a way that makes sense to them. This does not have to make sense to others and there is no right or wrong way of doing it. What is important is that the notes reflect the way the student has received and processed the information.

Condensing versions of notes is a good way of revising and can prove helpful to look at before going into exams. Being able to condense notes means that the student has come to terms with the content of the material and is able to make choices about the key elements.

Students may sometimes need advice about how to take notes and may benefit from an exercise on note-taking in class. You could give them a photocopied chapter or even a newspaper article and ask them to underline or highlight the key points, to condense the text and to try to organize it in an easy to remember way. This is an essential study skill. Even reading with a pencil in their hands, prepared to mark pieces of text which are confusing or interesting, will help keep them alert and processing the material.

Exams
Prioritize
It is impossible to try to study everything. Students need to choose which topics they have to cover and concentrate on these. If they have trouble choosing topics, they can ask a teacher to help them. It is useful to continue summarizing the information as they approach the exam, so that by the time they enter the exam they only have a few keywords on a card. These will trigger memory of the wider material to be remembered.

Mock exams
These are an excellent way of seeing how much information students can remember, discovering their strengths and weaknesses, and practising their exam timing. They can give themselves mock exams at home. Trying to remember something in a mock exam and failing provides a good incentive to go back to the material to see what they forgot, and they are less likely to forget this again. Practising answering exam questions is a good way to reduce anxiety.

Designing a study timetable
Students should write a list of all the subjects they are doing and prioritize them in terms of the ones which they know least about to the ones they know most about. They then need to draw up a timetable

and focus on the subjects they know least about, while at the same time revising topics they are confident about, so as to prevent feelings of panic and anxiety. Encourage students to keep the work well organized with each subject in its own folder.

Exam stress

Coming up to an exam

It is normal for students to worry before an exam, but it is important to convert the worry into action and get focused. Students will find their minds filling with thoughts about all the things that could go wrong. You need to impress upon them that just because these thoughts are recurrent, they are not realistic. Assure students that they are normal reactions and just the result of the pressure they have been under to do well. You can assure them that their teachers and examiners want them to do well.

Encourage students to take a *deep breath* or to try counting to ten to relax when they go into an exam. They need to read the *instructions* carefully and read the exam paper through to the end. Writing *short notes* at the beginning on the questions they are going to answer may stop them feeling anxious about not knowing enough to write. This is also good for jogging the memory. Encourage them to *adapt* what they know to the questions and to keep their answers relevant.

REMEMBER WRITES

- Use your best Writing
- Try to Relax
- Read the Instructions and questions properly
- Time each question strictly
- Have Everything you need with you
- Write Short notes first

Stress and worry

Keep it in perspective

Although it can be hard, it is good to advise students to try not to worry too much about the exams, as this will not help their performance. They should focus on sticking to their study timetables. Staying focused and organized rather than getting caught up in worrying will help them to do their best in their exams. There have been suicides linked to exam stress, and although achieving well at school is good for young people's future, you may not realize how anxious and stressed they are until it is too late. Young people can spend a lot of time worrying about the consequences of their exams, thinking about what course they will get into, what kind of job they'll get, whether they'll be satisfied, how much money they'll earn, or if their parents or friends will approve. Assure them that they can only do their best and it is not the end of the world if things don't go entirely as planned.

It is worth reminding them that stress and worry take up a lot of time and energy which would be better applied to the task at hand. Advise them that if they feel their anxieties about the exams are interfering with their work or the rest of their life, they should definitely find someone to talk to about it. Make sure that students are aware of counselling facilities both within the school and locally.

If young people feel that their parents have unrealistic expectations for them and are placing too much pressure on them to succeed, they should discuss this with them. If you, as a concerned adult, have witnessed signs of anxiety which could be debilitating, it may be worth your offering to facilitate such a discussion. If the young person cannot talk to their parents, and feels uncomfortable talking to a counsellor or guidance counsellor, perhaps they could try talking to a relative, family friend, brother or sister. They could even ask them to talk to their parents. The main thing is to encourage and inspire without causing undue stress and impeding their performance. In other words, support and guidance are more effective than provoking anxiety *per se*.

Time management

Try asking young people what they think time management is. Do they think they have a problem with time management?

The symptoms of poor time management include a sense of being rushed and hurried all the time, being late regularly, feeling low in energy and motivation, feeling like you're always trying to catch up, feeling irritated and impatient, not getting things done, being indecisive about what to do next, and always putting things off.

The central principle of time management is to spend your time doing those things you value or those things that help you to achieve your goals. But what are our goals and what do we value? Most people would admit to spending a great deal of time involved in activities which they neither value nor help them to achieve their goals. Try asking young people to think of these types of activities. Why is this? It is easy to think that it is because we are weak-willed, or lazy or inefficient. But often the real reason is that we are unclear about our values and goals.

Exercise on time management

This exercise will assist young people in identifying their highest priorities. Ask them to close their eyes and imagine their own funeral. What would they like people to say about them? What would they like their friends, family, teachers or classmates to say? You can then explore with them what this exercise says about the sorts of things that are important to them. For young people, as with older people, this exercise often helps to clarify what values are important to them, and will help them to decide if they are living their lives in a way that is in keeping with these values. It can help them to see what kind of person they want to be, and what they want to achieve.

We often want to be remembered as being a good friend, a loving son or daughter, someone who was there to listen, or as someone who was cheerful. We also like the people we respect to respect us too, and to respect what we are trying to achieve.

Knowing more about our values and goals can help us to plan a life around what we believe in. Suggest that students use a pie chart to design how they would like to divide their spare time. It may take a while to become clear about what their values are.

How to manage time well

> *Procrastination is the thief of time.*
> Edward Young.

Once your students are clear about what they value in life and what they would like to achieve, they will be good time managers if they never put off studying and thus spend time in limbo between working and relaxing; get into a routine that allows them to waste the least time hanging about; feel confident in their choices and follow through on that; break down large projects into smaller ones, thus making them less intimidating; accept that they won't be good at everything but this is no reason not to enjoy things; and set aside time to plan each week.

If your students are finding it hard to manage their time, suggest that they think about what's important in life, set goals to achieve this, write down an action plan, and set about fulfilling this in an organized way. Encourage your students to estimate how much time they spend per day on various activities by keeping a diary or time log. They may not have realized quite how many television programmes they watch or telephone conversations they make.

CONCLUSION

Preparing for exams can cause significant stress for many young people. In this chapter it was suggested that you:

- talk about the pressure to succeed and where this comes from
- ask them if it is affecting their well-being
- discuss difficulties getting down to study or putting in sufficient time
- discuss where, how and why they study
- offer advice on study skills
- discuss the role of nutrition and exercise in effective studying
- offer advice on taking notes and exam preparation
- reassure them on the importance of keeping things in perspective
- engage them in exercises on time management

Notes

1 Butler, G. and Hope, T. (1995) *The Mental Fitness Guide: Manage Your Mind.* Oxford: Oxford University Press.
2 Sigman, A. (1992) *Getting Physical – A Teenage Health Guide.* London: BBC Books.

CHAPTER 8

Interpersonal and communication skills

This chapter is about relationships, paradoxically one of the biggest causes and comforts in the stress process. Relationships form a central component in the stress process at all ages. Having people in our lives who provide emotional, physical and material support as well as advice can buffer the effects of stressful events. As they move from early to late adolescence, young people place increasing importance on peer support and approval. This is highly important and provides a forum for young people to discuss the multitude of novel thoughts and experiences through which they are journeying. Parents, relations, teachers, sports coaches and other significant adults in their lives are also hugely important in providing guidance, love and support during this vulnerable transition.

Unfortunately, when we are under stress we can become more difficult to be around; we can become irritable, distant or simply not there. This chapter aims to help you to communicate to young people that although they may find their relationships difficult they are probably their most important support and resource for combating stress. Students should be encouraged to discuss which relationships are particularly difficult for them and the ways in which they are stressful. There are suggested discussion points which should prove interesting and thought-provoking for young people. As with all discussions around stress and coping, it is useful for you to ask the young people to raise the issues first and form the discussion around a response to these issues. Ask them to think about the main problems they encounter in their relationships. Ask them to think specifically about their relationships with family, friends, teachers, other adults, boyfriends or girlfriends.

When you ask young people to list things that cause them stress, they are often quick to mention 'people stress', i.e. those individuals, be they parents, teachers, friends or classmates that are a source of conflict for them. Everyone has times when they feel down or annoyed by the actions of others. We feel they have behaved inconsiderately, aggressively or inappropriately. Unfortunately, these are often the people we see every day at school, at home or at work.

A useful exercise is to ask young people to think of five people who cause them the most stress or hassle. Give them a couple of minutes. Then ask them to think of the five people to whom they turn when they are under stress. Give them a couple of minutes. Now ask them if they found that there were at least one or two of the same people in both categories.

It usually comes as something of a revelation to young people that they rely so heavily on the very people who cause them the most stress. This is true for most of us, as relationships with parents, brothers and sisters, friends, boyfriends or girlfriends can cause real pain as well as bringing us joy.

Investing in relationships is important in order to help us maintain our mood and well-being and in helping us to cope with day-to-day events. It is highly important that young people are encouraged to draw on this support, as many stressful life events they have encountered and will encounter in the future can be eased through social support and advice. The suggestions contained in the rest of this chapter are aimed at ameliorating relations between young people and others. Reducing conflict and day-to-day tension through learning self-awareness, negotiation, assertiveness and listening skills can make it easier for young people to feel confident in turning to those relationships at times of stress.

Central to this book's message is that stress is about the way we view the world as well as our objective circumstances. Therefore, when it comes to people in their lives who are 'stressing them out', young people can learn to assume responsibility for their half in that relationship as they bring with them their own views, emotions and actions. Interactions with others often cause us to feel threatened, angry or upset, and we react in the same 'fight-of-flight' way described in Chapter 4. This rarely improves the situation.

Based on their personality and life experiences as well as their current circumstances, many young people show patterns in the way they deal with conflict with other people. Some young people will do anything to avoid confrontation. They are inclined to conceal their feelings from others and seek to appease them. They often blame themselves for breakdowns in the relationship. Others hide deep-seated feelings of insecurity by creating conflict. They can bully and act insensitively and are often unaware of how this comes across to others.

Relationships[1]

Ask students to think of a relationship which is causing them stress. Then ask them to think of something that would improve this relationship. Give them a few minutes. Ask them if they thought the relationship would improve if the other person changed their behaviour or attitude.

It is normal both for teenagers and adults to assume that if other people change, their relationships will improve. We usually think 'if my boyfriend would stop doing this' or 'if my mother wouldn't do that' things would be better. This seems obvious to us. However, by placing the onus for change on the other person we are, in fact, doing ourselves a disservice. We are losing our control on our own relationship and well-being. We are handing over that control to another person which means taking power away from ourselves. The important thing to communicate is that to improve our relationships we can only change ourselves. Others will then change the ways in which they relate to us.

Feeling confident enough to 'be ourselves' in a relationship can be difficult for all of us, but particularly for young people who are in the process of identity formation. You can discuss this with young people if they find it difficult. It is in fact the key to a good relationship. They will recognize that the relationships in which they feel they can be themselves are the ones in which they feel most comfortable, confident and happy. This does not mean that they can behave exactly as they wish if it means being rude or hurting other people. It also does not mean that they should always feel totally comfortable, because sometimes we learn a lot in relationships that are challenging. It just means that when we feel that others accept us we can express ourselves, and often the relationship is more satisfying as a result.

But how do we start thinking about our relationships, and how can we start to change them?

In adulthood we relate differently to different people, and this is particularly true for young people as any parent or adult working with young people knows. They can often be difficult with adults while friendly and cooperative with peers. Ask young people to think about a relationship which is causing them stress or sadness and to ask themselves when do they feel at their worst in these relationships and when do they feel at their best. Ask them if they have noticed patterns in terms of what happens in their relationships. These are crucial questions in helping them to work out what is going on in their interactions with different people.

Being aware of how we tend to respond to people and situations is a useful skill. Most of us have developed habitual ways of responding over time and may not even be conscious that we are acting routinely in a particular way. If young people can become aware of these tendencies they will be in a better position to decide whether reacting this way is helpful, healthy or brings them happiness in their lives. An example might be if some aspect of their work or appearance is criticized and they react as if their whole being has been attacked. They feel undermined, angry or worthless. Another example is if someone fails to make contact having arranged to do so, and they feel rejected and isolated.

These are normal reactions that don't tend to last for too long. If, however, they respond very strongly in this way every time this happens and the feelings last for some time, it is likely that they have developed a pattern of response. This can come from experiences in the past and usually reflects their view of themselves and their insecurities. However, it can be damaging to new relationships and stop them leading fulfilling lives. Being aware of our patterns of behaviour is the first step in analysing and deciding where they come from, whether they are rational and whether we want to change them.

Think about it

Try to encourage young people to think about problems within a relationship in specific terms rather than having vague feelings of discomfort. If there are unresolved issues, difficult emotions or feelings of dislike, then these will be easier to work through if they are clearly identified.

Take responsibility

As already mentioned, taking their fair share of responsibility within the relationship will give young people more freedom and control. This means that they don't allow others to make all the decisions, but rather that they participate, that they don't respond to others with aggression and that they don't place blame without acknowledging their own part in the relationship. Learning to be flexible and responsive is important to stop them getting stuck in habitual ways of behaving which can prove hard to break.

Watch how others change

You can suggest that young people try the following exercise. They can decide to change their behaviour towards a person who is causing them a great deal of stress. If they normally ignore this person, they can try being more attentive to what that person is saying and doing. If they normally act in a withdrawn and submissive manner, they can try being assertive and tell the person calmly how they feel. People may not respond in the way they would like, but at least they will be able to see that the relationship is not outside their control.

Solitude

Although relationships are important to our well-being, we should remember that spending time alone can also be a fulfilling and worthwhile experience. Many of the things we produce and of which we are most proud happen when we are alone, such as working on a project. Other things like listening to music can be even more enjoyable when we are alone. If we are at ease with ourselves, we will be at ease with others. Keeping a diary can be good for letting off steam and thinking about things which are important to us, particularly for teenagers.

SUMMARY

Developing healthy relationships means that we need to acknowledge that:

- We can only bring about changes in others by changing ourselves and changing the way we relate to them. We can change the way we behave around and towards them, the way we feel and think about them, and the way we express affection or anger.

- We have to give changes time to take effect. This is particularly true in relationships where there are more people involved.

Suggest that young people think about the sorts of things that always make them react strongly or perhaps unreasonably. This may tell them more about themselves or their past relationships than the current situation. Ask them to think about why the situation makes them angry and where this might come from.

Communication skills

It is difficult for many of us to express the way we feel. This can be particularly hard for teenagers who may feel self-conscious about what they want to say. They may feel too unsupported or angry to discuss things which are important to them. It could be argued that young men find this particularly difficult, but it varies greatly in both young men and women. Not being able to express how we feel can be stressful for many reasons. It can mean that others don't know what we want, that it is hard to get help when we are having trouble coping with a problem, and that, when we feel sad, we cannot talk about ways of feeling better. It can also lead to misunderstandings in our relationships.

Assertiveness

Feeling unable to assert ourselves can be very stressful because all the feelings which are not expressed can build up, making us hostile or resentful. They can also explode in bursts of anger or crying. Sometimes these feelings are stored up for a long time and are a source of silent hurt. None of these ways of coping with our feelings is good for our well-being.

Adults as well as teenagers often misinterpret the meaning of the term *assertiveness*. Try asking young people to define what it means to be assertive. Do they see themselves as assertive? Whom do they know who they would define as assertive and why? What often emerges in these conversations is that we are confusing assertive with aggressive behaviour. We think of people who insist on having their own way the whole time or who have a pushy manner as being assertive. In addition, adults may sometimes be afraid to talk to young people about being assertive as they fear it will make them more demanding or aggressive.

What is assertiveness?

The fact is that these assumptions are untrue. Assertiveness is really about being *fair to ourselves and fair to others*. Assertiveness means realizing that our needs, wants and feelings are neither more nor less important than those of other people, but rather they are equally important. This means that when we tell people about our needs, we should be open and accurate and not exaggerate. We are assertive when we stand up for our rights in such a way that the rights of other people are not taken away. When we behave assertively we are less likely to leave situations feeling bad about ourselves or leaving others feeling bad. Young people who are confident and assertive are more able to stand up to peer pressure, to relate democratically to others, to be self-aware and aware of others. They are more likely to see relationships as systems.

Why be assertive?

Being assertive means being able to ask for what you want, to express your likes, dislikes and interests freely, to talk about yourself without self-consciousness, to accept compliments, to disagree politely, to say no and to be relaxed around other people. Being assertive is half-way between being passive and being aggressive and, as with coping skills training, often requires thinking about things in a different way. You can discuss the following basic tenets of assertiveness with young people. These include the right to make mistakes, say no, express hurt and pain, not have to justify themselves to their friends, and to be alone. Do they feel they have these rights?

The bottom line is that young people are entitled to their own feelings and opinions. If they value themselves and trust their own feelings, they will feel more confident in expressing themselves regardless of whether their friends feel and think differently. This is an invaluable tool throughout life. They will probably even find that when they have confidence in themselves and start valuing themselves, other people will start to value them more and have more confidence in them. The trick is to stop worrying about whether other people like them and start focusing on being fair instead. The rest will fall into place.

All they need to remember is that being assertive is all about balancing their needs and the needs of others.

Negotiation skills

Negotiation forms a large part of all relationships throughout life. During the teenage years, young people must negotiate with parents, siblings, teachers, friends, boyfriends and girlfriends on a multitude of issues, including leisure time, pocket money, choice of friends, choice of boy/girlfriends, choice of school subjects, holidays and so on. Negotiation is a useful skill for young people to learn, not because it will teach them how to get more out of situations, but rather because it will teach them the rules of cooperation, to see responsibilities as linked to rights, the importance of trust as well as 'give and take' in relationships.

You can suggest to young people that in future circumstances which require negotiation or cooperation they try to:

- Be clear when they express themselves to avoid misunderstandings.

- See the situation from the other person's perspective.
- Be constructive – placing blame is rarely a positive way to proceed, so move on from where you are at.
- Accept responsibility – it is rarely helpful to start a discussion on the defensive or on the moral high ground. Suggest that they acknowledge their contribution to the argument or situation before moving on, even if they are only acknowledging it to themselves.
- Recognize individuality: different individuals become upset about different things or take different things in their stride. Similarly, some people need a good deal of intimacy while others need space, some people like to talk about their feelings while others prefer to remain silent.
- Think about how they would like to be treated in this situation and act this way – if they'd like understanding and warmth, then try to give this.
- Better out than in – it's a bad habit to allow themselves to bottle things up. Recent reports indicate that repressing emotions has all sorts of negative effects on our mental and physical health. Young men in particular need to hear that it is acceptable to talk about the way they feel.
- Keep a lid on insults – these usually cause arguments to escalate.
- Count to ten or go for a walk if they're getting angry. Anger rarely achieves anything in discussions. If they have grievances these should be expressed in a calm and constructive way that helps to change the situation.

In summary, good negotiation involves finding out what each person wants, trying to find the common ground, looking for alternatives that allow both parties to get what they want, being flexible and trying to give and take as much as possible. It is important that young people learn to be clear in how they communicate. This means expressing how one feels rather than retreating to a room to brood. This will help others see that they are hurt or angry.

It is worth discussing the assumption held by some young people that conflict with parents is inevitable. Although it is natural and often healthy for teenagers to argue with their parents while discussing differences of opinion over values, rules and so on, it is not necessarily inevitable. They may be surprised to learn that their parents would often rather work things out amicably and look for the common ground.

Listen!

Being a good listener is just as important as being listened to. Learning the importance of listening will help young people to provide support to others, making them more likely to receive social support when they need it. It will help them to understand where other people are coming from and so lessen the risk of misunderstandings, arguments and communication breakdowns. It will help them to show others that they care about them and so help nurture their relationships. It will also help them to learn from others.

You can suggest the following to young people to get them started on improving their listening skills:

- Make it clear to others that they are listening by using important signals such as looking straight at the person who is talking, maintaining eye contact, nodding or saying 'uh-huh'.

- Give simple feedback to show they are listening by acknowledging what the other person is saying; for example, 'did you really?', 'is that right?'.

- Summarize what the person has said to show they understand; for example, 'so you'll have to go back in then?'

These are easy ways to show we are listening. When discussions get heated we are less inclined to listen. However, learning to listen in these situations is a useful negotiating skill for young people to learn.

Suggest that they:

- Listen until the person is finished, as the end of their point might be different to what was expected.

- Articulate their agreement as well as their disagreement. If we fail to do this the speaker assumes we feel differently and can become agitated trying to get their message through.

- Be open – our assumptions of what someone wants out of a conversation can be different from theirs. Allow people to express themselves.

- Try to understand the real meaning of what people are saying, not just the words. People's tone of voice and body language can express different sentiments from what is actually said; for example, when someone says, smiling, 'about time you got here!', it may be meant as a light-hearted joke but could be taken as a criticism or attack.

Listening skills, in conjunction with assertiveness and a knowledge of the importance of social support, will help young people to get the most out of their relationships.

Social support

Many studies have shown that talking to people about how we feel can help us feel better. Simply expressing our feelings as well as engaging the advice and support of others is a hugely important way of managing stress.

As well as being a source of enjoyment and fun, relationships are a resource when we feel stressed. They can, however, be a resource we don't use, because the relationship is the problem, or because stress has made us feel too tired to talk or because we are reluctant to express our worries. When we are under pressure we often put a strain on our relationships and may not be aware we are doing this. This is commonly known as 'taking it out on others'.

Ask young people to think about those who can give them support when they need it. Ask them to think about whether, when they are under stress, they usually explain this clearly to the person, or tell them exactly how they are feeling. Is it possible that they have been expecting the other person to ask them first? Suggest in future they take the first step and tell these people when they are under pressure, and enable them to be supportive. Ask them to think about whether they have been irritable with those close to them, because of feelings of pressure and strain. If this is the case, it may be helpful to say they are sorry and to explain that their behaviour was not because of them, but because of the strain they are feeling.

Quite simply, young people need to know that they need other people around to help when they are feeling stressed, and so acting with hostility will deprive them of this resource. Suggest they find other ways to let off steam, like exercise, music, dancing, sports or keeping a diary. The most important thing is that they spend time with other people and don't cut themselves off, that they learn to talk about their problems and how they feel, that they spend time with people who care about them and respect them, ask for advice, tell people why they're feeling cranky and try to help others when they too are under pressure.

Bullying

Begin the discussion by asking young people to define bullying. Can it be verbal as well as physical? Are boys more likely than girls to bully or do they bully in different ways? Is there a particular age when bullying is more common? What should friends or classmates do when they witness bullying? What should teachers or parents do when they discover bullying? What would their advice be to others if they are being bullied?

Bullying is more commonplace than many people imagine. The figures produced by the Anti-Bullying Centre at Trinity College Dublin suggest that in Ireland 31% of primary and 16% of secondary school students had been bullied at some time. This amounts to nearly 200,000 children at risk of experiencing bullying. In the UK, two out of ten boys and three out of seven girls reported being bullied, from sometimes to often.

Bullies can be people at school, people they don't know, friends with whom they've fallen out, brothers or sisters, or adults. Being bullied can be very hard to cope with and can make young people feel sad, helpless, angry or scared. Young people should be aware that no one should have to put up with being bullied. A lot of people don't tell anyone because they are frightened, depressed or don't think anyone else can help. They might even feel that it is their own fault. Their self-esteem suffers, and every day becomes a battle to get through.

Bullying can be verbal or physical. It can be psychological when friends choose to ignore others and cut them out of the group. A young person might find themselves bullied because others are jealous, perceive him or her as different or because they refuse to go along with certain things. Usually, young people fear that if they tell on the bully, the situation will become much worse. They are often afraid that other people will see them as cowards, tell-tales or simply won't believe them.

It is important to assure young people that most teachers are trained to deal with these types of situations. They can talk through with them the different options they both feel are appropriate. You should encourage them to tell their parents, whose experience and insights will help them to cope better with the situation. Adults can advise them on a whole range of possible strategies. In addition, the bullies will have their own difficulties, and alerting adults to their behaviour may help them to address their own situations. In summary, if young people are being bullied, they need to take action using the advice of adults whom they respect and can talk to.

Why intervene?

Adults may sometimes feel that if they intervene they will undermine the victim, somehow retard their growth of coping skills or disturb their relationships with their peers. However, the consequences of bullying are too extreme to adopt a *laissez-faire* attitude. In recent years more research and initiatives have focused on bullying, in part because of severe cases linked to bullying, some of which have even led to suicides. Bullying is caused by aggressive behaviour which if unchecked in childhood can be sustained into adulthood. This can mean that violent, aggressive behaviour is carried over from one generation to the next. Failing to act can give a silent but powerful message that aggressive, violent or abusive behaviour is appropriate and acceptable. Parents may feel torn between reporting bullying to the school and following their own child's wishes, and so teachers may not always expect to learn about bullying from a child's parents.

When to intervene
Bullying has been defined as 'a repeated aggression, verbal, psychological or physical, conducted by an individual or group against others'.[2] Bullying is found in males and females of all ages and socioeconomic backgrounds. It can be short or long term but can always cause a great deal of distress to the victims. Teachers, parents and others can look out for bullying in the following symptoms: reduced ability to concentrate, poor or deteriorating work, fear of going to school or work, loss of confidence and self-esteem, aggressive behaviour, depression, anxiety, wanting to leave school or job, or attempted suicide.

How to intervene
It can be difficult for those caring for children to identify when and where bullying is taking place and sometimes to know what to do when they have discovered its occurrence. Many schools have now developed a bullying strategy and teachers will have been informed of this. This is essential in order to help teachers identify and tackle bullying. If promoted actively it will give a clear message to parents and students that bullying is regarded as a serious issue and not a 'natural part of growing up'. It will warn potential bullies of the consequences, and it will educate parents so that they know more about the causes of bullying and what to do when it occurs. It will help teachers to act within a recognized and appropriate framework of response.

The following recommendations refer to appropriate school actions where bullying has been identified.[3]

- Investigate the problem and take reports of bullying seriously.
- Respond to every incident, no matter how minor, and act immediately.

- Keep a careful eye out for bullying at high-risk times, such as break times, the beginning and end of the school day and when students are changing for sports.
- Monitor high-risk students, those who are likely to be targeted; these students may be different in some way, may keep to themselves or appear not 'to fit in'.
- Make sure that locations where bullying is likely to occur are monitored carefully. These include poorly lit corridors, cloakrooms, changing rooms, school yards and bike sheds.
- Try assigning particular teachers in turn to watch out for bullying.
- Reinforce non-aggressive behaviour by rewarding students who show caring behaviour.
- Educate students by showing a video or giving a presentation on bullying. Portray the bully as someone with difficulties and inadequacies to remove any status they might otherwise gain from bullying. Encourage students to report when they or others are being bullied. Assure them that they will be believed and helped and that confidentiality will be respected.
- Be supportive to other staff, set up a system to deal with bullying, talk to other staff about their own experiences of bullying in adulthood.
- If someone confides in you that they are being bullied, assure them that you believe them and take this seriously, that you will help and that the situation will end.
- Counselling is sometimes necessary for students who have been the victim of serious bullying. Discuss this with the child's parents.
- Discuss the situation with the parents of both the victim and the bully. Talk about possible causes for the behaviour and ways the children can address the problem. Causes of bullying can include experience of abuse and violence, poor coping skills, low self-esteem, not being able to keep up at school, parents being over-strict or being bullied by others.
- Always focus on the behaviour of the bullies and not the bullies themselves. Suggest more effective coping skills.
- When bullying takes place in groups, confront each of the bullies on their own. Help them to understand their own role and responsibility.
- Expect bullies to compensate the victim for anything broken or taken. Expect them to apologize.
- In serious cases of bullying, if parents refuse to cooperate invite external advisers and assessors to participate.

It is important to educate young people in defining bullying. They may not realize that they are experiencing bullying and may therefore fail to take appropriate action. If young people are being pressured to act in a particular way, to do things that they don't want to do, are being called names, teased, insulted, threatened, robbed or beaten up, these are all different types of bullying.

In summary, bullying is a serious, physically threatening and psychologically damaging occurrence that can interfere with healthy adolescent development and cause severe problems to young people at a vulnerable stage in their lives. Always be concerned, and act when you learn of such episodes.

CONCLUSION

Relationships cause considerable stress in adolescence as in adulthood. They are also often the best stress management resource we have. To encourage young people to maintain healthy relationships, it was recommended that you:

- ask them to recall difficulties they have experienced with people in their lives

- ask them to consider whether the relationships that cause the most stress are also the ones they turn to in difficult times

- discuss the importance of relationships

- persuade them to accept responsibility for their own role in their relationships

- encourage them to 'be themselves'

- ask them to look for patterns in their relationships that might be rooted in the past

- discuss the good and bad things about being alone

- ask them what they think being assertive means

- discuss how being assertive can help them in their relationships

- provide them with advice on negotiation and listening skills

- convey the importance of talking to others when they are feeling upset or down

- discuss bullying

As the next chapter is about self-confidence, it is often useful to suggest to young people that they do some research on the subject prior to your discussion. Ask them to ask ten people whether they consider themselves to be self-confident, and to ask some people whom they think are self-confident if they consider themselves to be self-confident, and if there are things they are not confident about.

Notes

1 Butler, G. and Hope, T. (1995) *The Mental Fitness Guide: Manage Your Mind.* Oxford: Oxford University Press.
2 ABC – Research and Resource Unit, Teacher Education Department, Trinity College Dublin.
3 Copley, B. and Williams, G. (1995) *The Teenage Years: Understanding 18-20 year olds.* London: The Tavistock Clinic.

CHAPTER 9

Treating yourself right

No amount of skills, strategies, ideas and information on learning to cope with stress will be of any use unless young people (1) value themselves, and (2) have the self-confidence to put these into effect.

Treats

'All work and no play . . .' has long been an adage which suggests how limiting and stultifying it can be when we deny ourselves playtime and enjoyment. In order to develop as rounded, happy people we all need to give ourselves rewards and to 'treat ourselves right'. Treats do not necessarily have to be things which aren't good for you. They are simply a recognition of efforts we have made and the need for us to take breaks in order to remain relaxed and stress-free.

Whelan (1993) talks about sources of energy in much the same way that we talk about treats. These sources differ for each of us and you can ask young people to think of things that make them feel happy, fulfilled and relaxed. These could include going dancing, spending time with friends, watching a video, listening to a favourite CD, going for a walk or taking a bath. Whatever our own sources of energy or 'treats', these allow us to continue to thrive and cope with life in a positive and constructive way. They somehow combat what can be referred to as energy drains, such as having too much work, strict deadlines, not spending enough time outdoors, arguments with friends or family, rejections, or things going wrong generally.

When you ask young people to think of treats, encourage them to think of treats which are just as good for them in the long as in the short term. Frequent drinking, smoking, eating fast foods or staying up all night are likely to leave them twice as drained, as their health will suffer and their energy levels decline. Similarly, acting inconsiderately, while it may bring short-term pleasure, may end up bringing them more stress in the medium term. Feeling happy, creative and well nurtured in turn gives us the energy to get stuck into other tasks like school work, projects, maintaining difficult relationships and so on. It's all a question of balance.

Ask young people to:

- Think about a difficult task they are facing and to plan a treat for having finished it. This works for small tasks too; young people can learn to associate one hour's study with half an hour's treat, such as chatting on the phone, watching television or just relaxing.
- Introduce the treat immediately after the task is completed to maximize the effect. This works well for studying and will make it easier to concentrate. It can work for other difficult situations, such as having to discuss a sensitive issue with someone. They can plan a swim or a video for afterwards.
- Think of small, regular treats that are harmless pleasure.
- Do the things they dread first to get them over and done with. Utilize the energy that comes with beginning a project to do the difficult parts first.
- Use the things they like doing as rewards. For example, if they're planning to go bowling, they could squeeze in some study time before they go rather than have to face it when they get back.

Boosting self-confidence

Try asking young people:

- What they think self-confidence is.
- What they think the symptoms of low self-confidence are.
- What they feel self-confident about.
- What they feel low in self-confidence about.
- Were they surprised by any of the responses to their survey of self-confidence?
- Did the people that they thought were self-confident consider themselves to be self-confident?
- Were there things that they were not confident about? Did that surprise them?
- Did they feel that other people have more self-confidence than them?
- How can they tell if somebody is confident or not?
- Are confident people always confident? Or confident about everything?

Low self-confidence can have a pervasive effect on a young person's life. Their thoughts, behaviour, feelings and the way they hold themselves are all affected. Having low levels of confidence can be a major obstacle for young people trying to live their lives. As the group 'The Smiths' put it, 'Shyness can stop you doing all the things in life you want to.'

Although it is normal for us all to feel lacking in confidence at some time, for young people this can be especially difficult, and a good discussion on self-confidence should help debunk a few myths and flesh out the area. It's a good idea to suggest that the questions you raise are also discussed with peers. The following is a list of the main ways that a lack of self-confidence affects us. These are experienced by everyone from time to time, but for some people they can seriously impede them from achieving things that they value. Try asking young people to think about which of these things is true for them.

Low self-confidence[1]

When young people feel low in self-confidence they tell themselves they can't do anything, they're not good enough, things are too difficult, they don't know how, they can't cope, and that they won't be any good. They feel apprehensive, nervous, anxious, stressed out, worried about difficult things that are coming up, frustrated and angry with themselves for not doing things better, afraid of the unknown and new situations, resentful of other people who find things easy, and disappointed and low.

They may be more withdrawn, keep a low profile, find it hard to make suggestions or put themselves forward, put things off, avoid taking on anything new or making changes in their lives. They may stoop, retreat into themselves, avoid looking people in the eye, fumble and fidget, have tense muscles, and feel tired.

Confidence is complicated

Confidence consists of many things. Suggest to the young people that they ask themselves what they are confident about and what they are not confident about. For example, they may be good drivers but bad at English essays, they may be good at fixing cars or minding children, but bad at maths. They will soon realize that there are things on both sides. In addition, without exception, confident people always have something they are not confident about. Suggest they ask someone whom they consider confident what they are insecure about. There will always be something. The lesson is to focus on the positive.

Seeing is deceiving

An important thing to communicate is how many people who appear confident are actually not so. What they are actually successfully doing is giving the appearance that they are confident. This is a good trick and one they can learn, because once we start behaving confidently, we often begin to feel more confident too. Their interviewees will always be able to think of something that makes them feel unsure of themselves. In fact the majority of people feel less confident than they appear.

Practice makes perfect

Wouldn't it be great if we always did everything right? Or would it? Most of our valuable lessons come from the mistakes we have made along the way. This is true for everyone. Young people should learn to believe that what's important is trying new things, learning and growing, and not the mistakes. Once they've been practising for a while, they'll improve at most things and their confidence will grow. Perhaps they might even see their mistakes as equipping them with funny stories to share with their friends. They should remember that they won't be the first to be in this situation, or the last. Try asking them to think of something they can do now that they couldn't do before.

Confidence in five easy steps?

1 If at first . . .

Suggest that if they are unsure about starting out on something, they give it their best shot for a while and see what happens. Ask them to think about the first time they tried to ride a bike or use a computer.

2 Talk the talk and walk the walk

It is amazing how emulating characteristics tends to trick our brain. If young people were even to try to pretend to be confident in stressful situations, their confidence levels would actually grow. Ask them to think of someone confident whom they know and respect and to consider how he or she would act in this situation. As everything is interrelated, any changes in our posture, thoughts, feelings or behaviour will influence each other and they will immediately begin to feel more confident.

3 Learn and move on!

We all tend to remember our mistakes in a negative light, but young people lacking in self-confidence can focus excessively on appearing foolish or feeling inadequate. An important lesson for life is to try to think about what we learned from the experience. Ask them to think of a mistake they have made and what they learned from this. There is no mistake that hasn't been made before, and it is only people who are afraid to try new things who do not make mistakes.

4 Don't beat yourself up!
There is nothing to be achieved from beating ourselves up having made a mistake. Once the situation is in the past and we have learned from it, we need to move on and not allow ourselves to be dragged down by the experience.

5 Be nice to yourself
If we don't give ourselves the same breaks as we give others we care for, our confidence levels will never grow. Young people should 'cut themselves some slack' and forgive themselves for their mistakes.

Boosting self-esteem[2]
Self-esteem is about how we see ourselves. It is a core aspect of our very being, often based on our childhood and adolescent experiences. It is central and inseparable from the way we handle events in our lives and how we feel about ourselves all the time. If we have high self-esteem we feel good about ourselves and when it's low we will feel bad about ourselves. Self-esteem is something that needs to be nurtured over time and it develops throughout our lives. It allows us to value ourselves and feel that our contributions are worthwhile. There are, however, things we can do to help increase our self-esteem. Young people cannot have enough self-esteem, as it brings not arrogance but real security. It's probably the best stress management tool there is.

Be the devil's advocate
When we suffer from low self-esteem we tend to be dismissive towards ourselves. We see ourselves as worthless and unliked. If we could only be rational and look at the evidence, we would often find it difficult to maintain this viewpoint. Suggest that young people, when they are feeling negative towards themselves, try to fight the bias and focus on their good points and acknowledge that they matter.

If you're the hardest judge that you could get – tell yourself to get real!
Statements which some young people will find familiar include: 'I'm unwanted', 'they don't like me', 'I'm in the way', 'I don't matter'. They can learn to recognize that these statements stem from feelings of low self-esteem, which does not make them true. Similarly, we often

acknowledge the achievements of others while dismissing our own, by saying they mean nothing or we were just lucky. If we tend to be critical about ourselves we can expect things to go wrong, which is unhelpful in facing challenges. If things don't go well, we can use this as evidence that we can't cope or aren't popular. In some ways these are self-fulfilling prophecies. Once they recognize that these voices are irrational, young people can gain the confidence to tell them to shut up.

All you can do is your best

There is a big difference between wanting to do well and torturing yourself when you don't do well all the time. Sometimes when our self-esteem is low, we make rules that are hard to stick to as they are unrealistic and impossible. Examples of this are:

- I have to get things right all the time
- I should always come first in the class
- I must always win at sports
- I'm not good enough
- Boys should never look weak
- I can't make a mistake
- If they realize I lack confidence, they won't want anything to do with me
- I shouldn't talk about it when things go wrong
- I can't change.

If we repeat these unfair generalized comments to ourselves all the time, we'll just feel bad about ourselves. Ask young people to think about what they may be saying to themselves which is undermining their self-esteem. Remind them that they can only do their best.

Nurture company that nurtures

Throughout our lives, but particularly in adolescence, we can be around people who undermine our sense of self-worth. If young people feel their self-esteem is low, ask them to make a list of the people who help them to feel good about themselves. Who are the people who make them feel bad about themselves? Suggest they spend more time with the former and in general avoid friends who undermine their confidence.

Self-esteem changes all the time. We all feel better about ourselves some days than others. Remembering this in itself is a worthwhile skill, as we can ride the bad days more easily. The most important thing is to be kind to ourselves and value ourselves.

Unhappiness and depression

It is an illusion that youth is happy,
an illusion of those who have lost it.
W. Somerset Maugham.

The relationship between depression and stress is highly complicated. Stressful life events as well as poor coping skills can lead to depression, and feelings of depression can create stress in the lives of young people through loss of social support and creating stressful events.

Many adolescents go through periods of sadness from time to time. For some, this can be more serious and depression may follow. Depression is a highly complex condition. It may be due to genetic, biochemical or hormonal predispositions, or rooted in early or current relationships and experiences. This section provides advice for helping young people who report feelings of unhappiness. It is important, however, that you are aware of sources of professional help and can provide young people with contact details of counsellors. They should be encouraged, if these feelings are prolonged and severe, to contact their GP or school counsellor.

Try asking young people if they have felt 'down' from time to time. If you are doing this in a group, the group will realize that this is normal and most young people have experienced this. Ask them what sorts of things make them feel sad and what sorts of things make them feel better.

The following can make young people feel depressed: their parents arguing, their parents separating, someone they know committing suicide, someone they know becoming very ill, falling out with a close friend, feeling too much pressure to achieve, feeling unable to cope, being bullied or feeling unattractive. Other causes include experiences of abuse, racism or poverty, difficulties around adoption, or fostering issues or addiction problems.

When these things happen at once, young people may find it more difficult to cope and will feel depressed for a while. They may not know why they feel sad. They may feel depression, anger, stress, pressure, fear, loneliness, confusion, guilt, shame, or a combination of these feelings. Feeling sad is an important response to things in our life or things going on in our mind. It can tell us that something is not right in our life or in the way we are thinking about our life, and we can use this as a sign to do something to improve this.

The key to recovery is to be aware that we are not happy and to do something about it. By doing something positive or talking to someone about the way we feel, we can definitely start to improve things. This is often difficult when we feel down, as life seems pointless and without hope. Depression can make it difficult to see the different options that are open to us. We find it hard to see that there are things we can do to make ourselves feel better.

It is sometimes hard to assess whether young people are depressed or just feeling down. This is important to know in order to help them to decide what action to take. It is a question of the intensity, duration and cause of the feelings (if they know), and the impact it is having on their day-to-day functioning.

Depression can mean feeling extremely sad or just numb. It is increasingly common in young people. The reasons for this were discussed in Chapter 2. It is likely that today's young people are experiencing more pressures, expectations and disappointments than in the past. They may feel increasingly isolated, as there seem to be fewer people, systems and beliefs they can rely on and life seems to change so quickly. They may feel that it is assumed they can cope with a great deal of changes and stressful situations alone. When young people encounter problems, they need stability and adults to rely on. They need people to support them, to help them to understand what they are going through and help them feel better.

The symptoms of depression are listed below. Try asking young people to think of these first.

Depression affects:

- *The way we think.* We believe we deserve the worst, blame ourselves for everything, see everything as meaningless, feel things will always be this way and can never improve, focus continually on problems, failures and negative feelings, hate oneself, lose interest in life and other people, have thoughts of harming oneself, and find it hard to concentrate and make decisions.
- *The way we feel.* We feel sad and unhappy, numb, hopeless, worthless, unattractive, helpless, irritable, tense, anxious and worried, guilty, as if we can't cope with things, under pressure, low in self-confidence and self-esteem, we take no pleasure out of anything, and we feel no sense of mastery or achievement.
- *The way we behave.* We do less, everything seems like a huge effort, we find it hard to get out of bed in the morning, we withdraw from meeting people socially or at work, we feel restless, we sigh and cry a lot.

- *Our physical well-being.* We eat, drink, sleep and smoke a lot more or less than usual. We may find ourselves waking early in the morning in a very low mood. We feel lethargic and exhausted.

What can young people do?
Talk about it

The most important thing, if we are experiencing these symptoms, is to express our feelings. Sometimes just talking about the way we feel to an understanding person can make us feel better. Research has shown that having someone to listen to us and help us to talk through what we're feeling is of huge benefit when we feel sad.

We can also express how we feel in other ways. Keeping a diary, painting or writing songs, poetry or short stories are examples of things that can help us to work through what has happened or is happening, and to reflect on what this means and often what we need to do to move on. They also allow us to express feelings we wouldn't want to share with others. We don't always feel the benefits immediately, but they usually come with time. Ask young people how they let off steam, if they find it hard to talk about feelings of sadness, what the obstacles might be, what might help them feel more comfortable, if it is harder for young men to talk about their feelings, if they keep a diary and to discuss their reasons.

If they're cynical about the positive benefits, suggest they experiment next time they feel down by choosing an understanding person whom they trust to talk to, and to think about how they feel afterwards. The best person is someone whom they find easy to talk to. Friends, brothers, sisters, parents, teachers, aunts, uncles, grandparents, GPs or counsellors can be very helpful in making them feel happier. It is important that they communicate the depth and duration of their feelings, so that these people will take them seriously as well as choosing an appropriate time to commence the discussion. Encourage them to arrange a time that will suit both people to sit down and talk, as they could easily misinterpret inconvenience as disinterest if they pick a bad time for this other person.

Young people are often unaware of how many of their peers feel the same way, and so talking to friends can be a useful source of support. You can also mention the availability of a counsellor at school if there is one. You can also provide them with a list of phone numbers and addresses of local and national help agencies (such as Childline or the Samaritans) and details of any school facilities.

Use their support systems

Many things may stop young people discussing their feelings with others. They may feel ashamed or worried about finding out the worst. They may feel weak and that they are to blame for their feelings of depression.

Next time they feel depressed, ask them to remember that support will help them through it by showing them:

- that someone cares about them
- that other people have felt and feel the same way
- that these problems have been experienced by others
- why they are depressed and the problems in life which have made them feel down
- different and more realistic perspectives
- different solutions to problems

Sharing problems with friends will also help them to do what is necessary to feel better. We need this help because depression can destroy our energy and motivation. Although there are many potential causes of depression, as well as talking to people we trust or seeking professional help, there are things that we ourselves can do to improve the way we feel. We need to look at the things we do, the way we think and the people in our life.

Young people who suffer from depression need hope and help. You need to encourage them to start by concentrating on small changes, to move them in the right direction away from their depression. This means focusing on the next step and trying not to look too far ahead. They need to make their goal simply feeling better. They won't feel marvellous straight away, but focusing on small changes in the way they think and behave will allow the process of feeling better to begin.

Ways of alleviating depression

These include:

- *Increasing what we do.* Although depression deprives us of energy and makes us feel very tired, setting ourselves small tasks is the first step towards feeling better. Doing small things like going for a walk or phoning a friend can help to lift our mood. Completing tasks helps bring a sense of mastery and pleasure.
- *Thought catching.* Young people need to be aware of their self-talk. This is probably making them feel worse and telling them they will never feel better. Once they are aware of this they can start challenging these statements. When we are sad, we

tend to remember sad times and appraise things more negatively. If they need to analyse what is happening in their lives, it is best to wait until their mood lifts to begin this.

- *Reality check.* If they can remember when they are feeling like this, that their perspective is distorted, this might help them to view things more clearly and prevent them from feeling even worse.
- *Switch off.* When there is nothing we can do to change a situation, it is often useful to just switch off. Going to the cinema, playing sport or just trying to have a chat about something else can give our minds a chance to switch off. This can give us the energy we need to recharge and start tackling the problem.
- *Be specific.* Feeling depressed makes us look at things in a very apathetic way and this can perpetuate these feelings. Suggest that young people try instead to think of positive things in specific terms; for example, instead of saying 'I've still got friends', name a friend or some friends and list specific things they have enjoyed or been through, or specific plans that involve both or all of them in the future. The most likely mistake that we can make when we are depressed is mistaking feelings for facts. Thinking or feeling things doesn't make them true.
- *The talking cure.* Talking to others helps in many ways. It is good to know there is somebody else who knows what you're going through and who cares. It can also help you to explore why you are depressed and what sorts of things in your life have been getting you down. A friend can help you think of ways of tackling these problems and will also have a more accurate perspective on your problems and on you than you do yourself. Telling someone else will also mean that you have someone to motivate you and to help you take on the activities which will help you feel better.

Thoughts of harming themselves

When depressed, young people may have thoughts of harming themselves. This is quite common. It does not mean that they are 'going mad', but you do need to take such thoughts seriously. If you mention to young people that this symptom is not uncommon, they are perhaps more likely to feel that they can tell someone about these thoughts and/or behaviours. Encourage them to discuss these thoughts with an adult whom they trust. They should not be afraid of how others will react. Young people are often reluctant to mention their thoughts for fear that others will disapprove, or fail to understand, or for fear that talking about them may actually make them easier to put into effect. In fact, talking about thoughts of harming yourself usually brings some relief. If they feel like putting these into effect, or making plans, they should seek help at once and talk to someone about how they feel.

How to help prevent depression

Because the causes of depression are multifarious, taking preventive steps will not rule out the possibility of young people suffering depression. Genetic, biochemical and sociological factors may determine this outcome. Anyone can get depressed, and they should not feel it is their fault or responsibility if they do. There are, however, certain basic preventive measures that may reduce the likelihood of becoming depressed.

HELPING TO PREVENT DEPRESSION

Encourage young people to:

- Get enough *sleep* – this will help them to feel on top of things and able to cope, and will also keep their mood positive.

- Remember that *drinking* may make them feel good for a while, but it is often followed by a low. Alcohol is a depressant. It can also help distract them from problems which should really be confronted and resolved.

- Eat well – not *eating* enough will make them feel irritable, depressed, tired and weak. Girls in particular are under a lot of pressure these days to stay slim. Eating a balanced diet will help them stay healthy, in a good mood and give them energy. All these things will help them to enjoy life to the full.

- Get enough *exercise* – this is one of the best ways of staying in good form. If they do start feeling down, it can help to alleviate these feelings and give them a boost.

- Make room for things they *enjoy* – these will help keep them happy!

- Spend time developing good *relationships* – so that they have people to turn to when they feel down.

It is also important to *lead a balanced life*. It is normal for us all to have times when things in one area of our lives are not going as well as they should (e.g. our homework, school, family relationships, or problems with friends or boyfriends/girlfriends). If all our happiness is bound into one of these areas we will be very vulnerable if things go wrong with that aspect of our lives. If, for example, our self-esteem depends on our being part of a couple, breaking up might make it feel as if the world is coming to an end. Similarly, if our school work is the most important thing in our life we may suffer extreme exam nerves and stress, as all our eggs are in this basket. It is therefore a good idea to have several parts to our life: school, family, friends, hobbies, interests and so on. Then, at times when one part of our life is not going according to plan, we can get pleasure and comfort from another part.

Worry and anxiety

Worrying is a vicious circle, as it just makes us feel more wound up and anxious. It puts us in a bad mood and drains us of energy. Most of the things we worry about never happen, or are not as bad as we thought they would be. Even when things turn out for the worst, worrying has rarely helped to achieve anything, and may even leave us feeling less able to cope when it happens.

Try asking young people to think of something they have been worried about. Has this worrying helped resolve the difficulty? How does worrying affect thinking, behaviour, feelings or physical well-being?

What worrying achieves

Worrying is only useful if it makes us aware of something that needs to be remedied, allows us to resolve the situation and move on. It is bad for us when it constantly fills our mind and we take no action or remain preoccupied. It wastes time and energy.

Worrying interferes with our ability to concentrate and to focus on other things, it makes it hard to take decisions and makes us concentrate on negative aspects of situations. It is also a habit that we can learn to break. When we're worrying, we pay less attention to the task at hand and so our work can suffer, and it can also make us feel less confident as well as confused, anxious and helpless. Physically, when we are worried, we lose our ability to relax and sleep properly. We can get tired and run down. It can give us headaches and make us feel tense.

How to get rid of worries[3]

Suggest that young people divide their worries into (1) those they can do something about, and (2) those they can't do anything about. For the first category, they should decide whether they can do something about it now or later, and plan to act on that. The second category includes all worries that are unimportant, unlikely or unresolved. Unimportant worries are those which they can't see themselves worrying about in five years' time or things which simply aren't worth the worry. Unlikely worries are those which are probably never going to happen. Finally, there is no point worrying about things which are unresolved. They should wait to see what happens and then decide what to do.

SUMMARY

There are only two choices when we find ourselves worrying:

1   Use a problem-solving approach and do something about it.
2   Stop worrying about it.

This advice might seem easier said than done. The following tips will help young people to banish worrying.

- *Distraction*. You can only pay full attention to one thing at a time. When we are busy we have less time to worry. It's important, however, not to misuse distraction as a way of avoiding the task of thinking about problems. If there is something young people can do, they should use problem-solving strategies to try to solve it.
- *Only in the daytime*. The middle of the night is often when our worries loom large and seem most disturbing. Encourage young people to ban night-time worrying. They should be disciplined with themselves and insist as soon as a worry pops into their head that 'This is not the time'. They can write down their worries and forget about them until morning, try visualizing a pleasant image, or try a relaxation exercise, such as progressive relaxation described in Chapter 6.
- *Back in their box*. Suggest that they think of their own image for dispensing with the worry, for example, putting their worries in a box and closing the lid. If they need to remember it they can write it down.

- *Fence them in.* If worrying is a major problem, you could suggest that young people even put aside a regular half-hour each day to worry. This will stop their days and nights being plagued by worrying. It can also help worrying to turn into problem-solving and thus become more productive.

Worries are usually false predictions

People often believe they are worried about something they have said and done. However, the root cause of the anxiety is usually a prediction about the way this will affect the future or about being unable to cope in the future. Worrying can be alleviated if you can encourage young people to examine these predictions and challenge them.

- *Question assumptions.* Ask them to think about what they are really worried about. Is it really about having offended a friend by not telephoning, or are they more concerned that they will be rejected too readily by that person? Challenging these assumptions will allow them to take apart the worrying messages they send out.
- *Talk about it.* As with feelings of stress and depression, discussing their worries will give them the support, advice and relief often necessary to discard those worries. Other people can ask questions to help them identify what the worry is about, and can offer different and often more realistic perspectives. They can also practise asking themselves the questions they want to ask someone else, and try to answer it themselves. This can encourage self-reliance and self-confidence in young people.

CONCLUSION

In order to manage stress effectively, young people need to value themselves, and so this chapter discussed ways of boosting self-confidence and self-esteem. In addition, depression and anxiety may arise through poor coping skills, or may be a source of stress in the lives of young people. It was suggested that you discuss:

- treats or sources of energy
- what self-confidence is, where it comes from and how to increase it

- what self-esteem is, where it comes from and how to boost it
- the symptoms of depression
- ways of coping with depression
- ways of preventing depression
- thoughts of self-harm
- how to limit worry and anxiety

Notes

1 Butler, G. and Hope, T. (1995) *The Mental Fitness Guide: Manage Your Mind.* Oxford: Oxford University Press.
2 Ibid.
3 Ibid.

CHAPTER 10

Discussion and conclusion

Introduction

This chapter seeks to (1) summarize the aims of the book, (2) highlight important points to remember when instigating programmes for stress reduction, (3) discuss the role of socioeconomic factors, (4) summarize advice on stress management for young people, and (5) place stress interventions in the context of a changing world.

The aim of the book

This book aims to give those working with or in contact with young people the necessary information, techniques and ideas to discuss the issue of stress and suggest ways in which young people can cope better with the stress in their lives. Part 1 seeks to provide the context for these discussions in outlining our current knowledge about stress in young people. A good understanding of the most contemporary model of stress allows us to see the connections between all aspects of this process, including life events, daily hassles, self-esteem, feelings of control, social support, perceptions of stress, coping strategies, personality, age, gender, culture, and physical and mental health. It teaches us that no one of these factors on their own will lead to feelings of strain but that they act as a system leading to either positive coping and adaptation or feelings of pressure and failure to cope. Part 2 provides more practical advice about raising pertinent issues and relating useful coping strategies to teenagers.

Chapter 1 provided compelling evidence that many psychological, behavioural and physical outcomes have their origins in stressful events and daily hassles. This relationship is mediated by social and personal factors, such as social support, self-esteem, age, gender, culture, perceptions of control and negative affectivity. The important role of coping was also discussed, and it was argued that problem-focused coping has a protective function in steering individuals through stressful situations. There is, however, a place for emotion-focused coping in situations where the individual has less control.

Chapter 2 discussed contemporary theories of adolescence and asked whether stress in teenagers really is increasing. Evidence was provided for an increase in stress-related outcomes such as eating disorders, suicides, substance abuse, exam stress, depression and anxiety in young people. Societal developments which may account for these increases were discussed. A detailed discussion was provided on the key factors which contribute to adolescent stress. These include life events and daily hassles, coping, social support, personality factors, relationships with peers and family, puberty, transitions, emerging sexuality, school and exams, coping with depression, parental problems, and unemployment. An emphasis was placed on risk and resiliency research to identify factors which protect teenagers from maladaptive outcomes.

Chapter 3 discussed the efficacy of stress reduction interventions in reducing or preventing symptoms of stress in teenagers. Those interventions which have been successful in alleviating symptoms in adults were discussed first. Interventions which have been used effectively with young people include life skills training, social skills training, social competence training, exercise training, problem-solving skills and stress inoculation training. Details were given of resources currently available to practitioners for use with groups of young people. These offer advice on group dynamics as well as suggestions on the content of courses. Further reading on tackling stress in schools and counselling for young people was also suggested.

Chapter 4 gave advice on location and tone when discussing stress with young people. It discussed issues of confidentiality, role changes, ownership and gender issues. It was recommended that young people be encouraged to talk about sources of stress in their lives, resources, and symptoms and outcomes of stress as well as the benefits of learning to cope more effectively with stress.

Chapter 5 focused on mental ways of coping with stress. Fundamental to this discussion was exploring the link between events, thoughts and feelings. It was recommended that young people be encouraged to keep a stress diary to explore the relationship between their internal self-talk and feelings of strain and worry. Appraisal was identified as playing a key role in the maintenance of stress-related symptoms. Advice was given on learning to plan ahead, preparing for stressful events, keeping things in perspective, thought stopping, coping skills training, learning how to relax, problem-solving, the importance of humour and different coping strategies.

Because good physical health plays a key protective role in the stress process, Chapter 6 provided information on nutrition, exercise, sleep, breathing, relaxation and the effects of alcohol consumption. Dieting can cause a great deal of stress to the body and make it difficult to cope with normal everyday demands. It was suggested that assumptions around body shape were explored. Advice was also presented on coping with premenstrual syndrome. Key to this chapter was teaching young people about the effect of their physical health on the way they perceive situations, i.e. whether they feel they can cope.

Many young people find it difficult to cope with the stress which arises from exam situations. Chapter 7 provided advice on study skills and time management. First, however, a discussion was recommended on assumptions around achievement and well-being. Young people should be encouraged to discuss the pressure they feel they are under with regard to succeeding. The effects on concentration of diet and physical activity were discussed. Advice was also provided on note-taking and exam preparation.

Learning how to manage relationships well is an important skill in stress management, as they provide much needed support at difficult times in our lives. Chapter 8 aimed to facilitate discussion around the meaning and role of relationships in the lives of young people. It encouraged them to use these relationships as a resource, and also to accept their responsibilities for maintaining the relationship. Young people were encouraged to look for patterns in the way they relate to others which might be rooted in the past. Advice on assertiveness, negotiation and listening skills was provided. Coping with bullying was also discussed.

Chapter 9 presented advice around nurturing and sustaining self-confidence and self-esteem. It also looked at depression and ways it can be understood, prevented or alleviated. It is important that young people recognize the symptoms of depression and are aware of basic recommended courses of action. These include talking to people they trust, and making initial small changes in their thinking or behaviour. A discussion on thoughts of self-harm was also provided. Finally, some basic techniques for conquering worrying were presented.

Programme implementation
In the words of Black and Frauenknecht:

> primary prevention stress-management programs for asymptom-
> atic adolescents are currently non-existent, although sorely

needed to alleviate detrimental effects of excessive stress. (Black and Frauenknecht, 1990, p. 89)

The majority of evaluative studies which examine the effects of interventions in adolescence are non-comparative by design. The effects of a stress management course with a lecture-discussion format compared to a skills-based course (which incorporated biofeedback training) have been evaluated. Participants on the former programme demonstrated greater reductions in anxiety and subjective stress. Stress management programmes which include problem-solving, coping skills, cognitive skills and general life discussion have all demonstrated significant efficacy in alleviating adolescent distress.

Perhaps the most well-known and widely used stress management programme is Meichenbaum's stress inoculation training. This programme has been used with some success with young people, and incorporates relaxation, cognitive restructuring and assertiveness training. The *Stress Management Programme for Secondary School Students* (McNamara, 2000) has also demonstrated long-term benefits in participants.

Many studies examine differential outcomes in treatment and control groups, but fail to include comparative interventions. It is therefore difficult to dismiss in these studies the potential influence of core or non-specific elements which are shared by any intervention. These include rapport with the participant, suggestion, expectation of relief, treatment credibility and compliance. In other words, people taking part in a course would expect to feel better for doing so, and this expectation may lead to an improvement in symptoms. Shared elements such as an organizational acknowledgement of adolescent difficulties and issues, taking time out, relaxing, space to reflect, sharing experiences, social support and peer counselling are extremely important components for interventions with young people. These are the basics on which further skills and information are layered.

Following extensive research on happiness and well-being, and a review of mood induction and cognitive therapies, Argyle and Martin (1995) recommend that interventions which would enhance well-being should incorporate four components. These are 'persuading people to make different attributions for good and bad events, trying to change the content of ruminations, and increasing optimism and self-esteem' (p. 96).

Furthermore, an intervention study can only show that it has achieved more than general relaxation effects by its strict adherence to the stringent design desiderata proposed by such authors as Stiles *et al.*, who urge that future research should include a

> combination of greater specification of treatment components, via manualization and dismantling strategies, with greater differentiation of outcome measurement, via behavioral assessment and other measurement of specific therapeutic effects. (Stiles *et al.*, 1986, p. 171)

This means that until we have strong research designs which isolate the different components of interventions, we will not know which components are effective over and beyond the non-specific elements listed above.

The importance of accurate assessment is reiterated in an important recent publication, edited by Takanishi and Hamburg (1997), in which Hamburg writes: 'without credible evidence of benefit, we cannot be sure that the adolescents are receiving the help they need' (p. 130). Six key dimensions to successful programme implementation and assessment are outlined by Hamburg.

The first of these refers to adequate assessment of the specific needs of the target population. Second, selection of an appropriate programme site is discussed in terms of accessibility, acceptance and adequacy of space. The school as an appropriate forum was discussed in Chapter 3. Considerable attention should be devoted to choosing an appropriate location within each school which would best facilitate these criteria. For young people who are not attending school, more informal locations such as youth cafés or youth centres may be preferable.

Third, Hamburg discusses the importance of the relationship between the 'action researcher' and the system through which the intervention is to be delivered. The relationship between service providers and the researcher should be highly reciprocal. Detailed feedback reports should be presented at regular intervals to service providers and (when appropriate) to students. Course materials should be made available for school use and talks provided for parents, teachers and students on stress and its effects, complete with book lists, address lists and information handouts.

A fourth recommendation is the provision of manuals for the use of trainers or teachers. Hamburg also refers to procedures for data collection and the importance of securing an adequate information management system. Data collection in real-life settings is always a difficult component of applied research. Every attempt should, however, be made to standardize and maximize data collection. Finally, Hamburg recommends a multi-method, multi-measure approach to evaluation. As is suggested in Chapter 3, evaluation of these interventions should combine self-report ratings with independent ratings and objective data.

Research into the development of stress reduction programmes is increasing but differs on four major dimensions, namely in its focus on individual or environmental change, its focus on specific or general stressors, the types of skills taught, and the emphasis on competency enhancement or problem prevention. This book has focused on individual-based, general stress management, incorporating a variety of coping skills aimed at competency enhancement in an asymptomatic adolescent population. It is also important to examine ways in which the effects of such a programme would be enhanced by (1) the simultaneous delivery of such a course to parents and teachers, (2) tackling environmental stressors identified by the community as stressful to young people, (3) delivering the course to populations which differ in their exposure to risk, and (4) continuing to dismantle treatment components so as to retain only key components with proven efficacy.

More research is required to identify individual and group differences which might influence programme success in order to provide the most appropriate programmes to groups of young people from different backgrounds. Programmes which seek to reduce adolescent distress by improving school environments appear to represent a fruitful and worthy avenue for future research.[1]

The socioeconomic dimension to research

The socioeconomic dimension to this type of research merits comment. Much of the research on risk and resilience, together with the literature on primary prevention, suggests that interventions such as these should target individuals who are at a social or economic disadvantage. However, although school representatives and service providers may be highly enthusiastic about the opportunity this kind of research affords, many of these schools are unable to set aside time for the facilitation of the programmes. When students are invited to take part in the courses after school time, a low response rate may follow, making the provision of courses in these schools unfeasible. Many students at these schools have part-time jobs or are obliged to take care of younger siblings. Therefore, inclusion of stress management within the outlined curriculum is necessary to introduce many of these skills to young people in a formal setting.

More information on socioeconomic status, age and race is needed to identify the different types of stress, ways of coping, moderating factors and outcomes in different populations. It is likely that while generic stresses, such as negotiating transitions, familial conflicts, goal attainment and relationship formation, are general across all groups, other sources of stress will be relevant to young people from different geographical, educational, social and economic backgrounds. More research is needed on the types of stress management projects which are most effective with different populations.

There are also many societal changes required to alleviate stress in young people. These include, among others, changes in education and training, improved counselling and psychological services, continued research on youth needs, programme evaluation and policy change, a continued focus on children's rights, improved recreational facilities, drugs awareness programmes, economic policies and legislation which support children and families, nurturing educational environments, pro-youth urban planning, and good childcare facilities. In summary, we should be supporting young people through adequate education, physical and mental healthcare together with family, economic and social support. Young people also need to be afforded more flexible trajectories which allow them to develop and feel included and respected through alternative routes in education, training and employment.

Young people may be under stress because of structural inequalities, racial prejudice, where they live and other socioeconomic factors. It is clear that stress management is not going to undermine societal pressures which militate against all young people getting the same advantages in life. However, teaching people how to feel self-confident, how to look after their mental and physical health, how to learn efficiently and, most importantly, to discuss issues which are upsetting them will give them highly important skills. Discussing issues in a group setting with their peers will teach them that many young people share similar problems and difficulties. They will also learn that things which are relatively easy for them may be highly stressful for others.

OVERVIEW OF STRESS MANAGEMENT FOR YOUNG PEOPLE

Of the many suggestions contained in this book, in order to help them to manage their stress levels it is recommended that young people should:

- Use their *support networks* and talk about difficulties as they emerge.

- Be aware of *people* or *organizations* that they can talk to about specific problems.

- Lead a *balanced lifestyle* which has varied components (e.g. school, family, friends, homework, leisure, hobbies, recreation, rest and time alone).

- Get lots of *exercise*, particularly aerobic exercise. They can try walking, running, cycling, swimming or dancing. A brisk walk when they are studying or before an exam will help them to think more clearly and improve their memory.

- Eat a *healthy diet* and avoid too much caffeine, sugar and fats. This causes internal stress and makes us more irritable, tired and likely to feel that we can't cope. Foods which contain carbohydrates, like pasta, bread, potatoes and cereal, act as natural tranquillizers to help us feel calm. Getting enough vitamins from fruit and vegetables also helps us to stay healthy and increase our capacity to cope.

- Try some *relaxation* every day or when they feel stressed. They will need a quiet place, to be sitting upright, with good posture, and deep breathing. If they suffer from stress, they should get into the habit of doing breathing, stretching and relaxation exercises regularly.

- Get enough *sleep*. Young people need up to nine hours a night and should try to get into good sleep routines.

- Remember the importance of *appraisal*: to feel stressed we must interpret things as a threat and assume that we do not have the resources to deal with the demands. We can use coping skills, relaxation, positive appraisal, problem-solving, and remember our social and personal resources.

- Utilize *good study skills*, which basically involves remaining calm, focused and organized.

- Manage their *time* so that they divide it up between the things that are important to them. Try to get straight down to work so that they don't spend time hanging around feeling guilty and unsettled. Get it over and done with and then relax.

- When they feel stressed, they need to try to identify exactly what it is that is bothering them, then treat it as a *problem* in need of a *solution*. They should think of as many solutions as possible and work out which one they would like to try first. If this doesn't work, move on to the next solution and so on.

- Be aware of the sorts of things that give them *energy* (e.g. friends, exercise, food, laughing) and the sorts of things that drain energy (e.g. depression, lack of exercise, feeling a loss of control, arguments) so that they can try to reduce those that drain energy.

- Try to remember their *resources* as well as the demands they face. These include people in their life, and things about them that they like (e.g. their sense of humour, a feeling of confidence in certain things or a hobby that they have).

- Try to keep things in perspective, think *positively* and have a sense of humour about life.

- Remember that the *people* they care about who could help them when stressed are often the people they are most likely to attack. They should try not to take it out on others when stressed so that these people will be there to help them when they need them.

- Remember that being *assertive* means being fair to oneself and to others.

Conclusion

A consensus exists that today's young people are experiencing more distress than the youth of previous generations. This is evident in increasing rates of stress, suicide, depression, eating disorders, anxiety and drug use. No such consensus exists regarding the optimum preventive strategy which would successfully combat these trends. Researchers on adolescent stress are generally in favour of the development of stress reduction interventions. Johnson writes:

> a major task for the future will be the development of inter-vention programmes for helping children cope with stressful events. Although preliminary work in this area has been carried out, the development of such coping skills programmes largely remains a challenge for the future. (Johnson, 1982, p. 250)

Others agree, arguing that the 'development of effective and powerful prevention strategies is necessary'[2] and that the need for health education and life skills training, both now and in the foreseeable future, is so compelling that it should be as universal as possible.[3]

The implications of the issues discussed in this book are important. First, with regard to present adolescent mental health rates, research suggests that adolescents comprise, on average, one in three of all psychiatric referrals.[4] This book argues that adolescent distress may be significantly reduced by learning skills in stress management. Second, we need to think about the way in which we are preparing young people for predicted changes in the job market. The impact of these changes on mental health is a highly pertinent research area for psychology. Recent research supports the relationship between long-term unemployment and mental health problems, such as depression and low self-esteem. Conversely, within the workforce there is also a growing concern regarding levels of stress, with the Royal College of General Practitioners in the UK calling for the teaching of 'stress-proofing' skills to avoid burnout within the work environment.

This book is important given the dearth of both formal and informal resources for practitioners in helping young people to cope with stress. Many of the skills included have been shown to bolster self-esteem and improve academic performance and well-being while reducing anxiety. It is argued, therefore, that learning these skills in school would increase the competency of young people to cope with stress both in the job market and in periods of unemployment.

It is further argued that stress management training may address the lacuna within intervention research whereby interventions focus exclusively on either personal competencies or the social environment. Stress management training appears to ameliorate individual resources by teaching effective coping strategies while enhancing the environment through the improved social resources provided by group meetings and received training in social skills.

It is argued that the inclusion of stress reduction programmes within the school curriculum can successfully buffer adolescents against present and future stressors. These conclusions have far-reaching policy implications. The World Health Organization (WHO) has recently supported life skills education within schools and has published two important documents presenting the rationale, conceptual base and course materials for life skills training.[5] This is indicative of the scale of recognition which now exists regarding the need for competence enhancement and skills training in schools.

An imbalance remains, however, regarding this recognition on the one hand, and the lack of resources or methodologically sound evaluation studies of appropriate interventions on the other. This book aims to provide those working with young people, and in a position to implement programmes on stress management, with guidelines around implementation and evaluation. It is hoped that in so doing it redresses this imbalance and provides a useful guide to supporting teenagers through this crucial and difficult life stage, as well as providing them with skills that will remain with them throughout life.

It is time to prioritize the needs of young people and to acknowledge that current levels of stress are unacceptable. Together with providing a safer, more supportive and challenging environment for today's youth, we can take the knowledge provided by research and our experiences of working with young people and teach them skills that will stay with them throughout the exciting future that lies ahead.

Notes

1 Comer, J. (1991) 'The Comer School Development Program'. *Urban Education*, **26**, 56–82.
2 DuBois, D. L., Felner, R. D., Brand, S., Adan, A. M. and Evans, E. G. (1992) 'A prospective study of life stress, social support, and adaptation in early adolescence'. *Child Development*, **63**, 542–57 (p. 542).
3 Hamburg, B. (1990) *Life Skills Training: Preventive Interventions for Young Adolescents*. New York: Carnesis Council on Adolescent Development.
4 Houlihan, B., Fitzgerald, M. and O'Regan, M. (1994) 'Self-esteem, depression and hostility in Irish adolescents'. *Journal of Adolescence*, **17**(6), 565–77.
5 'Part I: Introduction to life skills for psychosocial competence' and 'Part II: Guidelines: the development and implementation of life skills programmes' issued by the Division of Mental Health of the World Health Organization.

References

Chapter 1

Aldwin, C. M. (1994) *Stress, Coping and Development: An Integrative Perspective*. New York: The Guilford Press.

Cannon, W. B. (1932) *The Wisdom of the Body*. New York: Norton.

Cohen, S. and Hoberman, H. M. (1983) 'Positive events and social supports as buffers of life change stress'. *Journal of Applied Social Psychology*, 13(2), 99–125.

DeLongis, A., Folkman, S. and Lazarus, R. S. (1988) 'The impact of daily stress on health and mood: psychological and social resources as mediators'. *Journal of Personality and Social Psychology*, 54(3), 486–95.

Eysenck, H. J. (1991) 'Type A behaviour and coronary heart disease', in M. J. Strube (ed.) *Type A Behaviour*, pp. 25–44. Newbury Park: Sage.

Faragher, B. (1996) 'Life events, coping and cancer', in C. L. Cooper (ed.) *Handbook of Stress, Medicine and Health*, pp. 159–75. London: CRC Press.

House, J. S. (1981) *Work Stress and Social Support*. Reading, MA: Addison-Wesley.

Holmes, T. H. and Masuda, M. (1974) 'Life change and illness susceptibility', in B. S. Dohrenwend and B. P. Dohrenwend (eds) *Stressful Life Events: Their Nature and Effects*. New York: Wiley.

Israel, B. A., Schurman, S. J., Hugentobler, M. K. and House, J. S. (1992) 'Case study no. 3: A participatory action research approach to reducing occupational stress in the United States'. *Conditions of Work Digest*, 11(2), 152–63.

Kahn, R. L. and Byosier, P. (1992) 'Stress in organizations', in M. D. Dunnette and L. M. Hough (eds) *Handbook of Industrial and Organizational Psychology*, pp. 571–650. Palo Alto, CA: Consulting Psychologists Press.

Lazarus, R. S. (1966) *Psychological Stress and the Coping Process*. London: McGraw-Hill.

Lazarus, R. S. and Blackfield Cohen, J. (1977) 'Environmental stress', in I. Altman and J. Wohlwill (eds) *Human Behavior and Environment: Advances in Theory and Research. Volume 2*, pp. 90–121. New York: Plenum Press.

Moos, R. H. (1995) 'Development and applications of new measures of life stressors, social resources, and coping responses'. *European Journal of Psychological Assessment*, 11, 11–13.

Rotter, J. B. (1966) 'Generalized expectancies for internal versus external control of reinforcement'. *Psychological Monographs*, 80, (whole no.), 609.

Schroeder, D. H. and Costa, P. T. (1984) 'Influence of life event stress on physical illness: substantive effects or methodological flaws'. *Journal of Personality and Social Psychology*, 46(4), 853–63.

Selye, H. (1956) *The Stress of Life*. New York: McGraw-Hill.

Steptoe, A. (1989) 'The significance of personal control in health and disease', in C. L. Cooper (ed.) *Handbook of Stress, Medicine and Health*, pp. 205–33. London: CRC Press.

Theorell, T. (1996) 'Critical life changes and cardiovascular disease', in C. L. Cooper (ed.) *Handbook of Stress, Medicine and Health*, pp. 137–58. London: CRC Press.

Wagner, B. M., Compas, B. E. and Howell, D. C. (1988) 'Daily and major life events: a test of an integrative model of psychosocial stress'. *American Journal of Community Psychology*, **16**(2), 189–205.

Warr, P. (1989) 'Individual and community adaptation to unemployment', in B. Starrin, P. Svensson and H. Wintersberger (eds) *Unemployment, Poverty and Quality of Working Life*, pp. 26–44. Berlin: Stigma.

Chapter 2

Allen, S. and Hiebert, B. (1991) 'Stress and coping in adolescents'. *Canadian Journal of Counselling*, **25**, 19–32.

Bushness, J. A., Wells, J. E., Hornblow, A. R., Oakley-Browne, M. A. and Joyce, P. (1990) 'Prevalence of three bulimia syndromes in the general population'. *Psychological Medicine*, **20**, 671–80.

Carnegie Council on Adolescent Development (1989) *Turning Points: Preparing American Youth for the 21st Century*. New York: Carnegie Council on Adolescent Development.

Chisholm, L. and Hurrelmann, K. (1995) 'Adolescence in modern Europe. Pluralized transition patterns and their implications for personal and social risks'. *Journal of Adolescence*, **18**, 129–58.

Coleman, J. C. (1995) 'Adolescence', in P. Bryant (ed.) *Developmental Psychology*. London: Longman.

Coleman, J. S. (1961) *The Adolescent Society*. New York: The Free Press.

Coleman, J. C. and Hendry, L. (1990) *The Nature of Adolescence*. London: Routledge.

Daniels, D. and Moos, R. H. (1990) 'Assessing life stressors and social resources among adolescents: applications to depressed youth'. *Journal of Adolescent Research*, **5**(3), 268–89.

Donovan, A., Oddy, M., Pardoe, R. and Ades, A. (1986) 'Employment status and well-being: a longitudinal study of 16 year old school leavers'. *Journal of Child Psychology and Psychiatry*, **27**(1), 65–76.

DuBois, D. L., Felner, R. D., Brand, S., Adan, A. M. and Evans, E. G. (1992) 'A prospective study of life stress, social support, and adaptation in early adolescence'. *Child Development*, **63**, 542–57.

Emler, N. (1995) 'Adolescence', in A. S. Manstead and M. Hewstone (eds) *The Blackwell Encyclopedia of Social Psychology*, pp. 9–14. Oxford: Blackwell.

Erikson, P. and Rapkin, A. (1991) 'Unwanted sexual experiences among Middle and High School youth'. *Journal of Adolescent Health*, **12**, 319–25.

Fombonne, E. (1995) 'Eating disorders: time trends and possible explanatory mechanisms', in M. Rutter and D. J. Smith (eds) *Psychosocial Disturbances in Young People*. Chichester: Wiley.

Frydenberg, E. (1997) *Adolescent Coping: Theoretical and Research Perspectives*. London: Routledge.

Frydenberg, E. and Lewis, R. (1991) 'Adolescent coping: the different ways in which boys and girls cope'. *Journal of Adolescence*, **14**, 119–33.

Frydenberg, E. and Lewis, R. (1993a) 'Boys play sport and girls turn to others: age, gender and ethnicity as determinants of coping'. *Journal of Adolescence*, **16**, 253–66.

Frydenberg, E. and Lewis, R. (1993b) *Manual, the Adolescent Coping Scale*. Melbourne: Australian Council for Educational Research.

Gore, S., Aseltine, R. H. and Colten, M. E. (1992) 'Social structure, life stress and depressive symptoms in a high school-aged population'. *Journal of Health and Social Behavior*, **33**, 97–113.

Hall, G. S. (1940) *Adolescence. Volume 2*. New York: Macmillan.

Hamburg, D. and Takanishi, R. (1989) 'Preparing for life: the critical transition of adolescence'. *American Psychologist*, **44**, 825–7.

Hamilton, S. and Fagot, B. (1988) 'Chronic stress and coping styles: a comparison of male and female undergraduates'. *Journal of Personality and Social Psychology,* **55**(5), 819–23.

Hauser, S. and Bowlds, M. K. (1990) 'Stress coping and adaptation', in S. Feldman and G. Elliott (eds) *At the Threshold: The Developing Adolescent,* pp. 388–414. Cambridge, MA: Harvard University Press.

Heaven, P. C. L. (1996) *Adolescent Health: The Role of Individual Differences.* London: Routledge.

Hurrelmann, K., Engel, U. and Weidman, J. C. (1992) 'Impacts of school pressure, conflict with parents, and career uncertainty on adolescent stress in the Federal Republic of Germany'. *International Journal of Adolescence and Youth,* **4**, 33–50.

Jessor, R., Donovan, J. E. and Costa, F. M. (1990) 'Personality, perceived life chances and adolescent health behaviour', in K. Hurrelmann and F. Losel (eds) *Health Hazards in Adolescence,* pp. 25–43. New York: Walter de Gruyter.

Johnson, J. H. (1982) 'Life events as stressors in childhood and adolescence', in B. Lahey and F. Kazdin (eds) *Advances in Clinical Child Psychology,* pp. 220–50. London: Plenum Press.

Knapp, L. G., Stark, L. J., Kurkjian, J. A. and Spirito, A. (1991) 'Assessing coping in children and adolescents: research and practice'. *Educational Psychology Review,* **3**(4), 309–34.

Lazarus, R. S. and Folkman, S. (1984) *Stress, Appraisal and Coping.* New York: Springer.

Leadbeater, B. J., Blatt, S. J. and Quinlan, D. M. (1995) 'Gender-linked vulnerabilities to depressive symptoms, stress and problem behaviours in adolescents'. *Journal of Research on Adolescence,* **5**(1), 1–29.

Magura, M. and Shapiro, E. (1988) 'Alcohol consumption and divorce: which causes which?' *Journal of Divorce,* **12**, 127–36.

Mechanic, D. and Hansell, S. (1989) 'Divorce, family conflict and adolescent well-being'. *Journal of Health and Social Behaviour,* **30**, 115–16.

Millstein, S. G. (1989) 'Adolescent health: challenges for behavioral scientists'. *American Psychologist,* May, 837–42.

Olbrich, E. (1990) 'Coping and development', in H. Bosma and S. Jackson (eds) *Coping and Self Concept in Adolescence,* pp. 35–47. London: Springer-Verlag.

Patterson, J. M. and McCubbin, H. I. (1987) 'Adolescent coping style and behaviors: conceptualization and measurement'. *Journal of Adolescence,* **10**(2), 163–86.

Patterson, J. M. and McCubbin, H. I. (1991) 'Adolescent coping orientation for problem experiences', in H. I. McCubbin and A. I. Thompson (eds) *Family Assessment Inventories for Research and Practice, Second Edition.* University of Wisconsin-Madison.

Petersen, A. and Leffert, N. (1995) 'What is special about adolescence?', in M. Rutter and D. J. Smith (eds), *Psychological Disturbances in Young People,* pp. 3–36. Chichester: Wiley.

Phelps, S. B. and Jarvis, P. A. (1994) 'Coping in adolescence: empirical evidence for a theoretically based approach to assessing coping'. *Journal of Youth and Adolescence,* **23**(3), 359–71.

Reese, F. L. and Roosa, M. W. (1991) 'Early adolescents' self-reports of major life stressors and mental health risk status'. *Journal of Early Adolescence,* **11** (3), 363–78.

Robson, M., Cook, P. and Gilliland, J. (1993) 'Stress in adolescence: theory and practice'. *Counselling Psychology Quarterly,* **6**(3), 217–28.

Rodriguez-Tome, H. and Bariaud, F. (1990) 'Anxiety in adolescence: sources and reactions', in H. Bosma and S. Jackson (eds) *Coping and Self Concept in Adolescence,* pp. 167–85. London: Springer-Verlag.

Rosella, J. D. (1994) 'Review of adolescent coping research: representation of key demographic variables and methodological approaches to assessment'. *Issues in Mental Health Nursing*, **15**, 483–95.

Schaffer, D. (1974) 'Suicide in childhood and early adolescence'. *Journal of Child Psychology and Psychiatry*, **15**, 275–91.

Seiffge-Krenke, I. (1993a) 'Coping behaviour in normal and clinical samples: more similarities than differences?' *Journal of Adolescence*, **16**, 285–303.

Seiffge-Krenke, I. (1993b) 'Introduction'. *Journal of Adolescence*, **16**, 227–33.

Seiffge-Krenke, I. (1993c) 'Stress and coping in adolescence'. *Journal of Adolescence*, **16**(3), 227–33.

Seiffge-Krenke, I. (1995) *Stress, Coping and Relationships in Adolescence*. Mahwah, NJ: Lawrence Erlbaum Associates.

Seiffge-Krenke, I. and Shulman, S. (1993) 'Stress, coping and relationships in adolescence', in S. Jackson and H. Rodriguez-Tome *Adolescence and its Social Worlds*, pp. 169–93. Hillsdale, NJ: Lawrence Erlbaum.

Siddique, C. M. and D'Arcy, C. (1984) 'Adolescence, stress and psychological well-being'. *Journal of Youth and Adolescence*, **13**(6), 459–73.

Silbereisen, R. K., Robins, L. and Rutter, M. (1995) 'Secular trends in substance use: concepts and data on the impact of social change on alcohol and drug abuse', in M. Rutter and D. J. Smith (eds) *Psychosocial Disturbances in Young People*. Chichester: Wiley.

Timko, C., Moos, R. H. and Michelson, D. J. (1993) 'The contexts of adolescent's chronic life stressors'. *American Journal of Community Psychology*, **21**(4), 397–420.

Winefield, A. H. and Tiggemann, M. (1993) 'Psychological distress, work attitudes and intended year of leaving school'. *Journal of Adolescence*, **16**, 57–74.

Zill, N. (1993) 'Long-term effects of parental divorce on parent–child relationships, adjustment, and achievement in young adulthood'. Special Section: 'Families in Transition'. *Journal of Family Psychology*, **7**(1), 91–103.

Chapter 3

Albee, G. W. (1986) 'Toward a just society: lessons from observations on the primary prevention of psychopathology'. *American Psychologist*, **41**, 891–8.

Benson, H. (1975) *The Relaxation Response*. New York: William Morrow.

Billingham, K. (1990) *Learning Together: A Health Resource Pack for Working with Groups*. Nottingham: Community Unit.

Black, D. R. and Frauenknecht, M. (1990) 'A primary prevention problem-solving program for adolescent stress management', in *Human Stress, Current Selected Research*, 4, pp. 89–109. New York: AMS Press.

Boardway, R. H., Delamater, A. M., Tomadowsky, J. and Gutai, J. P. (1993) 'Stress management training for adolescents with diabetes'. *Journal of Pediatric Psychology*, **18**(1), 29–45.

Bond, T. (1993) *Standards of Ethics for Counselling in Action*. London: Sage.

Bruggen, P. and O'Brien, C. (1986) *Surviving Adolescence: A Handbook for Adolescents and their Parents*. London: Faber.

Buckler, J. (1987) *The Adolescent Years: The Ups and Downs of Growing Up*. Ware: Castlemead.

Burningham, S. (1994) *Young People under Stress: A Parent's Guide*. London: Virago Press.

Caplan, M., Weissberg, R. P., Grober, J. S., Sivo, P. J., Grady, K. and Jacoby, C. (1992) 'Social competence promotion with inner-city and suburban young adolescents: effects on social adjustment and alcohol use'. *Journal of Consulting and Clinical Psychology*, **60**(1), 56–63.

Carrell, S. (1993) *Group Exercises for Adolescents: A Manual for Therapists*. London: Newbury Park.

Carrington, P. (1978) *Freedom in Meditation*. New York: Anchor.

Carrington, P. (1987) 'Managing meditation in clinical practice', in M. A. West *The Psychology of Meditation*, pp. 150–73. Oxford: Clarendon Press.

Carrington, P., Collings, G. and Benson, H. (1980) 'The use of meditative-relaxation techniques for the management of stress in a working population'. *Journal of Occupational Medicine*, **22**, 221–31.

Coleman, J. (1987) *Working with Troubled Adolescents: A Handbook*. London: Academic.

Compas, B. E. (1993) 'Promoting positive mental health during adolescence', in S. G. Millstein, E. O. Nightingale and A. C. Petersen *Promoting the Health of Adolescents: New Directions for the Twenty-first Century*. Oxford: Oxford University Press.

Compas, B. E. and Hammen, C. L. (1994) 'Child and adolescent depression: covariation and comorbidity in development', in R. J. Haggerty (ed.) *Stress, Risk and Resilience in Children and Adolescents: Processes, Mechanisms and Interventions*. Cambridge: Cambridge University Press, pp. 225–68.

Copley, B. and Williams, G. (1995) *The Teenage Years: Understanding 18–20 Year Olds*. London: The Tavistock Clinic.

Curran, D. K. (1987) *Adolescent Suicidal Behavior*. Washington, DC: Hemisphere.

Dwivedi, K. N. (1994) *Groupwork with Children and Adolescents*. London: Jessica Kingsley.

Elliott, M. (1991) *Bullying: A Practical Handbook for Schools* . Harlow: Longman.

Ellis, J. and Burns, T. (1987) *The Life Skills Training Manual*. London: Community Service Volunteers.

Field, T. M. (1992) 'Reducing stress in child and psychiatric patients by relaxation therapy and massage', in T. M. Field, P. M. McCabe and N. Schneiderman (eds) *Stress and Coping in Infancy and Childhood* (pp. 219–32). Hillsdale, NJ: Lawrence Erlbaum Associates.

Flanagan, T., Duffield, J. and Smart, S. (1987) *Working with Young Women: Adolescent Project Training Papers*. London: Adolescents Project.

Forbes E. and Pekala, R. (1993) 'Psychophysiological effects of several stress management techniques'. *Psychological Reports*, **72**, 19–27.

Goldberg, D. (1988*) The General Health Questionnaire (GHQ-28)*. Windsor: NFER-Nelson.

Gross, A. M, Heimann, L., Shapiro, R. and Schultz, R. M. (1983) Children with diabetes: Social skills training and hemoglobin A1C levels. *Behavior Modification*, **7**(2), 151–64.

Hamburg, B. (1990) *Life Skills Training: Preventive Interventions for Young Adolescents*. New York: Carnesis Council on Adolescent Development.

Hauser, S. and Bowlds, M. K. (1990) 'Stress, coping and adaptation', in S. Feldman and G. Elliott (eds) *At the Threshold: The Developing Adolescent*, pp. 388–414. Cambridge, MA: Harvard University Press.

Health Education Authority (1990) *Tackling Stress in Schools: A Practical Guide*.

Hurrelmann, K. (1990) 'Health promotion for adolescents: preventive and corrective strategies against problem behavior'. *Journal of Adolescence*, **13**, 231–50.

Klein, D. F., Zitrir, C. M., Woerner, M. G. and Ross, D. C. (1983) 'Treatment of phobias: behavior therapy and supportive psychotherapy: are there any specific ingredients?' *Archives of General Psychiatry*, **40**, 139–45.

Klingman, A. and Hochdorf, Z. (1993) 'Coping with distress and self harm: the impact of a primary prevention program among adolescents'. *Journal of Adolescence*, **16**, 121–40.

Lane, D. and Miller, A. (1992) *Child and Adolescent Therapy: A Handbook*. Buckingham. Open University Press.

Lazarus, R. S. and Folkman, S. (1984) *Stress, Appraisal and Coping*. New York: Springer Publishing Company.

Lehrer, P., Carr, R., Sargunaraj, D. and Woolfolk, R. L. (1994) 'Stress management techniques: are they all the equivalent, or do they have specific effects?' *Biofeedback and Self-Regulation*, **19**(4), 353–401.

Mabey, J. and Sorensen, B. (1995) *Counselling for Young People*. Buckingham: Open University Press.

Madders, J. (1987) *Relax and be Happy: Techniques for 5–18 year olds*. London: Unwin Paperbacks.

Markham, U. (1990) *Helping Children to Cope with Stress*. London: Sheldon.

McLeroy, K., Green, L., Mullen, K. and Foshee, V. (1984) 'Assessing the effects of health promotion in worksites: a review of the stress program evaluations'. *Health Education Quarterly*, **11**, 379–401.

McNamara, S. (2000) *Stress Management Programme for Secondary School Students*. London: Routledge.

Meichenbaum, D. (1977) *Cognitive Behavior Modification*. New York: Plenum.

Murphy, L. R. (1984) 'Occcupational stress management: a review and appraisal'. *Journal of Occupational Psychology*, **57**, 1–15.

Murphy, L. R. (1987) 'A review of organizational stress management research: methodological considerations', in J. M. Ivancevich and D. C. Ganster (eds) *Job Stress: From Theory to Suggestion*, pp. 215–27. New York: Haworth Press.

Nath, S. and Warren, J. (1995) 'Hypnosis and examination stress in adolescence'. *Contemporary Hypnosis*, **12**(2), 119–24.

Neinstein, L. (1991) *Adolescent Health Care: A Practical Guide*. Baltimore: Urban and Schwarzenberg.

Newman, J. D. and Beehr, T. (1979) 'Personal and organizational strategies for handling job stress: a review of research and opinion'. *Personnel Psychology*, **32**, 1–43.

Pelletier, K. and Lutz, R. (1991) 'Healthy people – health business: a critical review of stress management programs in the workplace', in A. Monat and R. S. Lazarus *Stress and Coping: An Anthology*, pp. 483–99. New York: Columbia University Press.

Rice, K. G., Herman, M. A. and Petersen, A. C. (1993) 'Coping with challenge in adolescents: a conceptual model and psycho-educational intervention'. *Journal of Adolescence*, **16**, 235–51.

Roskies, E. (1991) 'Stress management: a new approach to treatment', in A. Monat and R. S. Lazarus (eds) *Stress and Coping: An Anthology*, pp. 411–32. New York: Columbia University Press.

Rutter, M. (1994) 'Stress research: accomplishments and tasks ahead', in R. J. Haggerty (ed.) *Stress, Risk and Resilience in Children and Adolescents: Processes, Mechanisms and Interventions*, pp. 354–87. Cambridge: Cambridge University Press.

Schinke, S. P., Schilling, R. F. and Snow, W. H. (1987) 'Stress management with adolescents at the Junior High Transition: an outcome evaluation of coping skills intervention'. *Journal of Human Stress*, **Spring**, 16–22.

Seiffge-Krenke, I. (1995) *Stress, Coping and Relationships in Adolescence*. Mahwah, NJ: Lawrence Erlbaum Associates.

Shapiro, D. (1987) 'Implications of psychotherapeutic research', in M. A. West (ed.) *The Psychology of Meditation*, pp. 173–91. Oxford: Clarendon.

Smith, M. L. and Glass, G. V. (1977) 'Meta-analysis of psychotherapy outcome studies'. *American Psychologist*, **32**, 752–60.

Smith, M. S. and Womack, W. M. (1987) 'Stress management techniques in childhood and adolescence: Relaxation training, meditation, hypnosis and biofeedback: appropriate clinical applications'. *Clinical Pediatrics*, **26**(11), 581–5.

Smith, R. E. and Nye, S. L. (1989) 'Comparison of induced affect and covert rehearsal in the acquisition of stress management coping skills'. *Journal of Counseling Psychology*, **36**(1), 17–23.

Snaith, R. P., Owens, D. and Kennedy, E. (1992) 'An outcome study of a brief anxiety management programme: Anxiety Control Training'. *Irish Journal of Psychological Medicine*, **9**(2), 111–14.

Szirom, T. and Dyson, S. (1990) *Greater Expectations: A Source Book for Working with Girls and Young Women*. Wisbech: Learning Development Aids.

Thayer, R. E., Newman, J. R. and McClain, T. M. (1994) 'Self-regulation of mood: strategies for changing a bad mood, raising energy and reducing tension'. *Journal of Personality and Social Psychology*, **67**(5), 910–25.

Weinberger, G. and Reuter, M. (1980) 'The "life discussion" group as a means of facilitating personal growth and development in late adolescence'. *Journal of Clinical Child Psychology*, **Spring**, 6–12.

Weissberg, R. P. and Elias, M. J. (1993) 'Enhancing young people's social competence and health behavior: an important challenge for educators, scientists, policymakers, and funders'. *Applied and Preventive Psychology*, **2**, 179–90.

Wilson, N. (1988) *Lively Ideas for Life Skills Teachers*. Edinburgh: Holmes McDougall.

Wright, A. and Frederickson, N. (1992) *Stress in Schools*. London: University College London.

Yorde, B. S. and Witmer, J. M. (1980) 'An educational format for teaching stress management to groups with a wide range of stress symptoms'. *Biofeedback and Self-Regulation*, **5**(1), 75–90.

Chapter 4

Whelan, D. (1993) *Your Breaking Point: Effective Steps to Reduce and Cope with Stress*. Dublin: Attic Press.

Chapter 5

Ellis, A. (1984) 'The place of meditation in rational-emotive therapy and cognitive-behavior therapy', in D. H. Shapiro and R. N. Walsh (eds) *Meditation: Classic and Contemporary Perspectives*. New York: Aldin.

Chapter 9

Whelan, D. (1993) *Your Breaking Point: Effective Steps to Reduce and Cope with Stress*. Dublin: Attic Press.

Chapter 10

Argyle, M. and Martin, M. (1995) 'Testing for stress and happiness: the role of social and cognitive factors', in C. D. Spielberger and I. G. Sarason (eds) *Stress and Emotion, Vol. 15*, pp. 173–87. Washington, DC: Taylor and Francis.

Argyle, M., Martin, M. and Crossland, J. (1989) 'Happiness as a function of personality and social factors', in J. P. Forgas and J. M. Innes (eds) *Recent Advances in Social Psychology: An International Perspective*. Elsevier Science Publishers B. V. North Holland.

Black, D. R. and Frauenknecht, M. (1990) 'A primary prevention problem-solving program for adolescent stress management', in *Human Stress, Current Selected Research*, **4**, pp. 89–109. New York: AMS Press.

Johnson, J. H. (1982) 'Life events as stressors in childhood and adolescence', in B. Lahey and F. Kazdin (eds) *Advances in Clinical Child Psychology*, pp. 220–50. London: Plenum Press.

McNamara, S. (2000) *Stress Management Programme for Secondary School Students*. London: Routledge.

Stiles, W. B., Shapiro, D. A. and Firth-Cozens, J. A. (1988) 'Do sessions of different treatments have different impacts?' *Journal of Counseling Psychology*, **35**(4), 391–6.

Stiles, W. B., Shapiro, D. A. and Elliott, R. (1986) 'Are all psychotherapies equivalent?' *American Psychologist*, **41**(2), 165–80.

Takanishi, R. and Hamburg, D. A. (eds) (1997) *Preparing Adolescents for the Twenty-first Century: Challenges Facing Europe and the US*. Cambridge: Cambridge University Press.